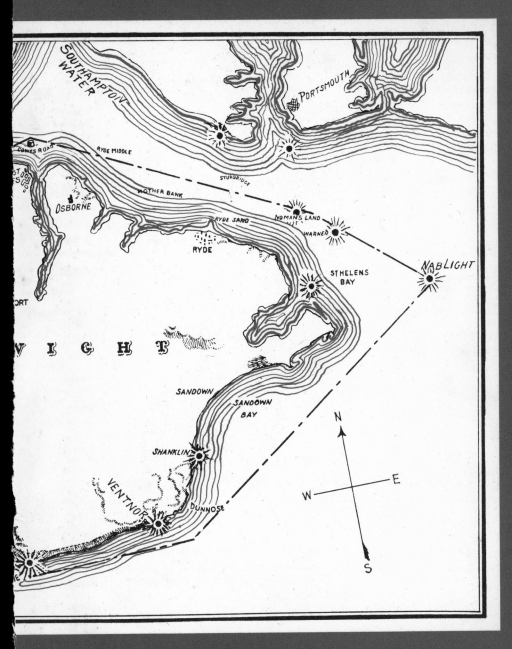

SOUTHAMPTON WATER

PORTSMOUTH

COWES ROAD

RYDE MIDDLE

STURBRIDGE

MOTHER BANK

OSBORNE

RYDE SAND

NOMANS LAND

WARNER

RYDE

St HELENS BAY

NAB LIGHT

W I G H T

SANDOWN

SANDOWN BAY

N

E

W

SHANKLIN

VENTNOR

DUNNOSE

S

COURSE OF THE ROYAL YACHT SQUADRON

AROUND TH‍‍‍‍‍‍‍‍‍‍‍‍ND,

SCENE OF THE *AMERICA* 51.

D1218639

THE
$30,000,000 CUP

THE STORMY HISTORY OF THE

DEFENSE OF THE AMERICA'S CUP

BY JEROME E. BROOKS

SIMON AND SCHUSTER

NEW YORK

1958

TO PATSY AND JOAN

SUNLIT COMPANIONS OF
OUR BEST SAILING DAYS

The author acknowledges with thanks permission of the New York Yacht Club to use its splendid library.

The occasional comments by Alfred F. Loomis which appear in this work are from *Millions for Defense; a pictorial history of the races for the America's Cup,* by Herbert L. Stone and Alfred F. Loomis (New York, The Derrydale Press, 1934).

Other quotations are from

Past Times and Pastimes, Earl of Dunraven (London, Hodder and Stoughton, 1922).
Sherman Hoyt's Memoirs, Sherman Hoyt (New York, D. Van Nostrand Company, 1950).
Lipton's Autobiography, Sir Thomas Lipton (New York, Duffield & Green, 1932).
Enterprise, Harold S. Vanderbilt (New York, Charles Scribner's Sons, 1931).
On the Wind's Highway, Harold S. Vanderbilt (New York, Charles Scribner's Sons, 1939).

Anyone interested in further details on the subject of this book will find the following of greatest value:

The Lawson History of the America's Cup, Winfield M. Thompson and Thomas W. Lawson (Boston, privately printed, 1902).
The Yacht "America," Winfield F. Thompson, William P. Stephens, William U. Swan (Boston, Charles E. Lauriat Co., 1925).
Traditions and Memories of American Yachting, William P. Stephens (New York, reprinted from *Motor Boating,* 1942).

CONTENTS

ILLUSTRATIONS

LIST OF ILLUSTRATIONS

THE
$30,000,000 CUP

1

"THE

FASTEST

YACHT AFLOAT"

A Cup which isn't properly a cup; a piece of silverware which would assay low as bullion; an antique which is no thing of beauty—that is the "old mug" which is the America's Cup.

Yet whatever imperfections this most famous of yachting trophies has in critical eyes are unimportant. They have never been important. For the Cup is a symbol and, as has very probably been said before, for symbols men have suffered and fought.

True, no blood has as yet been shed in contests for the Cup, though some men were, by accident, lost. Yet in those contests elements have been evoked which one expects in war and battle: national animosities and personal hatreds and sometimes the evidences of hysteria; sportsmanship, no-

3

bility—and cunning; contempt—and admiration. In no modern period has a sport been played with more intensity and stirred more drama than have the Cup matches.

The naval engagements were expensive. Impressive sums were cast upon the waters in behalf of the glittering symbol. In their stubborn efforts to retrieve it, the British spent what ran to twenty million dollars; some think much more. (It cost far less than four thousand pounds for England to fight off the Invincible Armada.) In its defense Americans have willingly, indeed eagerly, spent ten millions in hard currency.

Now, one might with reason have thought that this game of nautical aristocrats would remain fairly restricted, if not, indeed, private. It was largely men of great wealth who owned the contesting yachts, paid the high bills, devised the rules, and flew the burgees of exclusive clubs. But when the first challenge came, in 1870, and Americans discovered that *they* had the Cup, they moved on it en masse to take figurative possession. That trophy, won from the nation that once ruled the waves, was visible proof of a new supremacy.

Among the crowds which hovered protectively over the Cup were many who could not navigate a dinghy in still waters and those who quivered at sight of a running sea. Yet they, too, converged upon the Cup races, applauding—and criticizing, too—from the shore or from excursion boats. It was *their* Cup and they would defend it to the last yachtsman. And with equal enthusiasm the British demanded that extravagant yachtsmen get the thing back and as loudly cheered their champions on—or damned them.

The participants in challenge matches, almost startled at first at the spontaneous popular interest, were pleased as well. It made the game important. They had exceptional audiences. Actors always play best to a full house.

As a normal result of the Cup matches, over the years new types of hulls and rigs were developed, each designed to in-

crease the speed of racing yachts. The evolution finally produced boats of such character as to make them practically
useless beyond the specific purpose of a single match. In that
process they also became so expensive as to become impossible. Had not the rating (and associated) rules for Cup racers
been altered by due process, there could be no more matches
between such boats as those which fought it out in the thirties.
But the contest will go on, so long as yachtsmen strain to
capture and defend the Cup—and can afford the patriotic
and personal luxury.

On a day when it was good to be indoors, it being harsh
winter, a British nobleman sent off an invitation to an
American unknown to him. Though it was winter, the letter
was partly inspired by the thought that spring could not be
far behind.

The note was not something impulsively dashed off; that
would hardly have been correct. Its contents and its purpose
had been first discussed with the proper committees of the
highly exclusive yacht club of which the nobleman was commodore. He was Thomas Grosvenor Egerton, second Earl
of Wilton, a keen yachtsman, a skilled church organist, an
amateur surgeon, and the owner of several large and notable
schooners.

His note was addressed to John Cox Stevens, commodore
of the New York Yacht Club:

7, Grosvenor Square, London.
22nd February, 1851.

Sir,

*Understanding from Sir H. Bulwer that a few of the members
of the New York Yacht Club are building a schooner which it is
their intention to bring over to England this summer, I have
taken the liberty of writing to you in your capacity of Com-*

5

modore to request you to convey to those members, and to any friends that may accompany them on board the yacht, an invitation on the part of myself and the members of the Royal Yacht Squadron to become visitors of the Club House at Cowes during their stay in England.

For myself, I may be permitted to say that I shall have great pleasure in extending to your countrymen any civility that lies in my power, and shall be very glad to avail myself of any improvements in ship-building that the industry and skill of your nation have enabled you to elaborate.

I remain, Sir,
Your obedient servant,
Wilton
Commodore of the Royal Yacht Squadron

No hint in this that, perhaps, some of the huge fleet of the classic Squadron would welcome a test with Americans. No word that in Cowes, on the Isle of Wight, summer was a time for regattas, when trophy cups were liberally dispensed. Just a courteous message to say that his lordship would be at home should Commodore Stevens and his friends happen to visit Cowes.

There was significance, though, in the remark about "improvements in ship-building." British merchantmen who made New York a port of call had been telling with some enthusiasm, and envy, too, about an exceptionally fast pilot cutter. She was the *Mary Taylor* (the name of a current favorite in American theaters), from the design of George Steers, and had been launched in 1849. Young Steers—he was born in 1820—was wearing the laurels awarded to the best designer of small boats in the States.

Later, the British were to derive what comfort they could from the knowledge of Steers's paternity and training. The elder Steers, born in England, was apprenticed to a shipbuilder in Newquay and continued his career as a shipwright in the Royal Dockyard at Plymouth. When he became an American citizen he made himself useful in various fields. (He helped to construct the semaphore system between Sandy Hook and New York City which sent notice of incoming ships.) His chief occupation was in shipyards. Under his tuition young George, one of thirteen children, learned an exciting calling. George learned fast; before he was twenty he had won a prize offered by John Cox Stevens for a skillfully designed small boat.

Some years before George Steers was chalking down the curves of lines on a sail-loft floor for boats of his creation, or carving out wood models, the pattern for the fast Sandy Hook pilot boats had already been evolved. Steers had an uncanny perception of where the potentials for improvement lay. The *Mary Taylor* represented an improvement over the current boats of the harbor.

She would have been a novelty in England, with her long, sharp bow and greatest beam aft. For in the British Isles, where the art of shipbuilding was old, the designers' standard formula for hulls required that the bows and forebody be full, with lines converging to an easy run. This was the "cod's head and mackerel tail" principle. Americans had reversed the pattern. Their newly designed boats, therefore, knifed through the water while the British vessels "pushed it away."

George Steers was to provide a great shock to the convinced and stubborn old salts who thought the British craft the ultimate in hull design. Actually, a reformation had begun some years before 1850. The chief exponent of the long, hollow bow was an outstanding Scotch scientist, John Scott Russell. He developed a "wave-line" principle of hull design. Steers may have known about Russell's experiments, conducted in the 1840s. An iron cutter, the 50-ton *Mosquito* built on Russell's principles in 1848, was one of a very few new-style

7

yachts similar to the American design. In her first year she ran away from all others in her class. But the barnacle-studded mariners in British waters and the conservative builders, depending on rule-of-thumb methods, called her a freak. They credited her performance to the iron hull rather than to her long, hollow entrance. They were not ready for reformation. The Earl of Wilton had, at least, an intelligent curiosity about American improvements in shipbuilding.

He had a reply at last from Commodore Stevens:

New York, March 26th, 1851

My Lord,

I regret that an accident prevented the reception of your letter until after the packet of the 12th had sailed. I take the earliest opportunity offered to convey to the gentlemen of the Royal Yacht Squadron, and to yourself, the expression of our warmest thanks for your invitation to visit the Club House at Cowes. Some four or five friends and myself have a yacht on the stocks which we hope to launch in the course of two or three weeks.

Should she answer the sanguine expectations of her builder and fulfil the stipulations he has made, we propose to avail ourselves of your friendly bidding and take with good grace the sound thrashing we are likely to get by venturing our longshore craft on your rough waters.

I fear the energy and experience of your persevering yachtsmen will prove an overmatch for the industry and skill of their aspiring competitors. Should the schooner fail to meet the expectations of her builder, not the least of our regrets will be to have lost the opportunity of personally thanking the gentlemen of the Royal Yacht Squadron and yourself for your considerate kindness.

With the hope that we have the pleasure of reciprocating a favor so frankly bestowed, I remain,

Your lordship's most obedient servant,
John C. Stevens,
Commodore New York Yacht Club

It was clear from this that Stevens and his friends saw more in his lordship's note than a mere invitation to knock at the front door. If they called at all, they were going racing!

Stevens would have been an interesting man to know. His father, Colonel John Stevens, owned a good part of what is now Hoboken, having bought the expropriated farmland of a Tory sympathizer.

Getting to Manhattan from Hoboken, where John junior was born in 1785, meant ferrying across. The schedule depended too much upon the elements of nature. This was more than one should reasonably expect of a young man who sometimes yearned for the glories of New York after nightfall. He emancipated himself from the ferry in his early twenties by building a small sailing conveyance. There was no holding him back from the local seas thereafter. They were his natural element, his experimental playground.

He became a pioneer among American yachtsmen. What has been described as the first "true American yacht" was built under his direction. She was a two-masted, 56-foot pirogue (or piragua)—a type of Indian dugout not a stranger on the Hudson then. As she was something of a nuisance when building, Stevens broke a bottle of indifferent rum over her bow at a private launching and dubbed her *Trouble*. Not long thereafter he had built for him a catamaran twin-hull, appropriately named *Double Trouble*.

Stevens had a new schooner, the *Gimcrack,* in 1844. It acquired a fame which had nothing to do with her sailing ability. For in July 1844, in her saloon, the New York Yacht Club came into being. (There had been a down-east yacht club earlier, but that formed under Stevens' initiative was the first of the period to stay afloat.)

Eight convivial souls with sea water in their veins and all yacht owners joined Stevens in the new venture. Conspicuous among them was George L. Schuyler, more a scholar than

9

a keen sailor. His name was to become more closely linked with the America's Cup affairs than that of any other. Stevens, quite properly, was chosen first commodore of the club by acclaim. He held the post for more than ten years.

In 1850 the British, under Prince Albert's guidance, were excitedly preparing for the Great Exhibition to be held in 1851, the first world's fair of modern times. Before the buildings were up, a number of English businessmen had written, in late 1850, to merchant-correspondents in New York. They suggested that a New York pilot boat come over the following year, berth in the Thames, and then demonstrate its speed as a racer in English waters. They were well aware of the reputation of those boats. The Earl of Wilton, not being in trade, very probably knew nothing of this general invitation.

Through Schuyler, the letter reached America's premier sportsman, Commodore Stevens. (He was not entirely confined to yachting, though that was his major interest. He raced horses, introduced cricket to Americans, and built a baseball diamond near his home for the use of local clubs.) The invitation resulted in a syndicate formed to build "the fastest yacht afloat." Joined with Stevens were his brother Edwin, Schuyler, J. Beekman Finlay and Hamilton Wilkes. All were members of the New York Yacht Club.

Colonel James Alexander Hamilton, son of the more famous Alexander and Schuyler's father-in-law, is generally recorded in various publications, some of them official, as a member of the syndicate. He was not. In his *Reminiscences* he clearly states who were the five owners of the syndicate yacht. He does not include himself. He was, however, so intimately associated with the yacht which was to challenge the British as to give credence to the belief that he was part owner.

When it was suggested to the syndicate by Stevens and Schuyler that only George Steers could create the desired yacht there was no disagreement. At that period in his career

Steers had given up his own yard and was employed as a foreman by William Brown, a shipbuilder located at East River and Twelfth Street, New York.

The chance to design a yacht faster than the British or American best was met with bubbling enthusiasm by Steers. His excitement inspired his employer. The latter showed his own faith by appearing to forget that he was in business and that a business had to show profits. He made an offer which entitles him to top rank among American shipbuilders and a prime place among sporting men.

After a talk with George Schuyler an agreement was drawn by Brown in the form of a letter. Schuyler had drafted it. In it the builder offered to produce a "yacht rigged for ocean sailing" faster than "every other vessel brought against her." It would cost the syndicate $30,000. But if the boat turned out of Brown's yard was not speedier than any other in American waters, the syndicate need not take her. Hamilton Wilkes was to be the umpire.

Having gone that far, Brown's enthusiasm carried him on. The members could, if they wanted, take the proposed craft overseas, and if she did not show her stern to the best of the British of her size, the owners need not retain the yacht and could forget Brown's bill. This was on November 15, 1850. The yacht was to be off the ways by the first of April 1851.

Having just once reread Brown's letter, George Schuyler, on behalf of the syndicate, wrote an acceptance so fast that his pen nearly burned the paper. "The price is high," said his reply, "but in consideration of the liberal and sportsmanlike character of the whole offer . . . we have concluded that such a proposal must not be declined."

Had Brown sent the yacht, to be called *America*, down the ways on the promised date, he would have made further shipyard history. (Yards, generally, haven't changed since 1851.) Hamilton Wilkes, who had an almost boyish faith in his

11

endurance, did his best to speed the process of construction. He sat on the job during the winter building. (When he died of quick consumption in France, a year later, the cause was attributed to his constant attendance in the yard.)

In April the syndicate extended the delivery date to May 1 —"but we really mean it this time, Mr. Brown." Two days after the second promised date the *America* was actually afloat. When the owners stepped on deck to look her over they ordered an extra ration of grog for all hands and drank a hearty toast to Steers and Brown. She was beautiful. They loved her.

The marine reporter of the New York *Herald* came to look at her. "It is impossible," he wrote, "for the pen of the most graphic describer to convey anything like an accurate conception of the beauty and perfection of the *America*." And he had not been at the grog party.

With her clipper bow, sharp forebody, and broad beam (23′) well aft, she had particular grace in the most critical American eyes. (When the tradition-steeped British builders first saw her, they were horrified.) Her 81′ mainmast and her 79′ 6″ foremast were raked a few inches aft. Unlike the standard American flat hull with centerboard designed for shoal waters, she had a long, fixed keel. Her builder's certificate of registry included these figures: 93′ 6″ length, 22′ 6″ breadth, a fraction over 170 tons measurement. (The latter was the American version of the old Thames reckoning for tonnage.) Under full sail, with an area of 5,263 feet, she had a draft of 11 feet.

While it is only of academic interest now, it is a curious fact that the actual lines of the *America* are unknown.* And

* The closest approximation appears to be that drawn by the knowledgeable William P. Stephens, published in *The Yacht America,* 1925, and reprinted in his *Traditions,* 1942.

12

her tonnage has been something for later experts to calculate as best they can. Three or four measurement rules were then in use, and after one had a figure it could be either gross or net tons. The factor of tonnage was of importance in determining time allowance.*

It was May 17 before the *America* was fully rigged and ready for her trial by water. She had serious competition in the sloop *Maria*. That boat was the fastest smooth-water yacht in American waters—a record held throughout her racing career. She had been modeled by Robert Livingston Stevens in 1844, working with his brothers John Cox and Edwin, who owned her. The *Maria* was the largest pleasure craft to be launched in the States to her time. Her deck length was 110′, her built-up boom 95′ long and nearly 9′ at its thickest circumference. She was, in consequence of her "monstrous rig," a bitch to handle in a fresh breeze. It is no surprise to know that she was frequently dismasted. When the wind was on her she usually traveled with her hatches well under water. She was not regarded as safe in a seaway.

The Stevens brothers had spent over $100,000 on the *Maria* and for various alterations. Under the skillful hands of George Steers her original bluff bow had been lengthened and pointed, a change which improved her stability as well as her speed. The rate at which she traveled kept her crew vibrating. Her old sailing master boasted that she had been

---

* When the *America* was ready to leave for England the New York *Herald* had worried about the matter of allowance: "Without some modification of the English rule of measurement [the *America*] will labor under great disadvantage. [The British regulation of tonnage by Thames reckoning is explained.] By giving very great rake to the stern-post, and projecting their counters very far aft over their rudder-heads, they add great length to the vessel, without increasing her tonnage, as the length on deck is not taken into account. . . . The *America* measured by [the English] rule would be over two hundred tons."

13

clocked at 17 knots in smooth water. (That claim of speed has well been doubted. Except for an occasional burst, when the reading of the log on a brief run said 13 knots, the "skimming dishes" and the scientific J boats in Cup races rarely averaged more than 9 or 10 knots.) But the *Maria* was a flyer.

This, then, was the boat which was to test the *America* as "the fastest yacht afloat." The most conspicuous craft in American waters, whatever the *Maria* did made news. There was then far more general interest in her than there was in the unknown *America*. The new hopeful had no chance against her. She not only outsailed the *America* on all points but occasionally taunted her by running complete circles around her. Yet the *America* sped past all other boats in New York Harbor and even ran away from some steam vessels which tried to take her measure. During the trials it was found that her spars were too light. They were replaced.

Stevens and his associates understood the *America*. They knew they had a prize, even though "she hasn't found her feet yet." It would, after all, have been unreasonable to expect a keel schooner to beat a tuned-up centerboard sloop such as the *Maria* was, despite her builder's confident expectations. The *America* was designed for heavier work than the waters in which the *Maria* was so comfortable. The syndicate made Brown an offer: They would forget that clause about the fastest yacht afloat and would pay $20,000 for the *America,* "equipped and ready for sea by June 2d." When Brown agreed, and he was prompt about it, the owners who could arrange to leave began to pack for Europe.

They were impatient now, but there were the usual delays. Stevens had expressed the opinion that if they were on hand at Cowes early in the season "there would be plenty to compete for, with the probability of large cash wagers and special match races." A sporting man, well accustomed to wagers on a boat or a horse, he expected that the syndicate could retrieve the expenses of its beautiful new yacht. The placing of bets, and frequently very high ones on racing yachts, by owners and builders was even more open and customary then than it is today. It was understood, too, that the *America* was going abroad as a private enterprise, not as a representative of the New York Yacht Club.

It was not until June 18 that the owners were formally in possession of the *America*. Three days later the historic voyage to European waters started with a tow through the busy traffic of the East River to The Narrows. The New York Customs House papers listed thirteen men on board, six before the mast. The yacht's skipper was a top Sandy Hook pilot, hard-bitten, profane, likable Captain Dick Brown. George Steers, quite naturally, was a passenger. His brother James, also a shipyard man, and the latter's seventeen-year-old son, George, went along. The *America* was pilot-rigged for her transatlantic passage, wearing the working sails of the *Mary Taylor*. Almost all who saw her go saluted her, swore an affectionate oath or said a prayer. For the first time an American yacht was to cross the Atlantic to challenge the best of the British in their very stronghold. Their first port of call was to be Le Havre.

Barring bad weather and poor cooking, the crew and passengers were going to enjoy the trip. The crew's quarters were exceptionally comfortable, while those of the owners were described as splendid. There was a "tastefully fitted-up bathroom" below the cockpit. The "saloons were finished in carved rosewood, polished American walnut, and green silk velvet."

Provisions were plentiful. Purely for the purpose of "drinking the health of Her Majesty" while entertaining the distinguished guests who would certainly come on board, there were two dozen bottles of wine, "derived from the celebrated cellar of the late Mr. Bingham of Philadelphia." This was

15

Madeira bottled more than half a century earlier. Stevens himself had brought the hamper tenderly on board. Then Maria Stevens, his wife, in setting things to rights, artfully concealed the wine in a secret locker. In the excitement of last farewells she neglected to tell anyone, including her husband, who was not a passenger, where she had stowed it. Later, when Stevens went looking for the wine, he cussed someone unknown who he assumed had drunk toasts by himself. He never did uncover that choice cache, but he found out where it was when it was too late.

Nothing exciting seems to have occurred on the voyage over. The log which James Steers kept is a fairly prosaic account. One of his early entries notes that Captain Brown and some others "turned in rather qualmish." These mariners felt much more comfortable on the Sandy Hook run. Though they would not admit to seasickness, they finally indulged in "a little brandy, say about 10 drops." The record reports that the *America* passed all sailing vessels going their way. It includes expected details of weather, daily runs, praise of the cook on some days and criticism on others.

There seems to have been brandy to help wash down each dinner. But when they were an expected three days from France there was an alarmed note: "Our liquor is all but gone." Then, with two days still to go, "we had to break open one of the boxes marked *Rum*." (It was from Stevens' own stock and he was to blister the cabin velvet when he found that he had entrusted his rum to buccaneers. Bad enough not to find that Madeira!) James Steers felt they had a good excuse:

George had a belly-ache and all of our own stock was consumed; and we were not going to starve in a Market Place, so we took four bottles out and think that will last us.

Late in the evening of July 11 the *America* was piloted into Le Havre. The log has a proud entry: "From East 12th St.

to Havre" the voyage had taken 20 days, 6 hours, or "from land to land" only 18 days, 15 hours. The best run had been 276 knots in 24 hours, though the *America* was under working rig. They had had some rough weather—not much, yet rain almost every day. More annoying were five days and four hours of doldrums.

The owners of the *America* had thought it wise to drop the hook at Le Havre before going to England. They expected to surprise the British and they did not want their yacht too closely examined if there were to be races. Further, George Steers had decided before they left New York that some alterations were needed in the stem, which meant hauling out.

The Steers brothers reached Paris by July 13 and returned to Le Havre with Commodore and Edwin Stevens and Colonel Hamilton. George Schuyler had planned to join Stevens in France, but he was detained at home and Hamilton replaced him. The three men, after steamer passage, had waited tensely in Paris for two weeks before hearing from Le Havre. Not all Americans shared the confidence of Colonel Hamilton and her owners that the *America* could outsail the best of the British. As Hamilton tells in his *Reminiscences:*

I was earnestly urged by Mr. William C. Rives, the American Minister, and Mr. Sears of Boston, not to take the vessel over, as we were sure to be defeated. My friend, Mr. H. Greeley, who had been at the Exhibition in London, meeting me in Paris, was most urgent against our going.

He went so far as to say: "The eyes of the world are on you; you will be beaten, and the country will be abused, as it has been in connection with the Exhibition."

I replied, "We are in for it, and must go."

He replied, "Well, if you do go, and are beaten, you had better not return to your country."

Hamilton was not unduly upset. He wrote:

17

This awakened me to the deep and extended interest our enter-prise had excited, and the responsibility we had assumed. I remembered that our packet-ships had outrun theirs, and why should not this schooner, built upon the best model?

2

"NO
SECOND"

Through official introductions to the local naval authorities, arrangements were made for the *America* to go into government dry dock. Those in charge at Le Havre were impressed with the American yacht and eager to aid in her reconditioning so that she could go over and "beat the British." But there was no hurrying the shipwrights in the yard. It was generally understood among them that Americans were quite mad and that one was not to hear them when they demanded more energetic interest in the work at hand.

Finally there was nothing left to do. The prime gray of the *America*'s topsides had a smart coat of black and her trailboards forward sparkled with gold. There was a new coat of gilt, too, for the conspicuous spread eagle on her stern. Mainbooms, gaffs, mastheads and her inside bulwarks were painted white. If the *America* did nothing else, she would surely im-

19

press the British with her embellishments! Almost three weeks after she went into dry dock she was ready. It was then July 31. John Cox Stevens and his brother, Edwin, went on board. Colonel Hamilton and his wife, who had joined him on the trip to France, left for Cowes by steamer.

There was only a breath of wind, just enough with the current's help to move in the direction the *America* was to go. But when a fog set in, in the dark night, she anchored in the Solent, a half-dozen miles or so out of Cowes Road. As Colonel Hamilton was in Cowes by then, it was known that the American yacht was due momentarily. A prize cutter, the *Lavrock,* one of the British best, went looking for her in the early morning of August 1. The *America* was just making ready for the short run to Cowes.

Perhaps if Commodore Stevens had not been on board, Skipper Brown would have played it canny. Then some of those "large cash wagers" which Stevens hoped for might have been placed. But, as George Schuyler observed some years after the event, the *Lavrock* insisted on trying the *America*'s qualities right there and then. She was gracefully showing her own qualities. This was just too much, too great a provocation for a sporting yachtsman. A breeze of wind, perhaps six knots, which came along with the *Lavrock* made the invitation irresistible. Up went the *America*'s jib. At that moment began the great contest between American and British yachtsmen which has never ended.

"We were loaded with extra sails, with beef and pork and bread enough for an East India voyage, and were four or five inches too deep in the water." (This was Commodore Stevens' report, at his yacht-club dinner in October 1851, of the *America*'s first race in English waters.)

I have seen and been engaged in many exciting trials at sea and on shore . . . without feeling one-hundredth part of the respon-

THE *AMERICA*

Only foreign entry in the Royal Yacht Squadron regatta, August 22, 1851.
The winner of the race, she received a cup. *From a water color by W. G. Wood.*

ROYAL VISITORS ON THE *AMERICA*

Commodore Stevens is lending a hand to Queen Victoria. The Prince Consort is on Colonel Hamilton's left. Lord Alfred Paget, the Queen's clerk marshal, is facing the rest.

A nice conception by C. Chase Emerson, who executed an oil painting from photographs and drawings. The artist thoughtfully provided the *America* with a handsome and prominent wheel—but she was then steered with tiller.

George Steers,
designer of the *America*.
From a woodcut.

George L. Schuyler.
*From a woodcut copy of an
oil portrait by Leon Bonnat.*

Originally the 100-Guinea Cup or the Royal Yacht Squadron Cup;
then the Queen's Cup or the Royal Cup; later the America's Cup,
and now
THE CUP

sibility, and without suffering one-hundredth part of the fear and dread I felt at the thought of being beaten by the Laverock [sic] *in this eventful trial.*

During the first five minutes not a sound was heard save, perhaps, the beating of our anxious hearts or the slight ripple of the water upon [the America's] *swordlike stem. The captain was crouched down upon the floor of the cockpit, his seemingly unconscious hand upon the tiller, with his stern, unaltering gaze upon the vessel ahead. The men were motionless as statues, their eager eyes fastened upon the* Laverock *with a fixedness and intensity that seemed almost unnatural. . . . It could not, nor did not last long. We worked quickly and surely to windward of her wake. The crisis was past, and some dozen of deep-drawn sighs proved that the agony was over.*

Then the *America* dropped her hook a quarter or third of a mile ahead of the *Lavrock.* Twenty minutes later the Earl of Wilton and some of his family were on board to welcome the visitors. His lordship was at particular pains to make everyone comfortable. From the deck of his famous yacht, the *Pearl,* one of the first English cutters—she was built in 1815—and for long the speediest racer in British waters, the old Marquis of Angelsey studied the *America* carefully. "If she be right," said he, "then all of us are wrong!"

For the first time an invader, and under a rig and circumstances clearly not to her advantage, had fairly beaten a flyer among British yachts. Cowes was in a ferment. The London *Times* correspondent, in his comment on the agitation stirred by the *America's* victory, compared it with the "appearance of a sparrow-hawk among a flock of woodpigeons or skylarks. . . . The effect produced by her apparition off West Cowes among the yachtsmen seems to have been completely paralysing." That Stevens had damaged his hopes of the main chance when he made his strategic error was soon clear. Yet who among sporting yachtsmen could blame him?

21

After the polite preliminaries were over, Stevens posted a challenge at the Royal Yacht Squadron's clubhouse. Schooners were invited to test their speed against the *America*. Silence, broken by some heavy breathing. Cutters, anybody? No one ran up a code flag reading "Accept." Thereupon, in desperation rather than bravado, for the yachting season would soon end, the challenge went out to any British yacht of any rig. George Schuyler observed long after the event that, after a brief wait,

it was intimated to Commodore Stevens that if a sufficient amount would be staked to make it an object, what he desired could be brought about, whereupon our Commodore, with his usual promptness and regardless of the pockets of his associates had posted a challenge for [a purse] from 1 to 10,000 guineas.

Five thousand dollars in England then would have the purchasing power of fifteen thousand today (to give a rough equivalent). The larger sum proposed by Stevens was, to quote a wide-eyed British contemporary, "a staggerer."

The intimation Schuyler said was made to Stevens never did materialize. Yet, for a week or two thereafter, the waterside hummed with rumors that a group of yachtsmen were making up a large stake. In his original proposal, August 2, to race the *America* against any schooners, Stevens had addressed Lord Wilton. It was an open challenge to the British yacht fleet generally and was proposed on behalf of the New York Yacht Club. Almost a week thereafter the Earl replied, in elegant English, that he would advise all British yacht clubs of Commodore Stevens' proposal. He then went on to say that the member clubs of the Squadron "have offered a cup to be sailed for by vessels of all rigs and nations on the 13th instant." Would the *America* care to join?

It would take too long, wrote Stevens promptly on August 9, for anyone in his party to wait on what reply other British clubs might make to his proposal. Yes, he would enter the regatta to be held on the 13th

provided I am allowed to sail the America *in such manner as her rig requires: yet as the issue of a regatta is not always the test of the merits of the vessel engaged in it, I now propose to run the yacht* America *against any cutter, schooner, or vessel of any other rig in the Royal Yacht Squadron, relinquishing any advantage which your rules admit is due to a schooner from a cutter but claiming the right to sail the* America *in such manner, by such booming out, as her raking masts require; the course to be in the English Channel with not less than six knot breeze . . . some day before the 17th instant; the distance to be not less than twenty nor over seventy miles out and back and in such a direction as to test the quality of the vessels before and by the wind.*

Although it would be most agreeable to me that this race should be for a cup of limited value, yet if it is preferred, I am willing to stake upon the issue any sum not to exceed ten thousand guineas.

A day or two later Stevens withdrew the *America*'s entry for the August 13 regatta. He indicated that he wanted first to hear whether any single yacht would be put up to meet his challenge for a race before the 17th. The Squadron members might reasonably have been annoyed at this. If they were, they were courteously silent. The most aristocratic yacht club in the kingdom, the Royal Yacht Squadron was prepared to go far beyond routine politeness in its treatment of a foreign visitor. The *America* was to be permitted to "boom out," despite a contrary rule, and the Squadron waived its regulation prohibiting entry in its regattas of a syndicate-owned yacht. The Royal Victoria Yacht Club at Ryde had already barred the *America* because of her multiple ownership. (The Squadron was, indeed, far more democratic than the New York Yacht Club was to be later in its original attitude to a British challenger.)

23

From the time of its arrival at Cowes there had been daily press comments on "the Yankee clipper . . . that glorified pilot boat," the stir it had caused among yachtsmen, and Stevens' persistent efforts to find a champion yacht willing to place a sizable bet on a single race. There was, too, occasional comment on the contempt expressed by ordinary boatmen in Cowes waters over the timid owners of yachts. These local salts had offered to rig a boat and race the *America* if yachtsmen could be found to put up enough of a stake to make it worth their while.

The London *Times,* on August 16, had something to say on the subject. It is difficult to believe that the English would

allow the illustrious stranger to return with the proud boast to the New World that she had flung down the gauntlet to England, Ireland, and Scotland and that not one had been found to take it up.

If so inconceivable a situation became fact, "then there will be some question as to the pith and courage of our men."

This provocative call to arms evoked a most feeble response. It came first from Robert Stephenson, a noted engineer, who offered to match his 100-ton schooner, *Titania,* for a £100 stake on August 28. This yacht, iron-built and new, was not regarded as in a class with champions. Stephenson knew it, but he was not going to let the *Times* down. He thought, too, that by example he would stir his timid compatriots. He did not stir them. For the most part they remained glued to the club porches, studying the Yankee phenomenon through telescopes whenever she moved from her anchorage. Then came another tentative challenge, but it was proposed for a date too late for Stevens. When he suggested that the second challenger join the *Titania* in the scheduled race against the *America,* his offer evaporated.

The first reaction of the American owners to the trivial stake suggested by Stephenson was that they would take their yacht home. They were more than annoyed; they felt cheated. It was undoubtedly the better sense of Colonel Hamilton which prevailed on them to enter at least one regatta of the Squadron. All of the *America*'s racing in English waters to that time had been unofficial. It had merely served to demonstrate her superiority over any and all of the yachts in Cowes waters.

The request which Stevens, by this time an experienced marine secretary and ship's clerk, then sent to Lord Wilton was to prove most fortunate for the future of Anglo-American yacht competition. It must have been sent with a touch of irritation, and Stevens felt it would be his last in the rapidly closing yachting season. There was to be another Squadron regatta on August 22, a race around the Isle of Wight. He desired to enter the *America*. The Squadron's standard trophy for the event was its "ordinary" cup, worth a hundred guineas. Stevens made no mention of it. He did say:

The fact that this vessel is owned by more than one person is so well known as to render it almost unnecessary to state it; yet I do so when she is entered, to avoid the possibility of seeming to contravene the rule of the Royal Yacht Squadron.

But Stevens reserved the right not to sail on the twenty-second if the wind was too light. The Squadron's regatta committee promptly agreed that the *America* should come in on its own terms and thus "not deny the visitor a fair race."

Apart from other characteristics which set her apart, the *America*'s sails had excited the greatest interest. They lay flat, unlike the traditional baggy cut of British yacht sails. (Said the old school, apparently brought up by tentmakers, "Give her a bellying sail to drive her.") The *America*'s sails of machine-made cotton duck were laced to booms; British sails

25

of loose-woven flax canvas were loose-footed. The consequence of these variations from the cut and fit of British yacht canvas was to the clear advantage of the *America*. When going to windward, she could point much closer than the craft wearing their baggy suits of sail.

The *America* had reached Cowes still rigged as the pilot boats were at home. George Steers decided that she would do better with a flying jib. He went to one of the top shipbuilders at Cowes, Michael Ratsey, for a jib boom. Would Ratsey care to bet what the spar would cost that the *America* could outsail the Squadron's fleet? Bravely, Ratsey would. He chose the 161-ton schooner *Beatrice*. The next bet was placed by Steers with a sailmaker for the price of a flying jib. The latter's guess was simply that the *America* would not win; he did not trouble to name a victor.

Somewhat encouraged by these evidences of sporting plunging, Stevens and company began to think that perhaps not all British gambling blood had dried up. Someone advised them that a group in nearby Southampton was willing and eager to lay even money on the forthcoming race. When Stevens and Steers looked into it, they were informed that the group "booked" only against letters of credit. This hardly made sense to the Americans, who had ready cash for the hands of a stakeholder, and they offered to put it on display. The Southampton group disdained such vulgarity. No wager.

Any yachting center is a restless place. But from the day it was known that the *America* was entered in the Squadron's regatta, Cowes was in a state of unaccustomed turmoil. The landed gentry came to sea, to take up temporary residence on the island. Hotel and club registers seemed to have been copied from *Burke's Peerage*. And yachtsmen from all parts of the British Isles and some from the Continent, gamblers, and ordinary people infected by the excitement, converged on the spot. The little towns on the Isle quickly ran out of rooms. Some unfortunates, usually privileged, actually had to share quarters and some had to berth on boats.

There were seventeen yacht clubs in the United Kingdom, the first the Royal Cork, organized in 1720, "and not one of them," the London *Times* reported, "had ever seen a foreigner enter the lists in annual matches." Journalists were pushing their pens hard. They were, almost without exception, friendly to the visitors. They liked the two owners on board the *America,* and Colonel Hamilton, "three very cautious and gentlemanly persons—as downright cute and keen as the smartest in the States." They admired the challenging yacht, "a big-boned skeleton, but no phantom." *Bell's Life* (from the *Times*) gave its inland readers a close view:

> She has a low, black hull, two noble sticks of extreme rake, without an extra rope and is all together the beau-ideal of what one is accustomed to read about in Cooper's novels. When close to her you see that her bow is as sharp as a knife-blade, scooped away as it were outwards till it swells towards the stern, the sides gradually springing outwards as round as an apple, till a little forward of the mainmast, where she has her greatest beam. . . .

The day, August 22, a sunlit one, for which everyone seems to have been waiting saw Cowes a scene of further confusion. There was a new press of sightseers who had come to the Isle by steamer or sailboat or who had rowed across the few miles from the mainland. It was the *America* on which attention focused, despite the numerous fine yachts moving into position for the contest or already at anchor. The royal steam yacht, *Victoria and Albert,* took the Queen, her consort and family on board from their summer residence at Osborne House, Cowes. Then it went off to the immense pillars of chalk and limestone called The Needles at the west coast of the Isle. They anchored there, away from the overloaded harbor. The spot was not far from the end of the course

27

around the Isle of Wight. Of that 53-mile course the London *Times* had commented that it was

notoriously one of the most unfair to strangers that can be selected. . . . It does not appear to be a good race ground for anyone, inasmuch as the current and tides render local knowledge of more value than swift sailing and nautical skill.

Eighteen yachts were entered in the regatta. Two, the *Titania* (stationed as number 7) and the fast *Stella* (number 15), did not start. The trophy-winning schooner *Fernande* did not even take her station. No one seems to know what had upset the plans of these three entries, and later no one seems to have cared. (The *Fernande,* in a regatta on the fifteenth, had "lost" to the *America,* which, starting late over the course of the racing fleet, came in unofficially the winner.) The fifteen contestants were moored in a double line, three hundred yards apart, one of cutters, the other of schooners. There were seven of the latter, including the three-masted *Brilliant* of 392 tons. Of the former, the 47-ton *Aurora* and the 48-ton *Volante* were the smallest. There were to be no time allowances. It was an open race.

On board the *America* were twenty-one men, including a local pilot recorded only as Underwood, and six seamen lent by the owner of the schooner yacht *Surprise.* The latter were paired and stationed aft under the watchful eye of Captain Brown. The cook insisted on going along; he would have no amateurs messing up his galley.

The signal for "up anchor" in five minutes came at 9:55 A.M. At that, the huge spectator fleet went into action and, steaming or sailing cautiously on each side of the course, moved east by south. Skippers on the waiting racers were roaring orders, eager hands were laid to halyards and sheets, and husky seamen were bringing home their anchors. Gaff topsails and balloon jibs were greatly in evidence. There was

a mild westerly and the current was favoring. The spectator
fleet and the contestants at the start presented an exhibition,
wrote an enthusiastic correspondent, "such as the Adriatic
never beheld in all the pride of Venice!"

Last to get away was the *America*. There were two explana-
tions made for that tardiness; we shall probably never know
which is correct. Hamilton reported in his *Reminiscences,*
"Commodore Stevens . . . gave orders not to hoist our sails
until all the others were under way." Said Henry Steers *
twenty-six years later in a speech at the Seawanhaka Yacht
Club:

> *We constantly overran our anchor and slewed around, and we
> had to lower our sails; and so all the yachts got off ahead of us;
> however, we had a large crew and got our sails up very quickly.
> By the time we got to the Nab (12 miles) we had walked through
> the whole fleet except four—Beatrice, Aurora, Volante, Arrow,
> running wing to wing . . . these boats would steer close together,
> so that when we tried to get through them we could not without
> fouling, and had to keep cutting and sheering about, very often
> being near gybing. . . .*

This combination in restraint of sport might have been
serious. But a break came at Nab Light, off the east coast of
the Isle. Following instructions, the four leading yachts kept
it on their starboard. Following instructions, the *America* left
it to port. That saved her time and distance. She was not
alone in taking the inside course. The *Beatrice,* on which
Ratsey had bet a spar, was lost sight of fairly early in the race.

---

* This Henry is a puzzle. He was not in the Customs House list of persons aboard when the *America* left New York. James Steers's log clearly
indicates that it was George junior, not his second son Henry, who made
the passage across. But George died in 1873 and Henry's talk, according
to reliable records, was given in 1877. It may be that Henry, then fifteen, accompanied the Stevens brothers to Europe as a guest and was a
passenger on the *America* during her most famous race.

What was hoped for, a freshening breeze, came in the Channel. It blew enough for the *America* to part company with her new jib boom. "Damned glad it's gone," roared Dick Brown at the wheel. He never had liked the idea that a flying jib should be used in windward work. It was not Ratsey's fault, said the *Times* correspondent, that the jib boom was lost,

for not only did he recommend Messrs. Stevens to take a yellow spar instead of a white one they selected; but the boom was broken by mis-management on the part of the men when straining on it with the windlass, and did not snap from the action of the sail. The accident threw her up in the wind, and gave the advantage of about a quarter of an hour to her opponents, while she was gathering in the wreck. But it was of little use to them.

There was a drop in the wind soon after the mishap. The afterguard on the *America,* casting nervous eyes astern, saw the lighter vessels closing up on them. The pursuers were so eager to catch the *America* that they tripped themselves up. The *Arrow,* a cutter of 84 tons, only recently winner of the Ryde regatta, became tangled with the shore five hours after her start. The sailing committee's steamer soon dragged her off and the *Alarm,* a 193-ton cutter also an entrant in the race, chivalrously abandoned its hopes and saw the *Arrow* home. Not long thereafter, the cutter *Freak* and the *Volante,* during an inshore tack off the cliffs at Ventnor, fouled each other. The latter was disabled by the loss of her bowsprit and a damaged jib boom. And it had been the little *Volante,* new that year, which, it was observed, had "carried the hopes of all the professional watermen of the Solent."

Several starters, discouraged by the adverse current off St. Catherines, had gone about and gone home. By this time the *America*'s lead was incontestable. Behind her were the four boats still in the race: *Aurora, Bacchante, Eclipse* and

Brilliant. Ahead lay only blue water and victory. Then came a shock. Far in advance of the *America,* after a turn in the course, a smart cutter appeared. Reporters on the steamers following the race commented later that many passengers were convinced that she was the *Aurora.* But they had no explanation of how she had got so far ahead. The *America* bore down on the unexpected craft, which was then two miles ahead. In an hour or so she was caught and passed. It was then learned that she was the *Wildfire* out of the Royal Cork Club and that she had started on the course long in advance of any-one else just because she liked parties. She had very nearly brought about the collapse of the *America's* afterguard, men of stout hearts and strong bodies.

A hint of haze was rising as the *America* reached The Needles for the run home. The signalman on the waiting royal yacht saw her first and reported it to his superior officer. By due process of protocol the information was conveyed to Queen Victoria.

"The American boat has been sighted, madam."

"Oh, indeed! And which is second?"

By reverse process the question was conveyed to the signalman.

His glass swept the horizon. After a pause the answer reached the proper officer. He quivered a little. "I regret to report that there is no second."

As they reached the *Victoria and Albert* the *America's* ensign was lowered. Those on deck removed their caps, stood for a moment at attention, and then each made the sort of bow a sailor would give on the weather side of a deck. The London *Times,* in remarking on the incident next day, was not sure that this had been quite in order, any more, say, than a jockey on a racing horse saluting the royal box at passing. Still, upon reflection, it was decided that this evidence of respect to the Queen had been a very decent thing

31

to do, "not the less becoming because it was bestowed by republicans."

There *was* a second—and a gallant one: the little *Aurora*. It is anyone's guess now whether she was 8 or 20 or 24 minutes after the *America,* which came to the finish slowly in a lazy wind and under a cloudy, darkening sky at 8:37 P.M., Royal Yacht Squadron time. George Schuyler, twenty years after the event, placed the *Aurora* 20 minutes, the *London Illustrated News* of the day 21 minutes, and several others then and later 24 minutes astern. The New York Yacht Club, some years after, accepted 8 minutes as the official figure.

The actual figure of the *Aurora's* time at the finish would hardly matter were it not for the fact that, had time allowances applied, she might very well have been accounted the winner. A scale devised by George Holland Ackers (owner of the three-masted *Brilliant,* which crept in at 1:20 A.M. on the twenty-third) and known since 1843 as the "Graduated Time Tables"—the first of its kind—was the accepted allowance table of the period. Under Ackers' scale the *Aurora* would have been allowed 18 minutes. Under the New York Yacht Club's tonnage rule she would have had more than an hour.

Well, it had been a Yankee victory and a notable one, for it was to shake British yachting circles profoundly. Yet, despite its decisiveness and official acceptance, there was some grumbling and discontent over defeat, or patronizing acknowledgment of the *America's* victory. Even in a much later period it was remarked that the victory proved little. "The *Freak* and *Alarm,*" said one commentator, "both formidable cutters were out of the race early." Some able American authorities, in our own times, have thought that the *America's* victory was a "fluke" because of accidents to her rivals or because she had cut inside of Nab Light. Actually, what she had gained by taking the inside passage she had lost when her jib

32

boom went awry. And she was well ahead when some of the fastest boats in the race fouled themselves up. Her later history was to prove that the *America* was well entitled to her victory. She was superbly designed and superby handled, and was one of the soundest, noblest craft ever built.

The owner of the *Brilliant,* and quite correctly, too, protested over the *America*'s passage inside Nab Light. The protest was withdrawn when it was found that she had been within her right. The Squadron's instruction cards issued to entrants were, through some carelessness, in two forms. These seem to have been indiscriminately handed to the yachts' skippers. No one appears to have noticed that they differed on a vital point. "The cards containing the names and colours of the yachts," *Bell's Life* reported, "described the course as being merely round the Isle of Wight, while the printed programme stated that it was to be round the Isle of Wight and outside the Nab." The *America* had received the former; the *Brilliant* and others, the latter.

Some of the open disappointment came from the merely envious, the losers of bets, or those who just disliked Americans. The Steers brothers heard murmurs of "Yankee trick" and "skimming dish" (the latter surely a wrong appellation for a boat with a deep, fixed keel) in reference to the *America*. Michael Ratsey, a yacht builder whose renown went well past Cowes, was plainly upset. "In ninety days," said he, "I can build a boat that would beat the *America*." He would wager £500 on the outcome of a match. "For that I won't wait," replied Stevens. "Make it £5,000 and the wager is on." No answering signal.

The *Liverpool Journal* introduced a solemn note into the general debate. True, it made use of the situation in its general disagreement with British policy in Ireland, which it thought the United States might soon annex! It said, in part:

The Yankees are no longer to be ridiculed, much less despised. The new world is bursting into greatness—walking past the old world, as the America did the yachts at Cowes. . . . America, in her own phrase, is 'going a-head,' and will assuredly pass us, unless we accelerate our speed.

Generally, the spirit which prevailed before and after the famous race was that splendid evidence of an age-old civilization universally known as British courtesy. Commodore Stevens, and Colonel Hamilton in particular, frequently commented on the "wonderful hospitality" accorded them. (Both were men of culture, with broad interests and associations, and they inspired the friendliness they met.) Lord Palmerston, then Foreign Secretary, had promptly ordered that the *America* be treated at all ports as a British yacht and had made the customs free to her. The owners and Colonel Hamilton had been elected honorary members of the Royal Yacht Squadron almost upon arrival. Speaking of the "manly spirit with which they accepted their defeat," Hamilton went on to say:

Their expressions of congratulation to us were in the most remarkable spirit; so much was this so, that I remarked to a lady, "Your friends do not seem to feel any mortification or even dissatisfaction at their defeat." "Oh!" said she, "if you could hear what I do, you would know that they feel it most deeply."

One of the delicate matters which had seriously disturbed Commodore Stevens and Captain Brown was the selection of a pilot for the difficult local waters. The American consul at Southampton found one, Underwood. Intimations from various quarters, though chiefly by Americans on the scene, cautioned Stevens about placing faith in Underwood and advised that a second pilot be engaged to oversee him. A communication from the British admiral commanding at Portsmouth, who must have been aware of the difficulty, offered to provide

34

an experienced man "for whose fidelity he would be responsible." But the generous offer was promptly declined. By then
Stevens and Brown (too canny in such matters to be deceived)
had developed full faith in Underwood's reliability. Hamilton later paid warm tribute to the decent man who took the
America on the tricky course around the Isle.

Despite the care taken of the *America,* she touched bottom
and lost her false keel while at anchor on the day preceding
her race with the *Titania.* An urgent request for assistance
was made to the admiral at Portsmouth. As a result she was
taken into the Navy yard there. The admiral ordered that
precedence be given to the needed repair. Commodore Stevens later spoke with enthusiasm of the "vigor and good will
exhibited, from the admiral down to the humblest mechanic"
in replacing the shoe. The job was perfectly and speedily
done. When, quite naturally, Stevens tried to pay for the work
his offer was courteously declined.

The day after the regatta of the twenty-second it was indicated to Stevens and Hamilton that if the *America* would
drop down off Osborne House, the Queen, the Prince Consort, and their party would visit them on board. When they
came, Colonel Hamilton was impressed with Her Majesty's
graciousness and informality. She made some intelligent inquiries about the stowing of ballast and went over the galley
with keen interest. At one point she showed herself completely at home when, with an understandable housewifely
impulse, she touched a dainty handkerchief to a shelf to re-
move a spot of dust. There was no dust. Thereupon she
beamed on the cook, who beamed on the Queen. Captain
Brown had tried to go into hiding, but he was ordered forth
and, bowing awkwardly, presented. Not long after the visit
he received a gold pocket compass from the Queen with a
note from her. She knew, it said, he would keep it as bright
as he did the *America.*

As a result of the visit there was a small addition to American folklore, a tale found in various works. It was told as fact that Captain Brown "ordered" the Prince Consort to clean off his boots on the cockpit mat before descending the main companionway. The boots of the Prince, it seems, were muddy. At the demand the royal visitor paused, startled. "I know who you are, sir," Dick Brown is supposed to have said, with mingled respect and authority, "but you'll have to wipe your boots." The story was, of course, a libel on the Prince's bootboy, his valet, the Prince—and on Captain Brown. It seems to have been devised by some Yankee romancer. It clearly came out of a patriotic though exaggerated notion to show that good, solid democrats among Americans knew how to deal with British royalty.

At the time repairs were being made to her damaged shoe in the Portsmouth Navy yard, the *America* was the center of hundreds of curious eyes. The admiral there, in response to numerous requests, asked Commodore Stevens if her lines could be taken. Stevens replied that he "considered the lines and model of the yacht to be the property of her builder and that he did not feel at liberty to permit them to be copied." Thereupon the admiral ordered that none under his command take advantage of the opportunity. (Later naval architects and historians were to regard Stevens' decision as unfortunate.)

Among the hundreds who watched the *America* being hauled out on a wet day and who studied her as well as they could were some highly curious yachtsmen and naval architects. One of the current rumors (which helped to salve some British feelings) was that a cunningly concealed propeller was responsible for her exceptional speed. The suspicious were reminded that the Stevens family were inventors of steamboat mechanisms and that the commodore himself was highly experienced as a boat designer and builder.

In relation to the rumor Hamilton noted in his *Reminiscences:*

Our crew amused themselves by saying to the boatmen, who came alongside with visitors (there were thousands, as people of all classes were permitted to examine the vessel): "In the stern sheets, under the gangway, there is a grating which the Commodore does not allow any person to open." And, indeed [the opinion that a propeller existed] was entertained by persons not of the lower classes alone.

James Steers, who had been invited on the famous cutter *Pearl,* heard expression given to the absurd belief. His host was Sir Henry William Paget, first Marquis of Angelsey, known as "the father of British yachting." Sir Henry was a remarkable old man who, despite the loss of a leg at Waterloo, was still an ardent sailor at 83. On a day of puffs the *America,* without foresail, ran past the limping *Pearl.* This was too much for her helmsman, who, ignoring Steers or forgetting his presence, remarked, "Your lordship knows no vessel with sails alone could do that."

The *America* found a soft spot and eased up. "Now," said the man at the wheel, "it is stopped." A puff sent the *America* skipping along. "Now it is going," the helmsman reported bitterly. James Steers went hurriedly forward to inspect the bowsprit. It would have been bad taste to break into loud laughter while at his host's side.

With both vessels back at anchor the Marquis ordered his gig and approached the *America.* Might he come on board? Permission granted, the old man murmured his greeting to Stevens and then went as hastily aft as a one-legged man can move. Stevens went with him, and just as well. For in his determined search for some secret propelling mechanism under the transom, the Marquis nearly went overboard. Stevens seized his guest, fortunately by his good leg, just in time to prevent an international incident.

37

3

OF

SHIPS

AND CUPS

Before the end of August there seemed to be no good reason why the *America*'s owners should stay in Cowes. They had won the race against the *Titania*. It was clear that there would be no more matches for cups or money. The *America* had better start for home before mid-September gales churned up the Atlantic. Captain Brown had the Queen's gift to show. Commodore Stevens had the Cup—and £100 winnings to share with the four other owners. No one in the *America*'s party expressed any particular interest in or enthusiasm about the Cup. It was just a little souvenir they had picked up in Cowes.

George and James Steers had not waited for the Cup race on August 22. (The former was eager to return to the States. He had several profitable contracts from British yachtsmen to build them schooners on the *America*'s model.) Before the great race the Steers brothers and Commodore Stevens barely nodded in passing. In the diary which continued the log of the Atlantic passage, James wrote, "I am much dissatisfied with Old Stevens . . . a damned old hog, bristles and all." While still at Le Havre he noted that "we have had to sleep on shore ever since we have been here. . . . He has not even asked us to take a drink since he came on board, but we take about two bottles every day."

Both brothers obviously enjoyed social drinking. One entry records that James did not feel well: "Nothing to drink all day." It may have been the Demon Rum which came between them and the commodore. James reported that the steward used to see "Old Pig" seated on the cabin floor at night, in his shirt tails, counting the bottles. "Where the hell does my liquor go to?" he would roar. The steward reminded him that "Messrs. Steers take some when they want any." Stevens was annoyed to discover that they, too, had a key to the liquor cabinet. He did not, however, speak to them about it. "If he does," James noted, "he will get hell or something worse."

The diarist wrote down that he thought "Johnny was very stingy." When George Steers told the commodore they were leaving, James told him "what he thought of him." (Just what he said is, unfortunately, not recorded. It must have been colorful.) The brothers engaged passage on the *Atlantic,* which sailed from Liverpool on August 20. Captain Brown urged them to stay, but in vain. When he went ashore with them at Cowes to have a parting drink, "he looked as though he had lost all his friends."

It has been stated that the Steers brothers had left their employment and business to take the voyage on the *America* at their own expense. This would, in part, explain their attitude to Stevens. It does suggest that the commodore could well have been more generous.

When it was learned that Stevens and his company were

making ready to return home, the Honorable (later Lord) John de Blaquière made an offer of £5,000 for the *America*. Several other offers had been made within the preceding few days. As that of De Blaquière was the best, it was promptly accepted. The total expenses of the invasion of Britain, according to the reckoning of Colonel Hamilton, had come to £750. There was, therefore, a little profit for the *America*'s owners. Stevens suffered a loss. The Bingham Madeira was still on board. When, in New York, he learned from his wife where she had stowed it, Stevens wrote the new owner, making him a gift of it. He could not refrain, however, from remarking on the pricelessness of the gift.

It could not have been easy to leave the *America* in the hands of a stranger. In a career of less than three months she had made history and made her name unforgettable. Captain Brown particularly must have hated the moment of parting. All who sailed on her drank a toast on her deck, as to something living, and then went home.

In the English *Yacht List* of 1851 was the statement that "Yacht building was an art in which England was unrivalled and that she was distinguished preeminently and alone for the perfection of science" in sailing. The comment was not to be repeated immediately. English yards were busy, from September on, converting yachts to conform to the *America*'s bow. Owners were convinced that that change alone would improve the speed of their craft. In almost every instance the revisions were exaggerated or useless. The consequent crop of hybrids and abortions was to plague their owners for years.

It may have been news of these alterations which gave credence to the rumor that the *America*'s new owner had reduced her raking masts and made other changes. Americans, who had abandoned all but sentimental rights in her, were annoyed. They were consoled when a guest on board,

Colonel John Winthrop of New Orleans, saw her in 1852. "She remains," he reported in a letter to the press, *"precisely as Lord de Blaquière purchased her,* in rig, sails, trim, hull, interior fittings-up . . . even to the very paint. . . . Her beautiful carved eagle still adorns her stern." She had been entered in a few races, winning some, losing once to the iron cutter, *Mosquito,* and had ridden out a savage Mediterranean gale without the slightest damage. It was a storm which had driven some of the British Navy aground.

The *America* was to turn up again, unexpectedly, in her native waters. Before that she was sold again, in 1856, to Viscount Templetown, who named her *Camilla.* He seemed to have little regard for her, for around 1858 she was run onto the mud flats in Cowes and laid up. She might very well have ended her career there. But in 1859 a yard owner, Henry Pitcher, bought her for junk. She was tightened and towed to the Pitcher yard at Northfleet near Gravesend on the Thames. There she was nursed back to health after surgery on her dry rot. In her revised state she had new oak frames, teak and elm planking. A yachtsman, Henry E. Decie, bought her in 1860. The builder's certificate when she was sold showed variations in over-all and keel length.* What happened to her later will be told where it belongs.

In his speech to fellow club members at the Astor House testimonial dinner October 1, 1851, Stevens spoke briefly of the *America's* victory. During his talk he said, "I am requested, by the gentleman owning this cup, to beg your acceptance of it as a testimony of their gratitude for the interest you have so keenly felt, and so often and kindly expressed." No one seems to know why there was no acceptance there and

* In an advertisement, 1858, of the *America* for sale the "length between perpendiculars" was given as 93′ 6″; over all, 102′.

then. In any event the club members seem to have forgotten that the offer had been made.

For a while the Cup adorned a mantel in Stevens' home in New York's Washington Square. From time to time it was polished and it acquired an extra gloss from frequent handling by Stevens' guests. They found it an ornament of curious design, with elaborate decorations of scrolls, panels and shields. A ewer in outward form, it was not serviceable as a pitcher or cup, for it had no bottom in its base. It had been ordered in 1851 by the Royal Yacht Squadron from the well-known firm of R. and S. Gerard, silversmiths of London. The silver content of the 27-inch high, 134-ounce Cup was a trade secret of its makers. There was nothing about the trophy to indicate that it was just one of the standard prizes annually offered by the Royal Yacht Squadron.

After all his visitors had heard the story of the great victory, perhaps several times, Stevens must have felt it was up to other syndicate members to take the thing and play narrator. The Cup thereupon took up residence in a succession of private homes. There seemed to be doubt about what should be done with it. Someone in the family of a syndicate member suggested that it be taken to a silversmith and converted into medallions. These would be appropriately engraved with an inscription of the *America*'s victory. They would make simply lovely heirlooms and something for grandchildren to show with pride.

Before anyone became committed to this barbarian notion, George Schuyler devised a letter presenting the Cup to the New York Yacht Club. A meeting of syndicate members was called. All were present except Wilkes, who was dying abroad; a friend with power of attorney represented him. After a few changes the draft was agreed to, rewritten, and signed by and for the five former owners of the *America*. That was May 1852. Curiously, Stevens forgot to send it off. Because of his

42

forgetfulness, as Schuyler explained later, "there was no record on the minutes of the gift or its acceptance."

Apparently, on the first leg of the journey to its new home, the Cup went to the residence of Nathaniel Bloodgood, later recording secretary of the club. As he was only its temporary custodian, he tucked it out of the way, hidden by a pile of books. Some time later, on a clean-up expedition, Bloodgood's sister, Maria, uncovered the relic. Just what she said about that dust catcher is not recorded in the archives. But whatever she said was effective; Bloodgood saw his duty and convoyed the Cup to the club. John Cox Stevens had died on June 10, 1857. When it was learned that the letter written five years earlier had never reached the club, the conveyance was dated July 8, 1857. It was this letter which became known as "the original deed of gift."

No document in the annals of sports was to become better known, to be more often revised or to arouse greater controversy. "Any organized Yacht Club of any foreign country," it stated, "shall always be entitled, through any one or more of its members, to claim the right of sailing a match for this Cup." The terms for races were elastic; arrangements for matches would be by mutual consent. A challenger was to state the customs-house tonnage of his yacht (boats had to measure 30 to 300 tons), its length (probably on deck), rig and name, and give advance notice of six months.

It is to be distinctly understood that the Cup is to be the property of the Club, and not of the members thereof, or owners of the vessels winning it in a match. [The conditions in the deed] shall forever attach to it, thus making it perpetually a Challenge Cup for friendly competition between foreign countries.

A little north of rocky Castle Point, Hoboken, were grounds frequented by picnickers from New York City. The site was known as the Elysian Fields, a designation derived

43

from the old Greeks, who reserved it for the place inhabited by the favored and contented among the dead. The name would have been a most inappropriate one for a spot where live people consorted and sported and piled up picnic debris, had it not come to mean any place where happiness was complete.

On his property in these grounds Commodore Stevens had set aside land for a little house which became the first home (1846) of the New York Yacht Club. In this spot of complete happiness the Cup was accepted with due ceremonies. Then the club secretary wrote to all listed foreign yacht clubs that it had taken possession of the Cup and suggested "spirited contest for the [sailing] championship." The recipients were assured that they could depend upon "a liberal, hearty welcome, and the strictest fair play."

This was not the first time the club had invited a challenge. In February 1853 it had told the yachting world that a prize worth $500 would be raced for in New York waters. There were no takers. Nor was there any other response beyond some acknowledgments to the notice sent out in 1857. For a little while the Cup was on display for club members. Then it went into Tiffany's vaults. The Civil War and some other momentous matters were to keep it out of sight.

On one of the panels which the Cup's makers had thoughtfully provided, the first historical notice was inscribed. This, it read, was the "100 Guinea Cup won . . . at Cowes . . . at the Royal Yacht Squadron regatta 'Open to all Nations.' " It was presented to the club as a Challenge Cup Open to all Foreign Clubs. The donors' names (the five owners of the *America*) are listed. The *America,* it is stated, had been built by George Steers. (He had died in 1856.) There were some curious omissions. That sportsman among builders of yachts, William Brown, is not mentioned. And in the list of yachts which the *America* "beat," the gallant little *Aurora* is ex-

44

cluded. Yet the Duke of Marlborough's schooner, *Wyvern*, is included. That boat had less right to be remembered than many of the others. For "staggering about in the rear," as reported by a contemporary, "she had hauled her wind" and had gone ignominiously home.

A dozen years after the Cup had been officially placed with the New York Yacht Club, interest in Anglo-American yachting competition was renewed. There had been a number of American racers in England in the early fifties. The *Truant*, a small centerboarder shipped over on a steamer's deck in 1852, won seven of the eight races in which she was entered. Under a later local ruling that centerboarders could race only with others of the type, she found herself alone, the only one with a movable keel in British waters.

The *Sylvie*, built by Steers at the same time as the *America* (mistakenly called by some a "twin" of the Cup winner though she was a centerboard sloop), appeared at Cowes in August 1853, ready to compete for high stakes. In her most important race, when the wind was light, she came in second. In 1854 the Royal Yacht Squadron excluded boats with "shifting keels" from matches with any of its fleet.

The defeat of the *Sylvie* gave some consolation to British yachtsmen, but the real revival of interest in competing with Americans began because of a quite mad ocean race from New York to Cowes. The year was 1866. It was the first transatlantic race. It had come about when the owners of two good-sized schooners, the *Vesta* and the *Fleetwing*, over an extra glass or two of port, were loudly arguing the merits of their boats. A match was arranged, $30,000 a side, for immediate "play or pay." When James Gordon Bennett (not long thereafter a commodore of the New York Yacht Club) heard of it, he insisted on entering his clipper, the *Henrietta*. That brought the stake to $90,000. Crews were found, the

45

boats made ready, and the race started in, of all months, December.

Of this "foolhardy affair" a modern commentator made the casual remark "that they got away with it, with the loss of but six seamen, washed overboard at night from the *Fleet-wing.*" The *Henrietta* arrived at Cowes first, about fourteen days after her start. In England the wide publicity given to this race was accompanied with reminders that Americans had actually taken a trophy away from the British. The reminder nettled readers. Someone, it was generally agreed, ought to do something about it.

In the fifteen years since the *America*'s victory there had been improvements in British yachts. They were faster and they had some new, experimental sails. Among them was the spinnaker, a triangular piece of canvas set on the side opposite the fore- or mainsail with a fair wind. It first appeared in 1866 on the *Sphinx* ("Spinx" to her hands, who dubbed the new sail "Spinxer"). British yachtsmen were now more confident about meeting any foreign challenge. But they were not quite ready yet to cross over to where the Cup reposed.

Not long after the *Henrietta*'s victory the biggest of American yachts, the 310-ton *Sappho,* slid off the ways of a Brooklyn yard. Her model had been whittled out by an ordinary mechanic, William Townsend, a foreman in Poillon's yard. She was not perfect but she was surprisingly fast, at least in American waters. Messrs. Poillon had built her on the gambling chance that she would win whatever wagers were placed on her in foreign waters. Such a vessel could then be easily and profitably sold.

That was not the way it worked out. When she raced on the *America*'s course around the Isle of Wight there were four schooners ahead of her at the finish. Just why the *Sappho* went into the race under her cruising rig and with the stone ballast she had carried across the Atlantic only her skipper knew. He should have been much less self-assured. Perhaps it was just as well. It needed just such an event as her defeat to inspire someone to invade America and try to bring back that tantalizing Cup.

The inspired was James Ashbury, owner of the schooner *Cambria,* newly built by Ratsey at Cowes. She had won the race in which the *Sappho,* "the clipper of them all," had entered. If this was the best the Americans had, why then the 100-Guinea Cup was as good as home again.

It was not that England lacked cups. The Isles were studded with trophies. But *that* Cup in New York was a provocation, an irritant to every Englishman expected to do his duty. The yachtsman who wrested it from the Yankees would sit forever in the British hall of fame. That Ashbury had some such thoughts in mind was revealed during his elaborate correspondence with the New York Yacht Club and his later actions. And, as remarked by that sprightly, admirable writer on yachting matters, Alfred F. Loomis, "England's approach to sportsmanship and her attitude toward America (then) both bordered on the bellicose." But, for that matter, the American sporting ethics of the day were not such as to win admiration from fair-minded yachtsmen.

4

STORMY

WEATHER

In October 1868 Ashbury began a correspondence with the New York Yacht Club which was to become protracted. It began with a number of proposals: The club should send over its fastest schooner, though one which would not exceed by ten per cent the *Cambria*'s measurement (188 tons by Thames reckoning); enter her in the 1869 Ryde or Cowes regattas, and then race the *Cambria* back to New York for a prize, say a service of silver or a cup valued at £250. The club should then hold three races around Long Island. If Ashbury's yacht won two, he would be entitled to the "America's Queen's Cup of 1851." (Ashbury just had to get that "Queen's" in there but some Americans, too, so misnamed it.) He went on to say that he would decline a challenge if a contesting boat were built subsequent to his letter. Further, he
48

would not participate in a race unless the club's choice was "a seagoing vessel, not a mere shell or racing machine."

That was about all. Americans wanted a challenge for the Cup. Well, here it was. What it really meant was that one of Mother Carey's chickens had appeared on the horizon.

The club took little time in saying "No!" They reminded Ashbury that they held the Cup in trust under terms devised by its donors. Only yacht clubs could challenge for that trophy, not individuals. After a series of letters that ran for several months Ashbury made a concession: he would represent the Royal Thames Yacht Club. This was followed by a cable in which he asked if the "*Cambria* would now be allowed to sail your champion schooner." Most of Ashbury's proposals had been ignored till then. To this direct request the club committee replied with some indirection. It did make it clear, though, that after "the necessary preliminaries have been complied with upon your arrival here" the *Cambria* would have the whole club fleet as competitors. By that time the 1869 racing season had ended.

The New York Yacht Club was not praised for its attitude. Conceded, Ashbury was self-important and demanding. Yet it was generally thought that the club had been unnecessarily stiff and had depended too literally on the letter of the deed. After all, the Cup had been placed with the club to invite contests. Something should have been arranged. Furthermore, as was pointed out then and later, the *America*'s race was an open one. It was not against a club's selected fleet acting as a unit but a contest with yachts in which each entrant was competing for the trophy individually. That generous sportsman, Commodore Stevens, it was remarked, would have opposed a mass defense of the Cup. The club committees must have been puzzled over this noisy aftermath of Ashbury's challenge. They did not, however, defend themselves publicly or deviate from their decisions. It was to take time

49

to set a club course through the hazards of public opinion.

Ashbury, the stubborn man, was on the scene again early in 1870—with a letter. The *Cambria's* compass pointed only to the magnetic Cup. The *Dauntless,* James Gordon Bennett's schooner and a prize-winning racer, was in English waters. A transatlantic match between the two vessels had been arranged, to start sometime in March. Would the New York Yacht Club agree to a race for the Cup in May, out in blue water?

If that could be agreed upon, it was to be understood that the club must match the *Cambria* only with fixed-keel boats. A rule of the Royal Yacht Squadron, to which Ashbury referred, excluded yachts with "shifting keels." (Centerboarders were common in the shoal waters of New York Harbor, then the hub of American yachting. Lighter vessels could be constructed with a movable keel, and such a device, when lifted, considerably increased speed when running free. With the board down, leeway was much reduced.)

Well, said the regatta committee in a friendly reply, it is good to know of Mr. Ashbury's continued interest in "the challenge Cup won by the *America.*" But look, it isn't really our Cup. We are only its trustees and it would be most improper to violate any condition of its terms or to bar from a Cup race any member yacht suitable for defense. As Mr. Ashbury is coming over anyhow, wouldn't he call, join us in a glass or two of port and have a chat?

Ashbury could hardly say no to that. The match with the *Dauntless* was fixed anyhow and, in preparation for that great trial, the *Cambria* had gone into several races. The *Sappho* turned up again. She had been "hipped" in an American yard. This widening below her waterline had improved her speed and she won twice against the *Cambria.* That did not alter Ashbury's plans. He felt committed now to race for the Cup though no terms had yet been agreed upon.

It was not until July 4, 1870, that the *Dauntless* was ready for the transatlantic run. She was, concededly, speedier than the *Cambria*. Yet it was the latter which won by 1 hour 43 minutes on a northern course eleven miles longer than that taken by the *Dauntless* to the south. The *Cambria*'s run was 2,994 miles and it took her 23 days, 5 hours, and 17 minutes.

New York yachtsmen had been in a quiver over the race. They had posted a man at Sandy Hook to telegraph the news to the city, from the station at the Hook, as soon as a schooner yacht's topsails were sighted. The announcement came to the clubs and news offices at last. Then everyone in town who could get away sailed or steamed out to the Hook to greet the *Dauntless*. When the *Cambria* came rolling in first, "majestic with her swelling sails," the shock was intense. The spectators forgot their manners; she sailed past a crowd held in gloomy silence. It was a thoughtful fleet that went home. If the *Dauntless,* fastest of ocean racers, had been beaten, the Cup was as good as lost.

If anything had been needed to bolster Ashbury's spirit, his victory over the *Dauntless* would have done it. But it had not been needed; the challenger was by nature a determined sea wrangler. In prompt discussion with the club's committee, he again demanded that centerboarders be excluded. His argument was fair. Why should the committee insist on anything so unreasonable, asked he, as matching "skimming-dishes" against a deep-keel craft heavy enough to cross the Atlantic? The discussion over that and other conditions of the race became heated.

On a vote of eighteen to one the committees involved in the affair had decided that any of the club's fleet could participate. Ashbury was thereupon presented with an ultimatum: there would be a single race on the club's regular inside course, and against any or all boats the committee designated—or no match. Ashbury chewed on this briefly.

51

Stubbornness, he decided, was no longer useful to him; he accepted the conditions.

The date for the first English challenge match was to be August 8. When the day came some parts of New York were deserted. The exchanges were closed and their members and those of most clubs, waterborne, joined the huge press of sightseers that hovered near the starting line or anchored at strategic spots. The shores were crowded with restless spectators. Twenty-three schooners, chiefly centerboarders, were entered. (Only fifteen reached the finish line.) Among the entrants was the *America* (now United States Navy property, as will be shortly explained), handled by midshipmen. She was on the line because of public sentiment that she be there.

The club had taken up residence at Clifton, Staten Island, in 1865, and the start was from a line near its headquarters. The course was laid from Robbins Reef through the Narrows to Southwest Spit Buoy, around Sandy Hook Lightship and back—a distance of over 32 to over 35 nautical miles.* (This was the club's famous "inside course," shifted from its original start off the first clubhouse anchorage at Weehawken.) It had everything: strong currents, sand banks, and traffic indifferent to racing yachts. "No fair and equitable trial," wrote William P. Stephens, "could be possible on either the Royal Yacht Squadron (around the Isle of Wight) or the New York Yacht Club courses."

A neighbor to the *America,* the *Cambria* had been given a courtesy position at the windward end of the line. The start was to be from anchor. A little before the signal there was an abrupt shift in wind—and the challenger was unenviably to leeward. It did seem like a bit of Yankee skulduggery! The

---

* According to the list of Cup matches published by the New York Yacht Club, though, one entry is "40 miles." Contemporary accounts indicate, however, that the inside course was usually 38 miles.

Cambria passing Sandy Hook lightship, winning the ocean race against *Dauntless,* July 27, 1870. *From a drawing by W. G. Wood after an original painting owned by the Royal Harwich Yacht Club.*

"The Race for the Queen's Cup," drawn by Charles Parsons for *Harper's Weekly*, August 1870. *Magic*, with everything aloft, is leading the fleet; *America* is the third boat aft; *Cambria* is the last of those heading for the lightship.

Columbia, with *Livonia* on a stern chase, running home up New York Bay.

From a drawing by L. A. Shafer, 1899.

W G WOOD.

Sappho about to pass through Livonia's lee in the fourth challenge race of 1871. From a water color by W. G. Wood.

club representative in charge of arrangements hastily reached the *Cambria* to ask Ashbury if he wished to change her position. The challenger thought he had better not. Who knew that there would not be another shift of wind?

The *Cambria* had a veteran crew, and despite her leeward position they got her away quickly at the signal. But they were not as fast as the *Magic,* a 92.2-ton centerboard schooner owned by Franklin Osgood. (She was spry for her age, having been born a sloop in 1857 from the plans of R. F. Loper. In 1869 she was practically rebuilt.) She won the start—and never gave it up. Last to leave was the *America.* She had done that nineteen years earlier, at Cowes, when she won the Cup. Perhaps it was just her style.

There was quite a fleet crowding the *Cambria,* but she rid herself of a number of them by the time she reached the lightship. She made a serious tactical error, however, by going too far toward Coney Island. As the current had turned, it took the *Cambria* on her weather bow and set her off her course. Furthermore, stated the *Spirit of the Times* in reporting on "The Great International Regatta. Race for the Queen's Cup":

She also incurred a little delay by being fouled by Tarolinta *which, being on the starboard tack ought to have kept away from her, by the rules, when she could not go to windward of her. Some think her head gear was a little damaged in this foul, and that the carrying away of her foretopmast (later) was the result of it.*

The loss of her spar had occurred when, about to jibe before running for home, the *Cambria* heeled under an unexpected puff. Had the loss not occurred she would still have been too late. She was clocked eighth at the finish line, tenth under her time penalty of 2 minutes, 41.9 seconds. The *Magic,* which came in first, had an unneeded allowance of over 9 minutes.

Captain Ronald Coffin, the top yachting commentator of the day, who had an intimate knowledge of the *Cambria,* praised the challenger as an exceptionally good yacht but he thought her rig clumsy. She had put up a fine performance; her misfortunes came from being to leeward at the start, in being caught in an unfavorable current, in being fouled, and in losing her topmast.

The question of the attributed foul was long a matter of dispute. Ashbury did talk about it, in England, but he made no direct protest to the New York Yacht Club at the time. That cast doubt as to whether the *Tarolinta* had really been at fault. Had Ashbury felt the right to do so, it was in character for him to have set up a howl. British yachtsmen, violently Ashbury partisans, made much of the published opinion that there had been a foul. They continued to bring up the subject for years thereafter as proof of poor sportsmanship by American yachtsmen.

The *America,* fourth at the finish, came in for criticism. She was 17 minutes elapsed (25 minutes, 20 seconds corrected) time behind the *Magic.* Out of sheer sentiment, it had been expected of her that she would make a brilliant showing, perhaps lead the fleet again. This excessive optimism showed ignorance or forgetfulness of her history subsequent to 1860.

After Decie had bought her, he sailed her as a yacht for a brief period. She appeared rather suddenly at Savannah in 1861. There was a rumor that she had taken some Confederate agents to and from England. That may have been. What was clear is that she had joined the Confederate Navy around that time and, under the name *Memphis,* ran the Federal blockade. She finally found herself in trouble; there was probably an enemy gunboat on her tail. Whatever the reason, her crew bored holes in her hull and sank her in the St. Johns River, some distance above Jacksonville, Florida. During a reconnaissance in that area, Lieutenant (later Rear Admiral)

Thomas H. Stevens, commander of the Federal gunboat *Ottawa*, was told by a native where a sunken ship lay. It seems highly appropriate that a Stevens, though unrelated to one of her original owners, should have found the *America*. He could have claimed prize money when he had her raised but relinquished his rights when it was decided that she should be commissioned.

They gave her back her famous name and she put to sea again. She was still fast, fast enough to bring some blockade runners in to Navy docks. In 1864 she went to Newport, Rhode Island, where she was used to train midshipmen. Then she was stationed at Annapolis. With the war out of the way, it was decided to refit her as a yacht, a sentiment which had enthusiastic public approval. By the time she had been restored to her former status and almost her original appearance, the final bill was nearly her original cost. No one objected; she was the darling of the many yachts on the Atlantic Coast.

Her performance in the first challenge contest for the Cup, her vicissitudes and her ten-year withdrawal from racing considered, was excellent. Her commander, appropriately enough, was the son of that Dick Brown who had sailed her to victory around the Isle of Wight. There were many who, after the *Cambria* match, took pot shots at the Navy for the manner in which the *America* was handled by midshipmen, her rig, and her delayed start. They were promptly answered with return fire from Navy personnel. Said one, the critics' "pretensions" that they were better sailors than a man-of-war's men

are as ludicrous as the piratical, swashbuckling, and sea-doggy airs some of these same harbor-hugging mariners love to assume

—a translation into reasonable English of what he really thought.

55

For more than a month after the regatta the *Cambria* participated in various races and cruises in American waters. There was nothing wrong with her hull, and as a contender she showed good fighting spirit. Ashbury donated several cups and acquired a number, though the *Cambria* was not too frequently a winner. The pioneer Cup challenger seemed more agreeable on closer view and he was accepted as a good sportsman. President Grant thought so; he was a breakfast guest on the *Cambria*. It seemed as though an *entente cordiale* had been firmly established.

But back in England Ashbury told whoever would listen —and apparently everyone would—that he had participated in the first challenge regatta "for sport and with faint hope of winning." He had gone into the race because he had been conveniently on the spot. Still bewitched by the Cup, however, and his role as England's champion, he had Ratsey produce a new schooner for him. She was much larger than the *Cambria,* being registered under Thames measurement at 280 tons and for racing at 264 tons. With an over-all length of 126′ her waterline was 107′. Her name was *Livonia.* One would have thought, at first appearance, that she was American-built. The best features of the fastest Yankee schooners had been incorporated in her. The cut of her jib was enough, however, to show where she had been born. She had the "greatest sail spread"—over 18,000 square feet—"ever carried by a challenger for the Cup."

Convinced that he had a winner, Ashbury asked if the New York Yacht Club would agree to a match between the *Livonia* and a single defender. He had consulted learned counsel and, apparently on their advice, he stressed the significance of the word "match" in the deed of gift. Some hint of what was coming had been indicated in an Ashbury communication at the end of January 1871. If the club should rule as before, he stated, then the *Livonia* would sail over the

56

course alone and take or claim the prize. If any doubt arose over "legality of the claim then [it will be] for the New York judges to determine upon the legal construction of the deed referred to." After the January letter the belligerence of this born litigant was eliminated from the correspondence with the club. It ran so long, however, that Ashbury asked that the required advance notice of six months be set aside. After a little wavering, the club waived.

Legal advisors on both sides of the Atlantic were in disagreement as to just what "match," as in the deed of gift, really meant. Several judges, attorneys and eminent sportsmen were consulted by the New York Yacht Club. In this impasse the only surviving Cup donor, George Schuyler, was asked to interpret what had been intended. His opinion was published in a letter of unusual interest in the *Spirit of the Times,* the foremost sporting journal in New York in that period.

Part of Schuyler's forthright comments read:

I think any candid person will admit that when the owners of the America *sat down to write their letter of gift to the New York Yacht Club, they could hardly be expected to dwell upon an elaborate definition of their interpretation of the word "match" as distinguished from a sweepstakes or a regatta; nor would he think it very likely that any contestant for the Cup, upon conditions named by them, should be subjected to a trial such as they themselves had considered unfair and unsportsmanlike.*

It seems to me that the present ruling of the club renders the America's *trophy useless as "a Challenge Cup," and that for all sporting purposes it might as well be laid aside as family plate. I cannot conceive of any yachtsman giving six months' notice that he will cross the ocean for the sole purpose of entering into an almost hopeless contest for this Cup, when a challenge for love or money to meet any one yacht of the New York Yacht Squadron in any fair race would give him as great a triumph, if successful. . . .*

57

To make quite certain that his basic opinion was not lost sight of, he went on to explain that, as he saw it, a match involved only two parties to a contest. Add one more and the affair became a "sweepstakes."

During the earlier course of the debate by letter between Ashbury and the club's committees it did seem as if a suit at law would have to settle the issue. Ashbury was to say later, "I had no thought of being guided by court legal decisions," but the spirit of litigation hovered over the entire issue. Schuyler's letter brought the controversy to an end. The club was, confessedly, not overjoyed at his opinion. Very well, they would match boat for boat but the defender would be one of four ready to race. The general idea, though unexpressed, was that a light-weather centerboarder would go in when conditions required a heavy-weather boat if it were needed. This may not have been exactly what the club members had in mind when they unanimously accepted a resolution to match vessel with vessel. But it was what the Cup and regatta committees thought should be the arrangement.

Originally, Ashbury had challenged on behalf of the Royal Harwich Yacht Club, of which he was commodore. By the middle of June he wrote to say that when he entered the match for the Cup he would represent twelve yacht clubs, all members of the Royal Yacht Squadron. He thoughtfully provided a list of them; two were Irish clubs. He wanted twelve races, one for each club. The Cup was to go to the club under whose burgee he won the seventh race—if he won seven. This was Ashbury being imaginatively egotistic rather than cunning.

For some reason not quite clear the club committees hit the topmast. (After all, it could hardly have made any difference if Ashbury had run up a different banner for each of twelve races. In the first match the club had piled on him en masse; he was now responding with a mass representation of clubs.)

It would have been a violation of yachting protocol if the
regatta committee had then written to Ashbury the opinion
they and the membership generally held of him. No wonder
the man, despite his great wealth, had never made some of the
most exclusive English clubs. No gentleman he, but a schem-
ing troublemaker. So they said, in more vigorous English.
Someone pointed out that Ashbury was taking publicity advantage of a situation in thus challenging for the Cup, that it
was done to further his candidacy as a Member of Parliament
from Harwich. (He was elected.)

A challenge had, however, been accepted. There had, therefore, to be an answer to this British nuisance. The sense of
the reply to Ashbury's announcement was that the club was
agreeable to a series of twelve races but only against a yacht
which represented the Royal Harwich Yacht Club. Ashbury
was asked to remember hereafter that the "deed of gift carefully guards against such sharp practice" as lay in his proposal. As Ashbury had already left England the reply was
held until his arrival.

The *Livonia* came to anchor in New York Harbor on
October 1 after some heavy going. While she was hove to in
mid-Atlantic a gale tore away her foreboom and bowsprit.
She was stout, though, and her hull showed no strain. In a
style which was distinctly his own, just before he received
the committee's decision in his New York hotel, Ashbury
had sent them a letter. It began:

*My ultimatum is that all 12 races must be sailed, not only as
a matter of right, but as I think, as an act of courtesy and consideration to me; seeing that the masts of* Livonia *were reduced
to cross the Atlantic, as yet the sails are unbent, the trim of the
vessel as a consequence requires to be found, and it will take 4
or 5 races to get the* Livonia's *exact time.*

The challenger and the regatta committee warily avoided
a meeting until the possibilities of agreement, through a

59

series of ultimata and rejections, were exhausted. The final decision was that there would be seven races over alternate courses, and no restriction on a centerboard boat if the club decided to use one or more. Each arrangement was a heavily fought compromise, though over the centerboarder clause Ashbury had almost lost his power of speech. The courses were to be inside, through The Narrows to Sandy Hook Lightship, the others outside from the lightship for twenty miles to windward.

Everything was settled now except Ashbury. Almost as an afterthought and for no discernible reason, he decided that he would race under the burgee of the Royal Albert Yacht Club, of which the Duke of Edinburgh was commodore. That brought a prompt reply and in a vein Ashbury knew meant finality. He would enter either as the representative of the club whose challenge had been accepted or not at all. "It's becoming cold," said Ashbury, thoughtfully. "Let's get it over with."

On the day of the first race, October 16, 1871, there was only a hint of wind. The 220-ton centerboard *Columbia,* built by J. Van Deusen and owned by Franklin Osgood, was the defending schooner. She came home well ahead of the *Livonia.* Two days later the same yachts competed on the outside course. The race was to cause a rumpus. Just before the start, the *Columbia*'s captain inquired of the race committee whether the stake boat at the turn was to be left to starboard or to port. He was told that the choice was optional. As an uncertainty had been expressed by an American helmsman, assumedly familiar with local custom, the committee might reasonably have seen to it that the challenger's captain also was informed of the rule. It did not occur to anyone on the *Livonia* to ask for advice, as in English waters it was customary to leave a turning mark to starboard.

An hour or so after the start in soft air, it blew a moderate

60

gale. The *Columbia* had been put in, as she was a light-weather boat. On the committee tug the nervous members began to fret over their choice. When near the stake boat, the *Livonia* was slightly ahead to windward but the *Columbia* held the weather position. In order to keep the mark on her starboard the *Livonia* luffed across the *Columbia*'s bow and finally jibed around the stake boat. The challenger had her big sprit topsail aloft and the wind came in a puff at that moment. It was a dangerous tactic and one which could have brought the topmast on deck. The *Livonia*'s rearguard were too well seasoned to have conducted so risky a maneuver for fun. Had they thought it permissible to do so, they would have held their course and passed the mark to port.

What happened was that the *Livonia* got herself in the wind's eye and staggered far to leeward. It took all of four minutes to straighten her out. The *Columbia*, meanwhile, had taken a proper luff around the stake boat, 1 minute and 10 seconds after the *Livonia* passed it, and went home on a close reach with a bone in her teeth. She was 5 minutes, 16 seconds elapsed time ahead of the challenger at the finish; 10 minutes, 33¾ seconds corrected time.

Although the accuracy of the course was questioned then and later, for many years the *Columbia* held the assumed record for speed in Cup races. She had gone the distance (some think thirty miles, some more) in 3 hours, 1½ minutes. Both yachts had reached around the course. No one had expected a centerboard schooner to stand up so well in heavy weather. She had proved that her type, reported an observer, was "something more than a mere racing machine, fit only to win in smooth water and zephyr breezes."

Ashbury lost no time in demanding that the race be rerun or, if not, awarded to *Livonia* because the *Columbia* had not left the stake boat to starboard. He also insisted that the course was only thirty miles, not forty as agreed, and he had

61

other objections. His demand was rejected. Captain Roland Coffin, who had been on the *Columbia,* thought Ashbury's protest a proper and reasonable one and that it should have been granted. The press, on the whole, supported Ashbury. This added to the annoyance of the club's committee. Ashbury, it reported later, had used his objections as "the foundation of communications to them through the press, which were of a disagreeable character generally, threatening to appeal to tribunals unknown to this club for redress against what he deemed unjust treatment."

The general sentiment was expressed by the author of *American Yachts,* J. D. Jerrold Kelley:

It would have been better if [the committee] had accorded a visiting yachtsman, who had twice pluckily crossed the ocean, the benefit of the doubt which did, and does, exist, as to the fairness of this competition. Mr. Ashbury did not claim the victory then but asked for another race, and Messieurs, you should have given it to him.

Unfortunately he fell into the hands of the scribes, and there was a rattling newspaper skirmish all along the line which settled nothing. . . .

The defender in the third race (October 19) was to be the *Dauntless,* but she lost some of her headgear while being carelessly towed to her position. The *Columbia* was hastily drafted, though her captain had been partly disabled through an accident and her crew was recovering from a night's victory celebration. Enough men were shifted from other boats to man the *Columbia,* and her owner took the helm. It was not entirely unexpected that she found herself in trouble and, disabled, came limping home more than 19 minutes later than the *Livonia.* It was to be the only victory of a challenger for a long time.

The next two races, October 21 and 23, were between old

rivals, for the *Sappho,* then owned by William P. Douglass, carried the defense. In the first of these, described as "the grandest race of the season," the defender, even with her top-sails stowed, made such speed that her deck was awash most of the time. She lost a 12-foot boat, required by club regulations, when a sea washed it out of the cockpit. The *Sappho* won both races, beating the *Livonia* soundly. The press, which was now explaining that the *Columbia* had lost the third race because her crew was not in good condition, gave no consideration to the strained, tired British crew which faced a fresh one on the *Sappho.*

In a later-day comment Alfred Loomis remarked that

In one short year (since 1870) American sportsmanship had begun to emerge from its Paleozoic ooze [but] we reserved the right to select our defender from a string of four yachts of varying weatherly abilities. Ashbury, who had only the sole challenger for all weathers, failed to see the justice of this arrangement. He was prejudiced.

As five races had been run, said the New York Yacht Club, and the *Livonia* had lost four, the second Cup challenge match was over. Ashbury worked with a different set of figures. He now claimed the second race and had won the third. That meant three to two. He issued the last of his postmatch series of ultimata. He was taking the *Livonia* out to the starting line on the next two days for "races number 6 and 7." If there were no defender representing the club, he would claim the Cup by default.

"Well," said the various committees involved, in substance, "have fun. We're not coming to your party." The *Dauntless* was playing around the starting line when the *Livonia* came out. Together they went over the course but in a private match. The challenger lost. On the following day they planned to race again. There was, however, so heavy a sea

63

running that the *Livonia* parted from her anchor, and two men were washed out of the *Dauntless;* one of them was lost. No starting or stake boat would take her station. The match was called off. Ashbury considered, though, that he had been at the station to meet a defender and that the New York Yacht Club had defaulted. He would be obliged if the committee would now wrap up the Cup, to which he claimed "legal right," and deliver it to his hotel.

That demand resulted in the most deafening silence. Thereupon Ashbury went home, an aggrieved man. From his tight little isle he continued to pelt the club, for its "unfair and unsportsmanlike proceedings," and Yankee yachtsmen, who were "too cute" to be dealt with by British sportsmen, all of whom were gentlemen. If he ever went over again for the Cup, he would demand that "the law courts of New York . . . be required to express official judgment on the advice of eminent Queen's counsel, without whose favourable opinion as to my rights I should not have sailed."

Though Ashbury had now reached the silly stage in these proceedings, in the main, British sporting journals supported him in his attacks on "Yankee cunning." Yankee editors conducted a counteroffensive. By that time the New York Yacht Club felt that it could live quite happily without the yachting trophies Ashbury had presented it and they were returned as freight. Ashbury thereupon became a pamphleteer and a most indignant one. Following receipt of a bristling piece, the club indulged in an angry protest to the Royal Harwich Yacht Club under whose burgee Ashbury had raced. "There are certain acts," said they in part, "which a gentleman cannot commit." One had hardly to read between the lines to understand that the club, as a body, thought Ashbury one of those Things which creep around in bilge water.

Not all was mere invective. Thoughtful writers in England who held no animosity toward Americans expressed their annoyance at the patent unfairness of reserving four carefully selected boats to defend the Cup. "It is surprising," wrote a noted commentator on yachting, "that such good sportsmen as Americans should not have seen the one-sidedness of" that arrangement. Along the British waterfronts there were rumblings that the Navy was being made ready to take possession of the Cup. The war went on for years—with words.

A symbolic trophy, intended by sportsmen to serve as a means of "friendly competition between foreign countries" had now acquired a tarnish. For the time being it was an irritant, intensifying national animosities.

Ashbury could hardly be regarded as a reformer in any field, yet his offensive against the New York Yacht Club was to prove socially useful. The noisy arguments, the meddlesome press, and the spirited interest expressed by the public, particularly Americans, gave the club committees cause for serious thought. As a result of what may have been painful reflection, they became less autocratic and fully aware of what the word "sport" really meant. The match of 1871 was the last in which a challenger had to meet more than a single defending yacht in a Cup race.

As the club through its committees appears not to have announced that decision then, no one rose to cheer. There were friendly enough matches after the Ashbury naval engagement. But many years were to pass before the Cup was restored to the place its American donors had intended for it. The man who did most to set the Cup high as a trophy gave his name to a yachting era. He was Sir Thomas Lipton.

5

MARINE
CIRCUS

Events associated with Cup matches were hardly ever to be dull—except many of the races. The Ashbury episodes were merely a little more noisy than the concomitants of some succeeding challenges. The skirmishes of 1871 had a normal effect upon most Americans, whether yachtsmen or not. To them the embattled Cup had lost whatever character it once had as a mere trophy. It had acquired special qualities which inspired nationalistic fervor. The time was not far off when it was to receive the tribute of being known as *The* Cup—a term which everyone understood in a sporting world studded with trophies.

For a while, however, it was to be frequently called the "Queen's Cup," or the "Royal Cup"—both wrong—and other names. Hamilton Morton, a former secretary of the New York Yacht Club, tried, in 1874, to fix the name when he composed a hundred bubbling quatrains, published as *The America Cup, a Nautical Poem*. This was one of several pieces, too, which attempted to elevate everything associated with the Cup to a plane of dignity entitled to serious treatment. The two matches which followed Ashbury's last were, though, to disturb the intention of these earnest people. Both affairs were to introduce, quite unintentionally, some elements of comedy if not farce.

They began when an unexpected challenge came from Canada. No one in American yachting circles had assumed that a challenge, should there ever be one again, could originate in any place but England. The request for a match was sent by Major Charles Gifford, acting on behalf of the Royal Canadian Yacht Club of Toronto. Gifford was its vice-commodore. This was spring 1876. What added to the amazement of the New York Yacht Club was the suggestion that the Canadians had a schooner they thought good enough to meet a United States champion. That was aiming very high.

The club was happy to receive that challenge. It had been having serious difficulties in early 1876. There was a movement afoot to give up its station on Staten Island, warehouse its treasures and wait for better days. The panic of 1873 had set much of its membership adrift. When it was learned, however, that the club was dragging its anchors and heading for the rocks, a number of affluent yachtsmen came steaming to the rescue. The Canadian challenge had a revivifying effect on the club. It meant that the Cup had its old magnetism. The club would again become conspicuous in the world of yachtsmen. And, as this was 1876, it was planned to hold a Centennial Regatta additional to the Cup match. English yachtsmen were to be invited to participate in the national celebration. By then, it was assumed, they had recovered from the loss of their colony.

67

The designer and builder of the challenging schooner, *Countess of Dufferin,* was Captain Alexander Cuthbert out of Cobourg, Ontario. Unlike most of the men concerned with actual yacht production, Cuthbert was a keen helmsman who raced his own boats. He was not an original designer, and not nearly as imaginative or skillful as George Steers and later Americans in his field. But the boats he turned out had given him high repute in Canada. This seems deserved; they won most of the races in Great Lakes waters.

Upon Major Gifford's request, the regatta committee agreed to an extension of the six months' advance notice and was generally liberal in its arrangements. It hedged, however, in its answer to Gifford's query as to whether the *Countess* would have to meet a fleet, four boats or what. "A yacht," the committee replied, "would meet the challenger each morning of the match." This was comforting; they had said "a" yacht. A meeting of club members was soon held; nearly two thirds voted for a single (and sole) defender.

Outside the club other yachtsmen and most of the press were demanding that the defense be carried by a fleet. They wanted no chances taken. That seafaring journalist, Captain Coffin, suggested that what the club did as trustees of the Cup was none of the public's business. The public did not agree. When they heard the decision that a sole boat would meet the challenger they loudly suggested that the club was controlled by renegades who were about to commit barratry or treason.

The club, by now nobly advanced in sporting ethics, refused to be influenced by the clamor without its gates. Major Gifford received the welcome news that the *Countess* would have to meet a sole defender and that the latter would be chosen well in advance of the Cup match. One race would be over the inside course, a second outside, and if a third were necessary it would be over a course mutually agreed upon.

But if Major Gifford thought the suggested courses unsuitable, he could join the club on its annual cruise. The races then could be held off Newport, in August. Sweetness and light held the scene.

Meanwhile, the *Countess of Dufferin,* still on the ways, was in trouble. She was being built on an economy budget. It was insufficient. Her owners, men of limited means, were tempted to appeal to the Canadian public for help. Somehow they found the money with which to finish her without the tedious process which a popular subscription would have involved. When she was finally afloat, the Canadians thought her admirable. She was a "Canadian bean," a centerboard schooner with a long, narrow hull, 107' over all, and registered at 138.2 tons.

Towed to Kingston, Ontario, she acquired the mainsail which had been ordered there. When it was found to be oversize, a new spar had to be stepped at Quebec. A Kingston paper wrote of her, "She sits most gracefully in the water, and looks as saucy and rakish as the most enthusiastic sailor could desire." The flattering comments were continued by marine reporters from Nova Scotia almost down to Rhode Island: "as handsome a yacht as ever we saw"; "rakish bow gives her a dashing appearance"; "remarkable speed." Such favorable advance notices put the salts of New York Harbor in a frame of eager expectation. The *Countess* came in on July 18.

It was a day of disenchantment. Criticism was severe—and impolite. To the seaside critics the *Countess* was dowdy and disreputable. In comparison with the beautifully turned out yachts which embellished the harbor, the Canadian challenger was a "fresh-water fisherman" with sails that "set like a purser's shirt on a handspike," and with a "hull as rough as a nutmeg grater." A leading New York journal told its readers:

There is nothing foreign about her. Her shape is American. Her rig is American. Her steering gear is of New York manufacture. From stem to stern, inside and out, alow and aloft, she is simply a Yankee yacht built in Canada.

Captain Coffin put her under objective observation. It was his opinion that Cuthbert had copied the pattern of Pat M. McGiehan of Pamrapo, New Jersey, who had built some fast sloops. One of Cuthbert's models, the *Annie Cuthbert,* won a race against a prize example of McGiehan's design, the *Cora.* Thereupon Cuthbert, who thought the American builder the best of them all, "deemed that he had only to make an enlarged *Annie Cuthbert,* stick two masts in it, and come to New York and capture the Cup. She was," Coffin went on, "meanly rigged and canvassed." Despite angry Canadian denials, New York yachtsmen and sports writers continued to insist that the *Countess* was but a poor copy of typical Yankee schooners.

The Canadian owners of the challenger may have been depressed at the harsh criticism with which their entry was greeted, but they did not show it. They displayed tact and patience—no Ashburys they. Whatever defects the *Countess* had were external and obvious; Gifford and Cuthbert conceded that. What bothered them most were her sails. It was thought that their fit would be improved through recutting; at least they would not hang in folds. A New York sailmaker went to work on them but the operation was not wholly successful.

The New York *Herald,* in a bold moment, dared to suggest that, for the sake of the sport, it might be desirable if a challenger won. "It is evident that foreign proprietorship of the royal Cup would not be without the most beneficial results." But there were others who thought it undignified that the New York Yacht Club should race one of its champions against so poor a yacht as the *Countess* appeared to be. The club, had it been minded to do so, would hardly withdraw an acceptance of a challenge. The *Countess* had an opportunity to show what merit she had when she entered the club's Brenton Reef race. She was not officially a contestant. The course of 275 miles ran from Sandy Hook Lightship to Narragansett Bay and return. Among the entrants was the *America,* and on the run to the Reef the *Countess* arrived ahead of her by more than eight minutes. This, commented a critic, was "a darksome mystery of the deep." The course home, however, was a windward thresh and not at all to the liking of the *Countess*. She staggered in, finally—by that time the race committee had gone wearily home.

The Canadian owners thereupon asked for time to refit their boat. This would have meant a postponement of the day set for the Cup race and would interfere with the annual cruise of the club. When the request was denied, the *Countess* went on the ways and her crew and afterguard poured sweat into the job of polishing her from truck to keel. She also acquired a new foresail and a better suit of light sails.

The club's choice of defender was the *Madeleine,* originally a sloop when built in 1868. She had undergone some successful operations, having been "hipped," lengthened, and converted into a schooner. In her revised form she had been a consistent winner. Her owner was John S. Dickerson. She was about the same measurement and length as the *Countess*. On the day appointed for the first of the races, August 11, she appeared at the line as graceful and trim as a yacht could be. Sperm oil and tallow had burnished her copper bottom; her suit of sails was beautifully tailored; her topsides showed loving care. The other lady in the party, the *Countess,* despite her new cotton sails and the hard work that had gone into her a day or two before, still looked frowzy.

Instead of the traditional start from anchor, the yachts

71

were to come to the line sailing. This was, so far as American records show, the first instance of this innovation. There was an enormous press of spectators, most of them on excursion boats. The skippers of the sightseeing fleet, in their efforts to give the paying customers a clear view of what was going on, could hardly have been more troublesome. Twice, as the contestants were about to start, a boat steamed across their path, forcing them to go about. A few minutes later, when reaching for the line, the *Countess* found a brig anchored where that vessel had no right to be. When, in consequence, she luffed, it brought her right under the *Madeleine*'s lee.

That cost her more than thirty seconds in crossing. It was to make little difference in the outcome. Captain Cuthbert was at the helm and he would have done far better had he followed the *Madeleine*'s lead in a series of tacks out of the Narrows. As a result of following his own course, he ran into a full flood tide. That slowed the *Countess* considerably. The *Madeleine* was ahead by nearly ten minutes elapsed time when she reached the finish.

For the next race, August 12, Captain Cuthbert saw the wisdom of hiring a pilot who knew the peculiarities of the local waters. He was Captain Joe Ellsworth, a good man, too, but he might as well have stayed ashore. The wind was so light both yachts were towed out to the committee boat, anchored off Sandy Hook. It was a dull race; the *Madeleine* was 26 minutes, 13 seconds ahead of her rival when it was over. The *America,* then a mature lady of twenty-five, joined the party for fun. She, too, preceded the challenger by 20 minutes. Captain Cuthbert took it all philosophically, remarking that the *Countess* had done as well in time as the *Livonia,* "and money went into *her.*"

After it was over, the marine critics became more tolerant. Wrote one authority: "Canadians may congratulate themselves on having produced a remarkably fast yacht, one which, in her first attempt, has done herself no discredit." Cuthbert decided that he could improve the *Countess* by reducing her stern overhang and making changes in her rigging. The work was to be done in New York. Then he would challenge for the Cup in 1877.

Cuthbert and Major Gifford, soon after the match, were involved in a wrangle over their shares in the ownership of their yacht. The dispute had not gone very far when the sheriff hove into sight, laid on grappling irons and took the *Countess* to dock. The action had been demanded by some worried creditors. After a sheriff's sale, which reduced Cuthbert's share, the vessel was dry-docked at the foot of Stanton Street, New York, still in durance. The lug-foresail, valued at about $200, was left behind at Stapleton to satisfy five claimants. Somehow, probably on a night when the current was favoring, Cuthbert succeeded in slipping the *Countess* into the East River. Long before the sheriff was aware that he had been taken by pirates, the Canadians were well on their way home. The legal tangle was finally settled judicially and a Chicago yachtsman bought the now unencumbered *Countess*. Under the burgee of the Chicago Yacht Club she had a long career and achieved a superior racing record.

There were to be no more races between schooners in Cup matches after the 1876 event. American yacht designers were giving increasing attention to the sloop and the cutter, with their simplified rig, for racers. A number of reasons furthered the development of these types. Quite apart from other considerations, naval design had long been a field for study and progressive change. One of the great, triumphant achievements of man is the sailboat, a solid mass which can be directed through a volatile element without machinery to power it. Yet the achievement was incomplete; the "perfect hull and rig" were still to be attained. (Even in our own days competent authorities have wondered whether the combina-

73

tion can ever be found!) The search was to produce geniuses among designers.

In American waters a number of catastrophes gave impetus to the development of new designs in hull and rig. Two days after the *Countess of Dufferin* anchored in New York Harbor, a major tragedy emphasized the unseaworthiness of the then typical schooner yacht. The great schooner *Mohawk,* while at anchor with all her sails aloft and close hauled, was caught by a puff and capsized. Her owner, his wife, and others drowned below deck. The crew of the *Countess* helped to rescue those who went overboard. This was only one of several fatal knockdowns in that period.

The *Mohawk* disaster dates a change in American yacht design. William P. Stephens observed that

Prior to this date yachtsmen were committed almost unreservedly to the wide, shoal-bodied centerboard type of hull. The general type, with its dangerously low range of stability and its growing record of fatal capsizes, was faulty in the extreme.

What was now demanded was less breadth, greater depth of body and draft, and outside lead as ballast. True keel cutters were coming into favor, together with a new type of "compromise sloop" with a centerboard working through an outside lead keel and the rig of a cutter's proportions.

While these changes were taking place, Captain Cuthbert, on Lake Ontario, was conducting his own experiments. He finally succumbed again, after five years, to Cup fever. With a wood model as his guide (then a typical practice), he went to work on a challenger. When completed, she was a center-board sloop, 70' over all, 64' waterline, and 5' 6" draft with board up. Her name was Greek: *Atalanta,* swiftest of mythical maidens. She was still in frame when, on May 16, 1881, Cuthbert sent off his challenge through the Bay of Quinte Club, Belleville, Ontario. The New York Yacht Club was prompt in its acceptance. It suggested three races for the Cup and waived the requirement of six months' notice.

A correspondence followed. Would the New York club, Cuthbert asked, name its defender in advance or was that to remain a secret until the day of each race? The Cup committee considered this a fair request. It reported to the club's flag officers:

We do not doubt the right of the club to reserve an answer to this question or, under the terms of the deed of gift, to take the position that it is entitled to name a boat on the morning of each race, but our judgment is that the most liberal and sportsmanlike terms should be offered to the challenging yacht.

They went on with a recommendation that a sole boat, to be nominated as soon as possible, carry the defense. In acknowledgment the Bay of Quinte Club said it was delighted; look for us in September. Then the flag officers representing the holders of the Cup went in search of a defender.

The correspondence, ostensibly a private matter between the two clubs, aroused an interest not confined to yachting circles. Canadians, still smarting under the criticisms with which the *Countess of Dufferin* had been greeted, were eager for battle. The New York Yacht Club had been most fair in the treatment accorded the owners of the *Countess,* but the Canadian press conveniently forgot that. Less than two weeks after Cuthbert's challenge had gone off, the *Toronto Globe* angrily reported that the New York club "is again about to resort to the discreditable tactics it has formerly adopted in order to avoid all danger of a fair contest." Further,

It has never been open to doubt that the New York Yacht Club has adopted this elaborate system [naming its defender on the morning of the race] out of determination to retain the Queen's

75

Cup at all hazards. Nothing short of a whole flotilla of yachts would stand any chance in such a skin-game as this competition has made.

The tone thus set was eagerly echoed in other Canadian papers. They took it as their particular victory when a decision favorable to the *Atalanta* was announced. The American sporting press did not join in the celebration. It opened fire on the club, which steadily maintained its course. Said one journal, embodying the general opposition, it objected to "conceding advantages to which no challenging party is entitled. . . . This historic emblem is no prize-fighter's belt. Any craft challenging for this Cup . . . should sail against all of her class that could be mustered . . . these single-handed matches constitute a bad precedent."

Of the New York Yacht Club's fleet, chiefly schooners, there were only five sloops from which to select a defender. The single-stick type was still something of a novelty among American yachts. Any of the five, it was thought, was of uncertain quality. Had it not been for a serious social error on the part of her owner, then abroad, the club would have named the *Arrow,* a flyer among sloops. But the error made her unavailable; her owner was not a member of the club. The committee in charge planned to cable and ask if he would sell the *Arrow* to the club. Thereupon David Kirby, who had built the *Arrow,* suggested that he be engaged to turn out a sloop even faster than his masterpiece. The club was agreeable. With his eye on a carved model as guide, Kirby created the *Pocahontas,* a centerboard sloop. She set a precedent, one since maintained, in being specially built as a Cup defender.

The *Pocahontas* was an expensive failure. Authoritative critics came to the conclusion that, apart from being over-sparred, she was wrong in design and construction. During three trials in mid-October she made so poor a showing that she acquired the nickname "Pokey." In the final heat she was badly disabled. She never was a racer but, after reconditioning, enjoyed a long career as a cruising boat. The sloop selected as a result of the trials was the *Mischief,* owned by Joseph R. Busk. A native Briton, he had been a member of the New York Yacht Club for a dozen years. His clearly expressed loyalty was to the club in all matters associated with Cup defense.

A participant in the trials was the *Gracie,* owned by two club members. There was no question that she was faster than *Mischief.* But she had a disadvantage. Under the current rating rules, her time concession to the *Atalanta* would probably have to be about eight minutes. The *Mischief* had to allow less than three. Despite the practical reason which had influenced the committee in its choice, the owners of the *Gracie* set up a small tempest. They sent off a series of letters, written with sea water and vinegar, to newspaper editors. Their indignation inspired a wordy fracas, open to all. The club committee, when the argument was at its most intense, just went below and made no further comment on its choice. It was still the *Mischief.*

The selected defender was a rarity in American waters. Her designer, Archibald Cary Smith of New York, had built her of iron. Unlike the rule-of-thumb boats of the period and earlier, this "iron pot" was a development of scientific design. She had first been shaped on drawing board and plans. (This was a continuation of a radical departure in designing method which appears to have been started by Smith and Robert Center when they created the first iron yacht in America, the *Vindex,* in 1871.) The innovation in method was later hailed as the American beginning of scientific yacht construction. A quick look at the *Mischief* gave contemporary observers the impression that she was an English cutter rather than an

American sloop. Her hybrid rig could have belonged to either type. A centerboarder with 5′ 6″ draft (16′ with board down), she was 67′ 5″ over all with 61′ waterline.

At Belleville the *Atalanta* was belying her name. It was September 17 before she was afloat. In less than a month the yachting season in New York would come to its usual close. Taking the challenger through the St. Lawrence and down the coast—the route of the *Countess of Dufferin*—would be tediously slow. The situation called for desperate measures. Cuthbert took them. With his boat finally equipped, he proceeded to Oswego. A crew of four professional seamen was on board. At the entrance to the canal connecting with the Erie the *Atalanta*'s spars and rigging were unshipped. Her movable ballast was placed in one bilge, which canted the yacht enough to pass the locks, for which she was 16 inches too broad in the beam. With a list on her, the hobbled *Atalanta* was ignominiously towed by mules. In a week or so she was sluiced through the Erie Canal. At Albany her crew put her back on even keel, restepped her mast and set her otherwise to right. She came to rest in New York Harbor on October 30.

Those of the New York Yacht Club's membership who did not greet the news with hysterical laughter gave way to a collective shudder. The more conservative members tried hard to blot from memory the fact of the *Atalanta*'s inglorious entrance. It was clear that something had to be done to prevent a recurrence of anything so ridiculous as a challenging yacht towed by mules. True, the deed of gift said nothing about mules and towing but it was quite clear that it should. After the Cup race, it was decided, something had to be done about this.

Cuthbert had to work fast in New York. The club was being most tolerant in extending the dates for the races to early November. There would have been reasonable justifica-

tion for a postponement to next year's season. Racing in
November was hardly going to be fun. The *Atalanta's* stick
was reduced and there were other changes, including alteration of her headsails. As before, Cuthbert's purse hardly
matched his enthusiasm. The rough hull had to be left much
as it was; the revised sails, though imperfect, just had to do;
there was no time to make further improvements in her spars.
Except for the four men who had accompanied Cuthbert on
the inland voyage, the *Atalanta's* crew were amateurs out of
the Bay of Quinte Club. They were outclassed at the start.

Fog canceled the first race, set for November 8. On the
following day the contestants were at the line. The rejected
Gracie, though not invited, flaunted her charms around the
committee boat. The race was to be over the club's regular
course, from off Stapleton. Before the gun, the *Atalanta's* crew
poured out sweat hauling the heavy anchor. (The boat had
no windlass.) While they were bringing it home a stray willi-
waw hit them. For a moment it was thought the yacht would
capsize. The club's tug was promptly assigned to stay close to
the challenger. The wind was coming in mean, sharp gusts
which kept the *Atalanta* staggering. It seemed only fair that
the tug should rescue the club's guests when their boat was
knocked down, an event expected momentarily.

It did not happen, but Cuthbert's frequent luffs to prevent
it brought his boat home more than 31 minutes after the
Mischief. The *Gracie* did better. She went over the line 10
minutes, 10 seconds later than the *Mischief* and reached the
finish over a minute in advance of her. "So, you see!" signaled
the *Gracie* to the committee boat. "Gate crasher!" replied the
committee, in current code.

The hardy reporters assigned to the race (they had been
supplied with an extra ration of grog), after they thawed out,
had some sharp things to say about the *Atalanta* and her
crew's yacht manners. Among other comments: "She was a

man trap, with all the bad elements of the New York light draft sloop." They puzzled over why she had not capsized and doubted if the event could be called a race.

The *Atalanta's* men seemed not to be too upset. When the second race took place, on November 10, they made a better showing on the first leg. The challenger had crossed half a minute after the defender, with the wind aft. Yet she was not far behind at the mark, though she had lost her spinnaker boom in the heavy, rolling sea half an hour earlier. Going back was rough work in a gale of wind. Topsails came down and mainsails were reefed. After a little of that the *Atalanta* tucked in a second reef. She came home late—just under 42 minutes after the *Mischief.* The *Gracie* just couldn't stay away. Again she crossed ten minutes after the contenders; again she came in earlier than her hated American rival, but by only eight seconds' elapsed time.

The Cup series of 1881, if the *Spirit of the Times* was to be believed, was "a stupid comedy." That sporting journal had no sympathy for the loser. It informed its readers, few of whom had dared November's gales to watch the races, that the

tried and proved sloop [Mischief], *one of the fastest in the world . . . fully manned and magnificently handled, distanced the* Atalanta, *a new yacht, hastily built, totally untried, and miserably equipped . . . and bungled around the course by an alleged crew, who would have been overmatched in trying to handle a canal-boat anchored in a fog.*

If that was intended as an epitaph for the *Atalanta* and her crew, it failed its purpose. The crew went home and, being hardened sailors, presumably lived long and usefully. Captain Cuthbert, who apparently never read bad notices, stayed on in New York with his boat. He was, he said, puzzled by the *Atalanta's* poor performance. What he planned to do, he announced, was to study her and decide if she needed revision. Then, alterations or not, he would challenge again for the Cup in 1882.

That expressed intention brought various New York Yacht Club committees into a series of fireside huddles. The very dignity of the club, they felt, was at stake. They resented the general public opinion that the latest match had been a farce. And who knew what that odd character, Cuthbert, had in store for the next match were his challenge accepted. Only something bizarre could be expected of a man who used mule power to transport a racing yacht.

The quartet of matches in the decade since Ashbury's first challenge had lifted the status of the Cup to an exceptional plane as a trophy. Its trustees were determined to keep it there. It was generally agreed that further challenges would come and that each would undoubtedly require a specially built defender. That expense would be borne by the club— something the members seemed not to mind, but they wanted a good reason for it. A worthy challenger would be a good reason. Having come to these conclusions, the club returned the Cup to George Schuyler. That was merely protocol; they expected its return after he had devised a new deed to cover the renewed gift.

Schuyler must have invoked the spirits of the departed co-owners of the *America* when he composed the revised deed. It had been assumed by the donors of the Cup that "friendly competition" for it would involve only champion vessels and expert crews. A factor which had disturbed Schuyler had been disputes over various clauses of the first deed. It was time that its language was made clearer.

The new deed and the Cup reached the club early in 1882. It was far more explicit than the original document. The basic alterations and additions were these: Only a sole yacht was to be used as a defender; any challenging club must have a course on the sea or on an arm of the sea which served in its annual regattas; challenging boats had to proceed under sail on their own bottoms; no vessel which had been defeated in a Cup match could challenge again under two years unless there had been an intervening race for the Cup by another yacht, and, should it ever be necessary to dissolve the club holding the Cup, it was to pass it on to a club of the same nationality which would maintain its prestige as a trophy.

Captain Cuthbert was eager to challenge again and with the *Atalanta,* but not so eager that he would wait more than a year. In the spring he took his yacht back to Lake Ontario. (She raced for fifteen years thereafter, and successfully.) The Canadian clubs on the Great Lakes expressed their annoyance over the clause which excluded them. No other foreign clubs seemed to find the new deed objectionable. Americans were highly pleased over the "improved" deed of gift. Their Cup was back on its pedestal.

6

TWO
GENTLEMEN
OF BRITAIN

Since the Ashbury incident the English attitude toward the Cup seems to have been one of studied indifference, if not disdain. By 1884 they were willing to forgive and forget. In December of that year an announcement came that the Cup holders should prepare themselves for a challenge. The announcer was J. Beavor Webb, designer of (among others) the notable cutters *Genesta* and *Galatea*.

When, a little later, the challenge came in official form, it was for a naval twosome. A match was requested first for the *Genesta*, owned by Sir Richard Sutton. The suggested date was late August 1885. Then, if the *Genesta* were defeated, a second match was proposed for the *Galatea*. Her owner was Lieutenant William Henn of the Royal Navy (retired) and he would like to race for the Cup before September 17.

This unexpected dual entry was properly handled by the New York Yacht Club. It agreed to the *Genesta*'s challenge promptly and tentatively accepted that of the *Galatea* for 1886. When Webb asked that the match take place on courses "free from tides and shallow waters," a compromise was effected. Three races would be arranged, one over the club's inside course and two, if both were necessary, outside. Races were to be limited to seven hours. When the race committee denied Webb's request that standard English time allowances should apply, he suggested that they be based on a mean of tables current in England and the States. This, too, was not acceptable to the committee. Webb then thought that George Schuyler should be asked to arbitrate the matter. When he was called on, he gave it as his reasoned opinion that allowances must be governed by the rating rule of the club holding the Cup.

As has been several times observed by top authorities in the field of yacht racing, though frequently forgotten by yachtsmen, the relative speed of two boats is very largely controlled by the rule under which they race. Schuyler's decision put the 80-ton *Genesta,* which had been built to the English rule, at something of a disadvantage. Webb and Sir Richard took their disappointment with good grace. The tone of correspondence with the club throughout was extremely friendly. It implied that Sir Richard would prove a very welcome guest. This expectation was most pleasantly realized during his American stay.

When it became publicly known that a challenge through the Royal Yacht Squadron had been accepted, the New York Yacht Club heard from a nonmember. He was General Benjamin F. Butler, generally of Massachusetts, and since 1873 owner of the *America.* She had been auctioned in that year and had brought the ridiculous price, on a single bid, of $5,000. Her fittings alone were worth more. (The sale resulted

Madeleine running for the finish; Countess of Dufferin beating out to the lightship. From a drawing by L. A. Shafer, 1899.

Mischief leading *Atalanta* at the start of their first race. From a water color by Frederic S. Cozzens, 1883.

Mayflower showing the way to Galatea in the second challenge race of 1886. From a drawing by L. A. Shafer, 1899.

Edward Burgess, designer of innovations in Cup defenders.
From a woodcut.

in a futile inquiry by a Congressional committee. There had also been some doubt as to whether she had ever been cleared by a prize court, and this made her title uncertain.) It was the general's argument that, should the challenger win, she should not be permitted "to take the Queen's Cup until she had also defeated the original winner." He offered to put the *America,* which he had been using as a cruising boat, at the club's disposal. The proper committees thought this idea of "Bold Ben Butler" a noble one—and promptly stowed it.

American yachtsmen were well aware that the defense of the Cup was going to require special effort. The *Genesta* had a great number of victories to her credit, running against speedy British "knife-blade" cutters. That type had developed, from around 1860 on, through an evasion of the old English tonnage rule that governed time allowances. Basically, this rule went on the assumption that a boat's depth equaled half the beam. This imposed an excessive tax on beam. The evasion came about when the keel was abnormally shortened and waterline length substituted for that of keel. The result was a boat of extremely narrow beam with non-taxable deep ballast, most of it of lead carried outside on the keel.

The American centerboard sloops of the late 70s and early 80s had speed but were not regarded as invariably reliable in heavy weather. The differences between that type then and the English cutter were marked. The shallow-draft, centerboard sloop, broad in the beam and with flaring sides, had a tall mast stepped well forward. Its mainsail was laced to the boom and its long bowsprit was fixed. In the British keel cutter (a wall-sided boat) the short mast, set well aft, carried a loose-footed mainsail. Its bowsprit had a "reefing" device whereby it could be brought inboard. These were the major differences between the two types. The physical appearance of

85

the cutter, with its narrow beam and sharp lines, had given it a characteristic name in England: "plank-on-edge."

Something happened in 1881 which was to put American yachtsmen on edge. James Coates of Paisley, Scotland, the owner of a small cutter, *Madge*, had brought her across on a steamer's deck. She was only 46' over-all and had an 8' draft. When she went into contests against American sloops, even with a disadvantageous time allowance, she took seven races out of eight. Yacht builders in and around New York went quickly to work in unashamed imitation of the *Madge*. The first experiments were expensive because they were not as successful as had been expected. From these attempts there developed a compromise sloop.

For want of a better term it was, for the time being, called a cutter. It was thought to be best suited to American weather and waters. It had a centerboard and incorporated those elements of the "plank-on-edge" and "skimming dishes" which had proved of value. But the hybrid was concededly imperfect. As an evidence that yacht designing had advanced, the American rating rule based on the cubic content of competing vessels had been changed in 1882 to one which took waterline length into account. (Changes in measurement and rating rules were frequent and represent in themselves a long, tedious, and involved history.)

The excellent record of the *Genesta* abroad had made the New York Yacht Club wary but it was really the *Madge* which had alerted it to the seriousness of the challenge. It was to be said later that, had it not been for the *Madge,* the *Genesta* would have been confidently matched with an old-time sloop. That might very well have resulted in the return of the Cup to its place of birth. There was no cutter or sloop then owned by club members which could be seriously regarded as fully worthy to meet the challenger. From its own first city clubhouse at 67 Madison Avenue, the club displayed evidence of a distress signal. It took the form of a circular, in May 1885, addressed to all American yacht clubs. If owners of single-stickers of minimum 60-foot waterline wished to enter their boats for trials and make appropriate arrangements with the club in the event of selection, would they please advise—and quickly?

No one came forward. But in Boston a centerboard sloop, to be called the *Puritan,* was already being built with the expectation that it would become the defender. The syndicate by whom it was ordered—a group of ten headed by J. Malcolm Forbes—had placed the commission with a young man, Edward Burgess. While fairly new in the field, he had designed some successful small racers. He fell upon the opportunity with imagination and fervor. Then, as there had been no favorable response to the club's appeal, its commodore, James Gordon Bennett, and William Douglass, its vice-commodore, placed an order for a sloop with the designer of the *Mischief,* A. Cary Smith.

The Boston entry by a man who had no experience in designing big racers was treated with contempt in New York. Insofar as yachts and racing were concerned, New York regarded itself as the American center of all that mattered. Captain Cornelius McKay, writing for a Bennett paper, the *Evening Telegram,* gave expression to the general opinion of New York yachtsmen. He thought it quite all right for Boston to build a Cup candidate for, after the trials, its entry could be used to carry brick in local waters! It was thought pretty brash for a novice to attempt to compete with Smith, then the outstanding designer in America. Didn't Burgess know that Smith was applying the advanced theories of John Scott Russell's scientific "wave-line" principles?

Perhaps, in relation to young Burgess, Smith knew too much. William P. Stephens, a practical designer and the keenest observer on yachting matters, said of the former:

Though generally proclaimed a genius in naval architecture, he would be the first to repudiate such a title. All of his tastes and his early training lay in a different direction from naval architecture; he had no interest in mathematics or mechanics, and he lacked the technical training considered essential today for success in designing. [But he had] natural intelligence, and hard Yankee commonsense. His first and greatest effort, Puritan, was built on deductions as simple and logical as those which produced the One-Horse Shay.

The *Puritan* was launched out of her Boston yard late in May. The New York candidate designed by Smith, the *Priscilla*, a centerboard sloop, was afloat shortly thereafter. They both were close to the *Genesta*'s dimensions, except for beam. She had an over-all length of 96' 5", an 81' 7½" waterline and only a 15' beam. New York yachtsmen hastily revised their snobbish opinion at first sight of the *Puritan,* the "Boston bean boat." Burgess had recognized the importance of the outside lead ballast used in the *Madge* and had created a remarkable hybrid, a brilliant anticipation of the speedy racers yet to come. The *Puritan*'s keel of 51' held 48 tons of outside lead through which her centerboard worked. Unlike the conventional "skimming dishes" she had a draft of 8' 8" (20' with board down), with deepest draft aft. She measured 140 tons. Except that her beam was broad (22' 7" on a 94' over-all length), she incorporated the most valuable features of superior English cutters.

The performance of the *Puritan* in the trials against the *Priscilla* and others called forth frank admiration. Additional to novelty in yacht design, Burgess had turned out a remarkably fast boat. She sailed under the auspices of the Eastern Yacht Club and carried her designer's private flag. But this caused the New York Yacht Club no concern. A member of the syndicate which commissioned Burgess, General Charles J. Paine, belonged to the New York club. When the *Puritan* was chosen as defender, she was entered as a member's yacht. A Corinthian crew was selected for her. Each man was an expert handler of his own boat and all were intimate friends of Burgess and General Paine. Captain Joe Elsworth, widely known for his knowledge of local waters and of yachts in general, was appointed "honorary pilot."

Upon her arrival, the *Genesta* caused some uneasiness. A straight-stem cutter she was, said the knowing among marine reporters, "a slippery customer." She was exceptionally attractive, with long, easy lines, deep body, unusual and elegant fittings, and a show-piece interior, every part of which was utilized. Both she and the *Puritan* had ladies' cabins aft which were "simply divine."

The Cup match had been set ahead to September 7 but the first race was called. Fog and light wind brought it to a close after five dull hours. The next day was to provide some excitement, enough at least to give an unexpected thrill to spectators on the huge fleet which crowded at the starting line. It was a clear day, the eighth, and the wind out of the southeast would have satisfied any yachtsman.

When the gun signaled two minutes to cross, the contending yachts maneuvered for the starting line. Both were traveling fast, *Genesta* on a starboard tack, *Puritan* on a port tack. Though the defender was slightly ahead she was not far enough in advance to cross the challenger. As they converged, the *Puritan*'s helmsman held his course. If it was a scare tactic, it failed, for, quite correctly under the rule, the *Genesta*'s captain maintained his course. Only then the *Puritan* was luffed—and hard—but she was seconds too late. The *Genesta*'s bowsprit ripped into the defender's mainsail and snapped her bowsprit.

As long as a foul had taken place, it couldn't have been in a better location. The committee boat, *Luckenbach*, was right at the spot. The *Puritan* was promptly slapped on the stern

and disqualified. Then the committee steamed alongside the
Genesta to make solicitous inquiries. When Sir Richard asked
how much time was allowed for a written protest, "the race
committee," commented Alfred F. Loomis, "not without hesitation, and, indeed, not with consummate gallantry, offered
Genesta the race on condition that she sail alone around the
course" within seven hours. Then Roosevelt Schuyler, the
club's representative on board the challenger, suggested that
they be given enough time to rig a makeshift bowsprit with a
spinnaker boom.

Sir Richard wouldn't have it. "We are obliged to you," said
he, "but we want a race, not a sail over." That impulsive
reaction spontaneously warmed America's heart. "Hitherto"
(again quoting the quotable Loomis) "we had regarded challengers as ruffians and like ruffians we had dealt with them.
But now a wave of good feeling swept the country." And
when the challenger rejected an offer by the *Puritan*'s owners
to pay the cost of repairing the *Genesta,* Sir Richard became
the public's fair-haired boy.

After about a week's delay, the first completed race was
run. The contestants had been at their stations a few days
after the incident of the foul, but September was behaving
more as though it were blooming June. On September 14 the
yachts went over the inside course. Both started late; they
were more than two minutes away from the line when the
signal came. The wind was spotty but finally stayed around
10 knots or so. A steamer going about her practical business
and with no interest in yacht racing cost the *Genesta* a little
time when beating out of the Narrows. At the Spit Buoy, however, the *Puritan* was only three minutes ahead of her. The
huge excursion fleet paid such close attendance on the challenger that they interfered with her progress. But at the lightship she was still only a few minutes behind.

It was on the run home that the *Puritan,* even without her

spinnaker, showed her speed. The *Genesta* had her balloon jib topsail and her spinnaker drawing, but there was no catching her rival. The defender crossed the line 16 minutes, 47 seconds elapsed (16 minutes, 19 seconds corrected) time ahead. Each of the spectator vessels which had a cannon on board, a whistle, a bell or foghorn, let loose. They all loved Sir Richard—but they loved that Cup more. The challenger might have, and with reason, protested about the interference he had undergone from the side lines, but he took that unpleasantness in his stride. It was obvious to him that the New York Yacht Club was upset about the enthusiastic (and intrusive) spectators over which it had no control.

The race on the outside course, 20 miles to leeward off Scotland Lightship and return, on September 16, 1885, became a Cup-match classic. The wind, which had been light at the start, built up to a piping nor'wester of 30 and more knots before the finish. It was a spinnaker run out and that gave the race committee some nervous moments. The smart English cutter showed her stuff on that leg. When the boats started on the beat home, however, the advantage turned. The *Puritan* could point closer than the *Genesta*. An ugly sea was running and there were puffs that stepped up the breeze to 40 knots. The skipper of the *Genesta*, Captain John Carter, made the serious error of crowding sail on her. That put her lee rail under most of the time. It slowed her enough to put her 2 minutes, 6 seconds elapsed (1 minute, 38 seconds corrected) time behind the *Puritan* at the finish. That was the closest near-win of a challenger in the twelve races for the Cup.

More often than not, yacht races can be dull. But that second one was worth anyone's while. The *Genesta* had proved a worthy rival, the finest of the challengers. She would have won that race, as remarked by competent observers, if her load of canvas hadn't kept her partly under water. Sir Rich-

91

ard took his defeat as a good sportsman should. He would have liked to try again, but there was that business about the *Galatea's* precedence. American yachtsmen took up the gallant Englishman as one of their own. He entered the *Genesta* in several races, won a number of trophies, and twice defeated the *Dauntless* on ocean courses, once for the Brenton Reef cup. By the time he left for home, he had gone far in promoting that spirit of "friendly competition" for which the donors of the Cup had planned.

As a formality, the challenge of the *Galatea* had been withdrawn. The Royal Northern Yacht Club renewed it in 1886. No one disputed the choice of Edward Burgess again as designer of a new defender. General Paine bore the costs. When the Burgess sloop, the *Mayflower,* took the water, it was observed that she was not unlike the *Puritan.* Again there was outside ballast and a centerboard working through it. She was 100' over all, 23' 6" beam, and measured over 171 tons, which made her the largest of American sloops of the time. The *Galatea,* dubbed the "tin frigate" because she was built largely of steel, was slightly over two feet longer and practically of the same tonnage. The 81 tons of lead poured into her trough-shaped keel was her total ballast, and it was there to keep her from leaving the water and flying when she was under full sail.

During her trials the *Mayflower* was matched with the *Puritan.* It came as a shock to find that Burgess' first Cup racer ran away from his second. The quick reaction of some critics was that the young designer, having given his all for the *Puritan,* had lost his touch. The reaction was too quick and not one shared by Burgess or his sponsor. The *Mayflower* was taken out of the trials. Then her ballast was shifted, her spars and sails were somewhat revised, and she was given rigorous private tests. In a little while Burgess found what he wanted. When the *Mayflower* went into the trials again she justified her designer's faith in her. None of her competitors had a chance. One of them, the very "last of the rule-of-thumb" sloops, the newly built *Atlantic,* had been entered by a syndicate composed of Atlantic Yacht Club members. The *Mayflower,* in her perfected form, was to set a pattern for designers of some of the ablest American yachts.

Meanwhile, the *Galatea* had taken a leisurely passage across the Atlantic, reaching Marblehead on August 1. She had plenty of time to get to New York for the Cup match, and her easygoing owner, Lieutenant Henn, was in a dawdling mood. Quite by accident the *Galatea* ran into the fleet of the New York Yacht Club in Buzzard's Bay. The cruise committee boat came alongside to bid her owner a hearty welcome. They nearly fell overboard when a lady sailor came gaily up the *Galatea*'s companionway. She was Mrs. Henn and she was very much at home at sea.

She had made herself most comfortable for the voyage to America. The *Galatea*'s saloon had potted plants, draperies and table ornaments, and leopard skins on the floor. As the crew was composed of mere men, she had brought along her pets—several dogs and a monkey. The hired hands and probably the afterguard may have done some mumbling in their beards about that small menagerie, but Lieutenant Henn seemed not at all disturbed. A hearty, jovial Irishman, he had enjoyed a life of cruising after his retirement from the British Navy. When he tied up temporarily inland, there were several places he could call home. One was an estate on Paradise Hill, County Clare, and because of it his closest friends dubbed him "Paddy Henn, the Bird of Paradise." He had acquired a wide reputation as an authority on yachts and racing but his heart was really in cruising. It was undoubtedly at the urging of the *Galatea*'s designer that he had entered his sloop for a Cup match.

The experts who converged on the *Galatea* to study her

93

when she reached New York were generally of the opinion that the Cup was not going to take a sea voyage. That seemed a safe first judgment, based on the appearance of the boat. And everyone on her seemed so leisurely. Even when she was supposedly tuning up, no sail was crowded on her and sometimes she just cruised the shore, towing a small boat. Her skipper, Captain Dan Bradford, was a man very like Lieutenant Henn in temperament and not very excited about the prospect of a race. He handled the tiller, a fifteen-foot steel tube, as though he were lazy. All this was highly contrary to the feverish activity usually shown by a challenger's rearguard in American waters when preparing for Cup races. The suspicion arose, in consequence, that Lieutenant Henn was at pains to conceal the real speed of the *Galatea*.

That was enough to increase interest in the challenger. It brought out an enormous collection of everything afloat that could carry spectators on September 7, the day of the first race, on the inside course. On the *Galatea* the potted plants and other nonessentials of the saloon had been stowed on land. But not Mrs. Henn. She was on board with her dogs and her pet monkey, though they were not permitted topside during the race. That was only kindly—they might have been bored on deck.

The designer of the *Galatea,* J. Beavor Webb, was her helmsman. Captain Martin V. B. Stone commanded the *Mayflower.* Both yachts made a beautiful start; only a second separated them at crossing. There was a good deal of short-tacking on the beat out. As was no longer unexpected during a Cup race over the inside course, an oversize schooner was anchored right where both yachts wanted to go. The *Galatea* was forced to leeward of the intruder; the *Mayflower* was able to luff around her. The 40-mile race was not as exciting as the near-collisions of the spectator steamers and tugs which swarmed around the contestants. There was nothing wrong with the

94

Galatea; she was a superb boat but not as good a one as the *Mayflower.* It may have been the diet of American waters that upset the challenger. Some think she simply was not as expertly handled as her rival. It could hardly have been the animals on board or Mrs. Henn who were responsible for the result. Whatever the cause, she came across the finish line 12 minutes, 40 seconds elapsed time after the defender.

The second race was marred by fog and drizzle. Both yachts had started, but the *Galatea* lost the outer mark simply because it was not visible to her helmsman in the gray gloom. The contest was declared no race when both boats ran past the seven-hour limit. It looked better for a match on the eleventh, over the outside course, with a wind that stayed awhile around 12 knots. But it blew itself out too soon and the racers drifted home. It took the *Mayflower* 6 hours, 49 minutes to cover the 40-mile course. Then she was 29 minutes, 48 seconds elapsed time ahead of the *Galatea.* Lieutenant Henn, who became ill before the start, was confined below decks during the race.

Well, the Cup stayed in its shrine and everyone settled down again. Except Lieutenant Henn, who admitted to a slight racing fever. It took the form of a challenge for a private match with the *Mayflower.* After all, that inside course, fog, drizzle, and the crowding spectator fleet had been a combination of nuisances to the challenger. The *Galatea,* her owner thought, could do better than she had done. True, the *Mayflower* had had to put up with it all, too, but she was not a deep-keel boat and she had been designed for home waters. General Paine was agreeable to Lieutenant Henn's suggestion, and he kept the *Mayflower* in commission. The wind, however, went out of commission. After a week and more, the defender was dry-docked. Lieutenant Henn thereupon thought that a race to Bermuda and back against any American sloop would be fun. But no one else seemed to think so.

95

New York made the Henns welcome. They stayed until spring 1887. Then the two yachts which had raced for the Cup in 1886 went out for their private match. There was all the wind they wanted. Though the *Mayflower* won, she did not have too easy a time doing it. Lieutenant Henn was sure that the *Galatea* would have a better chance in a long ocean race. Again he challenged any American sloop for a run to Bermuda and return. No one wanted to go. Thereupon, from the editors' chairs and the reporters' desks came some angry questions addressed to American yachtsmen. What sort of boats are we turning out when they are afraid of deep blue water? Where is that heroic spirit which made America great? What will the British think of us? Do we really deserve the Cup? The response to these representative queries and some direct taunts provoked a collective yawn from the yachtsmen. Lieutenant Henn took Mrs. Henn, the dogs, the monkey, and the potted plants cruising.

7

A CASE

OF SCOTCH—

AND A DEBATABLE DEED

Yachtsmen in Scotland had drunk many a toast with their favorite beverage—it wasn't barley water—to the little *Madge* since her American conquests in 1881. If she had done so well, the wee thing, why could not a bigger boat bring back the Cup? And to Scotland. That would be a fine lesson to a certain tribe of southern beefeaters. Then the Cup could be put on display, free to all Scotsmen; a shilling admission to foreigners, such as Englishmen.

The idea became increasingly enchanting. It finally took the form of an indirect challenge. The Royal Clyde Yacht Club wrote to say that its vice-commodore, James Bell, was manager of a syndicate which would build a challenger and that she would be a little larger than the *Mayflower*. (She turned out to be very much larger.) It was thought that the

New York Yacht Club would like to know well in advance
that the boat would be in its waters sometime in 1887. The
reply of the club was characteristic. It sent a copy of the deed
of gift with a note to say that if an official challenge were
received, the club would give it due consideration. The ensu-
ing correspondence was not calculated to endear the clubs to
each other, but it remained polite. Finally an acceptable challenge came, and just in time to meet the clause in the deed
which required six months' advance notice. All it stated was
that the boat would be named *Thistle* and that her waterline length would be 85 feet. (That specific figure was to
assume great importance later.)

The designer of the *Madge,* George L. Watson, had been
commissioned by Bell's syndicate to turn out the *Thistle.*
Watson, one of the most brilliant men in his field, has been
called (and by those competent to know) "the father of scientific yacht architecture." While the 1886 Cup and other races
were on, he was a studious and keen observer of American
sloops. He had an imaginative sense of where he thought
improvements might be made. He had created, additional to
the *Madge,* a number of exceptionally fast yachts. The *Thistle*
represented an unusual opportunity for him. She was the first
boat to be built abroad (in Scotland) specifically as a challenger for the Cup, and he strove to make her "the perfect
yacht."

A change in the Thames rating rule which had resulted in
the "knife-blade" cutters was formulated in 1886. (An alteration of the rule, made in 1881, was as weak as it was ineffec-
tual.) The new rule, long urged by Dixon Kemp, yachting
editor of the London *Field* and a noted authority on the subject, was adopted early in 1887 by the British Yacht Racing
Association. It took account of length, and sail area. This
logical change put in discard the extreme tax on beam for
time allowance, and made possible the building of lighter ves-

sels of greater breadth. That meant that a challenger would be built to, or close to, the dimensions of an American defender. That meant trouble. It was generally agreed by the defense that Edward Burgess was the man to save the Cup. General Paine said that he would be delighted to pay the costs of a defender again.

For the first time since Cup challenge races began an element of secrecy was introduced. American yachtsmen were naturally eager to know as much as possible about the *Thistle,* but no one would tell them. The building of the challenger was treated as top secret, and anyone who asked questions about her abroad was regarded simply as an American spy. Near the end of April 1887, the *Thistle* slid off the ways. Even then she was under wraps; canvas covered her from stem to stern. This excessive canniness was a silly business for, within a few days, the shroud had to come off. When it did, it uncovered a boat regarded as beamy by British standards, for she had a breadth of 20′ 3″. Her over-all length was 108′ 6″ and she measured 253.94 tons—a giant of a yacht designed to carry sail and be driven hard. The chief novelty in her design lay in the fact that, while her bow was of the old clipper type and she had a standard straight keel, she had no forefoot. That made it a "rocker" keel. That variation from the usual pattern was to have a profound effect on the design of future racers.

When the news of the *Thistle*'s dimensions and her novel lines finally reached New York and Boston, yachtsmen admitted that they were alarmed. What worried them were Watson's reputation for turning out the fastest boats in British waters and the fact that Burgess was working against time. (He had not received his commission to build until the formal challenge had been accepted.) Burgess remained calm. His creation, *Volunteer,* a steel sloop, was turned out by Pusey and Jones Shipbuilding Company at Wilmington in a little over two months. That was a remarkable achievement. She took the water in June and was greeted with delight. Her designer, who could not possibly have known what Watson was up to, had also cut away the straight stem, and he had given her a clipper bow. As was usual in the American type, she had a centerboard. She measured less than the *Thistle*: 209.08 tons. With an over-all length of 106′ 3″ and an 85′ 10″ waterline, her beam was 23′ 2″.

The competing designers might well have worked from similar plans, so close were they in concept and practice. Both boats were the fastest single-stickers yet produced. The *Volunteer* was unrivaled in American waters. At her helm was Captain Hank Haff. (An almost legendary figure as a racing sailor later, he was affectionately known to American yachtsmen only as "Hank.") Abroad, the *Thistle* outfooted every one of the British flyers she met. Her sailing master, Captain John Barr, was regarded as the best in Scotland, which meant that he was one of the best anywhere. The records both yachts made during their trials convinced all observers that the races for the Cup would be very close. They were wrong—and there very nearly were no races.

When the *Thistle* anchored in New York, she received the usual welcome from the curious and from yachting experts. The latter were impressed: "big, sail-carrying brute," "slippery in light airs" (a wrong guess), and "a tough competitor." There were imaginative surmises about her hull, some of them printed, most of them conversational. Because of the wide curiosity over her underbody, a New York newspaper which would do anything for its readers sent a diver down to investigate. He did his work secretly, at night, but that did not prevent him from describing the *Thistle*'s hull to a waiting artist. This genius, though not associated with any known school, may be regarded as an advance expressionist; the sketch he turned in, which was promptly published, could hardly have been more imaginative and less accurate. It was gleefully greeted by the *Thistle*'s designer and her crew. The daily printed it with the explanation that the *Thistle*'s owners had put them to a great deal of trouble by building her with such secrecy. It knew that its readers would appreciate this further proof of its interest in them.

Her owners followed closely behind the *Thistle*. They came on a steam yacht and their mood was expansive. They brought with them a little band of bagpipers to blast out homeland airs. Because there could be no whisky so good as Scotch Scotch, they were plentifully supplied with that beverage. They announced to the reporters who met them that the liquor was brought to fill the Cup for a long series of toasts to America, to Scotland, and all hands in the races. They said they would offer the toasts before they took the Cup back with them. When it was pointed out that it would be more than difficult to drink from a vessel which had no bottom, they were undisturbed. If there were not enough time to have a bottom added to the Cup, they would just have to use glasses.

The measurer of the New York Yacht Club reported that the *Thistle*'s load waterline was 86.46 feet. This was 1.46 feet in excess of the figure given in the challenge. Upon receipt of the report the Cup committee put on quite a show. They behaved as though a variation between the declared length and the actual one was the ultimate crime. (After all, they knew that Watson knew the *Thistle* would be measured before the match. There had been no attempt at deception on anyone's part.) The committee observed that never in the club's experience (perhaps in all history!) had anything occurred as "serious as this great discrepancy." They questioned "whether the *Thistle* should be allowed to race."

This exaggerated performance pleased no one, except perhaps the actors. An error had been made, true, but it repre-

101

sented a matter which could easily be adjusted. Watson had given the challenger's length as it appeared on his plans, before her launching. That was her designed length. When she went out on her trials, she probably took on extra ballast for the sake of her trim. Apparently no one thought then to remeasure her. Had the indignant club committee leaned less heavily on the rules book they would have improved their own trim. George Schuyler, then seventy-six, was called in as arbitrator. He brought the unpleasant matter to a prompt close with his usual common sense. Watson, he decided, should have seen to it that the *Thistle*'s owners received fully accurate dimensions of the vessel. But he accepted the situation as an honest error. He did not think the extra waterline length "though of disadvantage to the defender" an excuse to disqualify the *Thistle*. The matter would be resolved by the necessary adjustment of time allowances. (In the adjustment the *Volunteer* had to allow the challenger 5 and 6 seconds!)

That settled, the first race took place on September 27. It was to be the last on the club's inside course, one detested by all challengers. There was only a light breeze and the intrusive spectator fleet took some of that away. On the steam yacht *Mohican,* which accompanied the *Thistle,* the private corps of *dudelsackpfeifers* played furiously throughout the race. It was remarked that there was more wind in their bagpipes than in the racers' sails. They ended on a doleful note, for the object of their affection had no chance in the light airs against the centerboard *Volunteer*. She was 19 minutes, 28¾ seconds elapsed time behind the defender. Part of the time was lost through a mistaken tack when Captain Barr was deceived by the current.

The *Thistle* was promptly towed to dry dock. Vice-Commodore Bell was convinced that her underbody was dragging something she had picked up and which held her back. There was nothing there. The artist who had sketched her bottom went into hiding for a week. Bell angrily protested that the inside course was a ridiculous one on which to test the merits of a keel boat. He made no public comment on the huge fleet of spectator vessels, though a protest on that score might well have been justified. At one point, in pursuing the defender, which had just completed a tack directly ahead of the *Thistle* several excursion boats backwashed the challenger. No one seemed able to control the skippers of these boats and they had become a dangerous nuisance. The *Volunteer*'s crew did their bit for fair sport and safety. They were prepared. Twice, when the spectator fleet got too close, some hands on the defender held up a large canvas on which was painted KEEP ASTERN!

In the second race on the thirtieth, there was enough wind —a steady 12 knots—to favor a good contest. From a start at Scotland Lightship, it was to be an outside course of 20 miles and return. The race began with both boats on a starboard tack in a heavy sea. They ran alongside each other for a quarter of the distance out. Then the *Volunteer* began to display her ability to point higher than her rival. She was beautiful to watch in working to windward. When running for home the *Thistle* showed that she was as fast as the *Volunteer*. By then, however, she was too far behind to catch up. It was the defender's race by about 12 minutes.

"Look for us again," said Bell, speaking for all the owners. "And we'll bring our bagpipers, too." (The latter had blown themselves out during the first race. Their ancient instruments hung limply around their shoulders; not a single skirl was carried on the breeze during the second race. But had the *Thistle* won . . . !) Bell would have issued another challenge then and there had the deed of gift allowed it. A year after the 1887 match the *Thistle* continued its notable career as a racer, in English waters. Then the Kaiser bought her. He had been influenced by his uncle, the Prince of Wales, a keen

103

yachtsman, to take up sailing. The two were still on speaking terms.

Because of the *Thistle*'s magnificent racing record in England, her poor showing during the Cup races puzzled many people. Perhaps it was that which made Captain John Barr, her master, the victim of slander. It was hinted abroad that he had been paid off by American gamblers. It was a cruel, unwarranted charge. Barr returned to the States in 1889— "the best-known imported skipper." No yachtsman in America put any credence in the slander. They gave proof of their faith in his integrity by frequently appointing him captain of their racing yachts. George Watson, after some thoughtful reflections on why the *Thistle* had done so badly in the Cup match, conceded a probable fault in design. (It didn't really clear up the matter, for, after all, she was winning races in her home waters.) He thought that the *Thistle* was quite as fast as the *Volunteer* but "her surface was so cut down that sufficient lateral plane was not left to hold her to windward [so] she drifted bodily to leeward."

The excess length of the *Thistle*, which had been so upsetting to the regatta and other committees of the New York Yacht Club, was chieflly responsible for a further alteration in the deed of gift. The club thus hoped to prevent a recurrence of such errors, with their attendant unpleasantness. A further reason, though not publicly expressed, was a lingering annoyance over the secrecy with which the *Thistle* had been built. Over such a situation the club, of course, had no control, but it felt entitled to better foreknowledge of what a challenger would be like.

The Cup went back to George Schuyler on October 3, 1887, with a request for a new deed of gift. This time the club indicated what it wanted the deed to say. A committee, including General Paine, was appointed to confer with

George Schuyler. The club secretary, John H. Bird, presented a draft of suggested changes and additions. His approach to the matter was a legalistic one. In consequence, when the Cup was returned three weeks after it had gone to Schuyler, the deed which accompanied it read like a mortgage. Its tenor upset many people and it had a most disagreeable effect upon foreign clubs. Because of it the Cup seemed no longer to be a trophy designed for "friendly competition." It seemed to have lost what, essentially, it had long represented: the irrepressible elements of the wind and the sea and the fellowship of sport for its own sake. Learned counsel had done a restrictive, formalizing job. In order to get to the Cup now, challengers had to navigate cautiously through "parties of the first and second part" and equivalent hazards.

Instead of six months' advance notice of a challenge the new deed required ten. Foreign clubs were to present a document, also ten months in advance, which stated the load-waterline length and beam, extreme beam, and draft of the challenging yacht. No arrangements for a match would be entered into by the club until such information had been received. (Heretofore matches had been mutually agreed upon before details such as that now required were known.) Should disagreement arise over the exact terms of a proposed match, three races would be held, but without time allowances. Centerboard vessels were not to be excluded; single-stick boats could not exceed 90 feet nor be less than 65 feet load waterline; boats of two masts or more had to have a load-waterline range of between 80 and 115 feet; races were to be held only on ocean courses free from headlands, "practicable in all parts for vessels of twenty-two feet draft"; a sole yacht was to carry the defense; the club holding the Cup was not "required to name its representative vessel until the time agreed upon for the start," and no consideration was to be

105

given to any other challenge "until the pending event had been decided." All terms of the new deed of gift were to be maintained by any club whose entry won the Cup.

The members of the committee who had devised the new deed were men of exceptional ability and all were keen yachtsmen. While the club had officially indicated its desire of what the document should contain, its committee members had full freedom to make whatever changes they thought best. Theoretically, when the committee agreed to the new deed of gift, the club was bound by its acceptance. It was not, however, ratified by a membership vote—a fact which called forth criticism later.

The changes and additions in the deed, and the strict terms now imposed, seemed essential and logical to the club committees involved in Cup affairs. The ten months' advance notice (which could be waived) made it unnecessary ever again to have a defender built under the pressure of limited time. And a longer period of trials was thought to be advisable because of the appearance of new and experimental types. The long advance knowledge of a challenger's dimensions meant that a comparable defender could be built. Should the Cup pass to a foreign yacht club, the New York Yacht Club might have to send a centerboard vessel to try to bring it back. In that event it did not want its typical sloops excluded because of the British rule against "shifting keels." And if the club sent a boat abroad to recapture the Cup, it wanted to avoid races on such courses as those it had itself long imposed on challengers. (The last explained the "ocean courses" clause.)

A few commentators of the period and one or two later were to say that the deed of 1887 was fair, clear, and practical, and that it permitted "sportsmanlike matches." They were and have been greatly in the minority. The general reaction, when the contents of the deed of gift were published and copies sent to foreign clubs, was one of protest. (The dissent abroad was violent.) *Forest and Stream,* one of the more conservative American periodicals, characterized the deed "An Act to Prevent Yacht Racing." The club, it stated,

acted illegally and unfairly, having no right to establish any conditions of its own. . . . The future of international racing centered in the question of whether the Cup was the common property of all existing yacht clubs or the private property of the New York Yacht Club, the privilege of competing for it being accorded foreign clubs as a favor and not as a right.

The highly respected London *Field* thought that the New York Yacht Club had shown bad faith. It questioned whether the club understood what it meant when it stated that matches "would be conducted on strictly fair terms." (The phrase or a form of it occurred in the letters which had gone out with successive deeds of gift.) What annoyed the *Field* most was the condition which required a winning club to agree to "covenant that the present unsportsmanlike conditions [of the deed of gift] shall not be altered."

American critics took the deed committee particularly to task for the clause which required the exact load-waterline length of a challenger long before a Cup race. What happened if, during her trials, it was necessary to add or reduce ballast for the sake of her trim? That subject alone stirred a good deal of argument. George Schuyler was asked for an opinion on that and some other clauses in the deed. He thought that critics were attaching too much importance to the load-waterline requirement. He defended "the right to know what the challenging yacht is like." He disagreed "most emphatically" that a vessel's lines would become known through information on her dimensions. What had concerned him most when working on the new deed with the committee, he stated, was the matter of courses.

107

I wanted it so arranged that in case of a disagreement as to the conditions of races, the boats would race on the sea without time allowance, and thus avoid the possibility of a challenger being left to the mercy of a club course where she would not have an equal chance to win.

Questioners appear not to have been satisfied by this explanation by the most respected of American yachtsmen and the last of the *America*'s owners. One of the major points of argument, relating to dimensions, had not been answered.

It was around this time that the secretary of the New York Yacht Club reported the receipt of various unfavorable acknowledgments from abroad. The Royal London Yacht Club and the Yacht Racing Association, to which all major European clubs belonged, expressed their regrets "that the terms of the new deed of gift are such that foreign vessels are unable to challenge."

Perhaps, even if it had not been the holder of the Cup, the club would nevertheless have acquired its great importance. It had been created and was maintained in the very center of American yachting activities. Among its members were numerous men of wealth, and its member fleet was extensive. But it was the Cup which had brought the club its widest fame. If foreign yachtsmen were now unwilling to compete for it, the famous trophy would become merely a piece of old silverware. Perhaps the new deed was in reality too restrictive. Thereupon various committees began a series of earnest consultations. A half-year passed before their report was submitted. They stubbornly adhered to the proposition that the conditions laid down by the deed of gift were intrinsically right. In view of criticism and the disapproval of foreign clubs, however, it would be advisable to modify it. (This was to be the first of a series of cracks in the protective armor laid around the Cup.)

"The party of the first part," said the club, and "whereas," and "be it resolved," and equivalent terms to show the seriousness of the situation—all of which led to a simple announcement. This indicated that the club was quite content with the conditions which had regulated the last three matches. They would apply, therefore, to any future Cup challenge races. But the club clung earnestly to the new deed. If a foreign club won the Cup under the present modification, it stated, it would be awarded the trophy only with

the positive understanding that it shall be held under, and subject to the new deed . . . inasmuch as this club believes it to be in the interest of all parties, and the terms of which are distinct, fair, and sportsmanlike.

After a little nibbling on the resolution which modified the deed, the English decided that it was digestible. They indicated that they would try it further when the Royal Yacht Squadron, in March 1889, challenged on behalf of the Earl of Dunraven. Beyond the usual formalities, all it said was that the Earl's boat was the *Valkyrie* and that its waterline length would not exceed 70 feet. The challenge came as a complete surprise and it was promptly accepted with pleasure. With the acceptance went a note to remind the challenging club that, should the *Valkyrie* win, the new deed of gift would have to be maintained without any modification. Thereupon the Royal Yacht Squadron rescinded its challenge.

From that point on Lord Dunraven, once a member of the British diplomatic corps, participated in correspondence between the clubs. He argued skillfully and stubbornly. For the sake of continued Cup matches it was a good thing that he was so convincing. The communications ended with an agreement which resulted in a second challenge from the Royal Yacht Squadron in November 1892. His lordship's new yacht

109

was the *Valkyrie II,* designed by Watson. All that the New
York Yacht Club knew about it officially, beyond its name,
was the fact stated in the challenge that its load waterline
was 85 feet. It was agreed that there would be time allowances if necessary. If the *Valkyrie* won, the Squadron would
accept challenges for the Cup under the modifications which
applied to the forthcoming match. However, no challenge
which conformed to the conditions in the third deed of gift
would be rejected.

By that time everyone in the New York Yacht Club concerned with the proposed match was pretty tired. They said
"Yes" in weary chorus. Had George Schuyler been there, he
would have applauded the acceptance. He was by nature a
mediator, and to him the word *sport* had only a pleasant,
social significance. In the summer of 1890, however, he had
died at sea and, as he would have wanted it, on board a yacht.

8

HAIL

THE HERO—

VALKYRIE II

Before Lord Dunraven's second challenge had been accepted, a dramatic new type of boat had made its appearance in American waters. She was slim, modish—and fast, "a masterpiece, and a revolution." Her designer was Nathanael G. Herreshoff. His boat was the *Gloriana* and she set a pattern which was to develop into the modern racing machine among yachts.

Cup matches had had a direct effect on yacht design. (The effect was to become more pronounced in the early twentieth century.) But improvements in racing boats were inevitable. Indeed, some of the most notable advances in yacht construction were applied to boats never intended as Cup entries. The soundness and stability of a vessel were understood, of course, to be fundamental in concept. But what had always been an

111

urgent consideration of yacht designers and builders, since their art began, was the element of speed.

Burgess and Watson, with their imaginative application of principles which held great potentials for increased speed, had had a profound influence on designers. Some of the more conspicuous examples of this influence came out of Scotland. They were the cutters produced by William Fife, Jr., of Fairlie. Two of his prize specimens had been visitors in American waters and had given their Yankee competitors a bad time. Herreshoff had learned a great deal from what Burgess and Watson had taught. He learned more from his observation of the Fife cutters. Perhaps he had not really needed these lessons; he was a genius in his own right. When he created the *Gloriana*, he was returning to an early love, sailboats. He was a born innovator and he loved the smell of wind. The Herreshoff firm, in which he was a partner, had been best known for its steam vessels.

In designing the *Gloriana*, a fin-keel sloop, Herreshoff threw away some long-accepted rules for boatbuilding. He reduced the waterline and increased the sail area. His novel craft was a few inches over 45 feet on the water with an exceptional overhang of 25 feet. She had practically no displacement; what gave her stability was her deep bronze-plated fin, which carried a bulb of lead styled like a fat Corona cigar. The *Gloriana* skillfully evaded the then current rule for load-waterline measurement. Because of that she, and the racing machines which followed her, became known as "the rating cheaters."

The critics, as was inevitable, turned out to jeer. They expected the first puff to lay the slender sloop on her beam ends. But after the *Gloriana* had outfooted the fastest champions in the seven races she entered during her first season, they stayed to cheer. Even more extreme models from Herreshoff's plans, most particularly the *Wasp*, followed the *Glori-*

ana. They maintained her designer's reputation for turning out the speediest sailing craft in American waters.

As Edward Burgess had died in 1891, a victim of typhoid at forty-two, Nathanael Herreshoff was the logical choice as designer for a new defender. He accepted a commission from a group representing the New York Yacht Club. Shortly thereafter a second syndicate from New York placed an order with him for another candidate. The first group, which included Frederick W. and William K. Vanderbilt, wanted an enlarged *Wasp* of steel with a fixed keel. The second group, headed by C. Oliver Iselin, ordered a deep-keel center-boarder.

Boston had its own ideas of what a Cup defender should be. John Paine, son of the general who had underwritten the two preceding defenders, designed a sloop of steel with two centerboards and of the ballast-fin type. She was the *Jubilee,* patterned after the *Wasp,* but with more extreme lines. And the successor firm of Edward Burgess had an order from a Boston syndicate to build yet another fin-keel steel yacht, to be called *Pilgrim.* The mass production of expensive yachts as potential defenders probably gave the impression abroad that Americans were seriously worried about their Cup.

When the *Colonia,* built for the club syndicate, took the water, she showed herself to be a most businesslike racing machine. So, for that matter, was Herreshoff's creation for the other New York group. She was the *Vigilant.* Among her novelties were a hollow bronze centerboard and the first use of Tobin bronze, on her steel hull. She was a mechanical wonder to those who saw her. Her board, which gave her a maximum 24 feet when fully down, could be raised or lowered from below deck by powerful differential lifts. This gave but a hint of things to come. Machinery was to intrude much more heavily in a sport which had long depended only on the physical energy of men.

113

As a result of a series of trials the *Vigilant* was the choice of the New York Yacht Club as the defender. There was nothing really wrong with the *Jubilee*. But luck was against her; she was the victim of a series of irritating accidents. No one was too happy about the *Vigilant*'s behavior in stays but it was felt she would become less lazy in her tacking after a little study and revision. The other contenders for the honor of defending the Cup just weren't in the running.

The *Valkyrie II* had left England just in time to get herself into a mess of heavy September storms. There was genuine worry over her safety, but after a month of beating her way across she dropped her hook in safe waters. That trip had shown her mettle but it had seriously cut into the time she needed for tuning up in local waters. When the yachting experts looked her over, they decided that she was not going to be easy to beat. She was "sweet and clean," a triumph of Watson's skill in designing. While she was under construction, Watson had also produced a sister ship, the *Britannia*, for the Prince of Wales. She was "the greatest racing yacht the world has ever seen"—a British opinion, and quite justified by her remarkable record as a prize winner.

All yachtsmen who could get to where the *Valkyrie* lay converged upon her. She was well worth attention. It was her owner, though, who commanded most interest. The press made much of him and reported his history in intimate detail. His father, a noted Celtic antiquarian, had hoped that his son would become a concert violinist, and, when still young, Lord Dunraven had acquired a high reputation as an outstanding fiddler. But the "wind's song" was a stronger call than the melody of strings. He went earnestly into the career of sailing, held a master's certificate, and wrote a valuable textbook, *Self-Instruction . . . Practice . . . Theory of Navigation*. He was also the author of books on travel, hunting, and Irish history. After experiences as a war correspondent, he entered politics and was a remarkably progressive one for his period. Sports were a significant part of his life. On his Irish estate he had a valuable stud and rode in many a steeplechase.

New York society thought he had enough charm to float the *Valkyrie*. For the sake of the upper circle of its readers the correct journals reported that he was Windham Thomas Wyndham-Quin, fourth Earl of Dunraven and Mount-Earl, of Dunraven Castle, Brigend, Glamorgan, Wales, and of Adare Manor (his birthplace), Adare County, Limerick, Ireland. The young men about town abandoned all other of their occasional occupations in order to imitate the young Earl—except in the exhausting business of sailing. On a day when he had a touch of gout—a constitutional ailment of British landowners—Lord Dunraven appeared on the street wearing a brown shoe and a felt slipper. Thereupon the coterie of male admirers, without bothering to acquire gout, adorned the highways in a similar rig.

The crew of the *Valkyrie* did not think his lordship charming at all. They had a little time off, after their hazardous Atlantic voyage, to adjust to New York's Indian summer and to enjoy the city's hospitality. Then Lord Dunraven put down his good foot: carefully supervised meals, just so much time ashore and, when back on board, a smelly, black preparation, the *"Valkyrie* cocktail"—a medicine for strong men. Drink it—or else; his lordship knows best. He was not going to lose that Cup just because any of his crew of thirty-five men was not up to form.

There were seventy men on the *Vigilant,* and they had more than numerical importance. As a total of live ballast, they represented over six tons. When lying on the weather deck, as they frequently were, they had a very definite effect on their boat's stability. (The number of men on board a racing yacht became a weighty matter for club committees, which finally worked up a rule as to how many were permitted each few feet on board.) The *Vigilant* was 126′ over all to the *Valkyrie*'s 117′ 3″, with 85′ 10″ waterline for the former and a foot over that for the latter. The defender, with a beam of 26′, had a draft of 13′ 6″; the challenger, whose beam was 22′ 4″, had a fixed keel of just over 16 feet.

The races were to be held off Sandy Hook, the best three of five to win. The first was to take place on October 5, 1893. In the very light air at the start, the *Valkyrie* showed herself to be livelier than the *Vigilant,* which was still pretty slack in stays. Instead of the grace period of two minutes under the old rule, the contenders were to cross the line on gun signal, ten minutes after a preparatory warning. This gave both helmsmen a welcome opportunity to display their skill, to the delight of the overwhelming spectator fleet. But what little wind there was just faded shortly after the *Valkyrie* rounded the outer mark. She was then 26 minutes ahead of her rival. When the race became a drifting match, it was called and the yachts were towed to their moorings.

The two completed races, October 7 and 9, were won without much trouble by the defender. Light wind killed the chance of a race on the eleventh. The third was run on Friday the thirteenth—and it was a lucky day for everyone who saw that race. There was never another like it in the whole long series of challenge matches.

A 15-knot wind out of the east had a feel of much more to come. Crews and afterguards prepared for a wet race. The *Valkyrie* had been remeasured because of the addition of ballast, and her allowance of 1 minute, 48 seconds was cut 15 seconds. At her wheel was Captain William Cranfield, whose tactical skill was widely admired. The *Vigilant* was under the command of Captain William Hansen. Nathanael Herreshoff was on board and not merely as an observer, for he was often at the helm. A few minutes before the time for

116

Genesta taking a bite out of *Puritan's* mainsail just before the start, September 8, 1885. *Genesta* lost her bowsprit. The defender's fault. *From a drawing by L. A. Shafer, 1899.*

At this moment in *Genesta's* career, September 14, 1885, the artists show her flying. Otherwise the mooring chains of the lightship may well have tangled with her very deep keel. The excursion fleet appears to be right where *Puritan* is heading. *Drawn by M. J. Burns and J. O. Davidson for* Harper's Weekly, *September 1885.*

Getting aft the main sheet on *Puritan. Drawn by M. J. Burns and J. O. Davidson for* Harper's Weekly, *September 1885.*

Volunteer (in foreground) about ready to pass *Thistle* shortly after the start of their second race. *From a water color by W. G. Wood.*

starting, the *Valkyrie* carried away part of a throat-halyard block. Captain Cranfield himself followed two men aloft to look at the nuisance. The main came down and the block was replaced. On the *Vigilant* the lifts couldn't get the center-board down. It was at last forced almost to where they wanted it. These minor annoyances suggested that this was the right day for trouble. While repairs were being made the race was postponed for more than an hour. After a careful look at the lowering sky, Captain Hansen had a reef put in the mainsail. Captain Cranfield took the hint and ordered one for the *Valkyrie*. Working topsails were set on both yachts.

Then they jockeyed for the starting line near Sandy Hook Lightship. The second signal was only seconds away—and the *Valkyrie* was in the wrong position, to leeward of the de-fender. Traveling fast, the challenger luffed hard just before the line and came out where Captain Cranfield wanted her to be, on the *Vigilant's* weather side. That skillful maneuver brought the English helmsman a spontaneous cheer. Then the boats beat out to windward, spray in their eyes, lee rails awash.

The *Valkyrie's* ability to point put her almost two minutes ahead at the outer mark, 15 miles from the start. She made ready for the run home. (It looked very much as if this were to be her day, for she was fast down wind.) That was when the real excitement began. The sea was slashing under a strong breeze, around 30 knots, with puffs rated at a moderate gale. It seemed that it would no longer be necessary for the *Valkyrie's* men to hold up an oversize sign reading KEEP FURTHER OFF to warn some crowding steamer. With her spinnaker sheeted home, she started away faster than the pursuing excursion fleet of about two hundred steamers and tugs.

On the *Vigilant,* then about 600 yards astern, the situation called for some quick action. Up went her spinnaker. Then

117

her balloon jib topsail was sent up in stops. Its halyard jammed in a hank. A hand scrambled to the topmast head and down its stay to release the fouled line. Two others went aloft, one to the sky at the topmast head, where he lashed the head and tack of the working topsail and prepared to send its halyard to the deck. His partner, hanging onto the wind with his teeth, hauled himself out on the gaff to help with the topsail and bring its sheet to deck.

While these seagoing monkeys were working aloft—they were up there for a quarter of an hour and more—another hardy character who may have felt that there was nothing left to live for had gone out on the boom. That spar was then almost athwart the beam and every so often it sliced the crest off a wave. They tried to make it easy for the man by slinging him from the masthead in the bight of a gantline and then dragging him along the boom with an outhaul. His orders were simple and direct: Shake out the reef; if the points are jammed, cut them, and don't annoy us by falling off that slippery round boom—you're wet enough right now. The helmsman had no intention of spilling a spoonful of wind out of the main, even though a half-gale was playing a tune on the shrouds.

When his job was completed, the rest of the crew laid beef on the throat and peak halyards and the mainsail was swayed up full. The balloon jib topsail had been broken out and then a small club topsail, already aloft, was tied in to windward of the lashed working topsail.

Yachting history has no record of such operations as those which had been performed on the *Vigilant* in that gale of wind. As a consequence of heroic efforts which had increased her sail spread, the defender leaped forward.

While most of the crew of the *Vigilant* were overworking, the *Valkyrie*'s afterguard was having a series of experiences calculated to induce nervous breakdowns. When they had ordered her spinnaker set, it went up loose. (This was traditional British practice. American yachtsmen went to the trouble of holding in their light sails with stops, until aloft.) There was a slight tear in the sail when she went up; no one knew why, but there it was. A concentrated squall went promptly to work on it. It wasn't up long enough to bellow out a brief chantey before it was ripped into useless shreds. With speed and energy entitled to better success, a light muslin spinnaker was run up in its place. It was a huge sail, and if it had not been so delicately made it might have held. But before it had its full of wind, the crosstrees caught it, and after a breathless few minutes it went the way of the spinnaker. The *Vigilant* was so close now that the afterguard on the *Valkyrie* could have laid a seabiscuit on her bowsprit. Quickly a third, smaller kite went up on the challenger, a balloon-jib topsail which the British termed a bowsprit spinnaker. It tried to do the work of a full-size sail.

With every stitch of canvas on her that she could wear, it seemed as though the *Vigilant* would leave the water and start flying. With that weight of wind on her it appeared certain that something must give. But she was superbly stayed. There was no sound from the taut men on both yachts. This was a moment which might never be lived again. The *Vigilant* came tearing on—and shot across the line 2 minutes, 13 seconds elapsed (40 seconds corrected) time ahead of the challenger. That was the closest a whole defender had come to losing a race.

It was, said Sir George Leach, an observer from abroad and a noted British yachting expert, "a splendid race, nobly sailed." It was, said the reporter of the *New York Times*, "probably the greatest battle of sails that was ever fought." Just who the men were—Norwegians, Swedes, Americans—

whose deeds on the *Vigilant* were so valiant seems now to be forgotten. They made yachting history. What they did was conspicuous partly because such dangerous operations were rarely called for in the sport of yachting. Commentators of the day gave them high praise.

And the *Valkyrie* was praised for being the first challenger to beat a defending boat while racing to windward. It was willingly agreed that the *Valkyrie* would have won had she been able to make full use of her spinnakers. Captain Cranfield explained after the race that he had not dared to shake out his mainsail reef because the *Valkyrie*'s mast was "badly sprung." In his judgment it would have been extremely dangerous to load it further in that heavy wind.

Well, the eighth challenge for the Cup was over, with a dramatic, classic finish. Lord Dunraven, and rightly, maintained his faith in his yacht. He was, he said, going to try again some day with a boat of equal merit, and he hoped that he would have as worthy a rival to meet. His only complaint was that the *Valkyrie* "was greatly interfered with by excursion steamers. . . . As a total result," he concluded, "I do not consider that the merits of the two boats have been determined."

What happened to the rival yachts in the following season is of interest. The *Valkyrie,* after being recommissioned in New York, went home. The *Vigilant,* now owned by George and Howard Gould, was sent across to test the English in their own waters. Her sailing master was Captain Hank Haff. It was arranged that the *Valkyrie* and the *Vigilant* would race each other again. Early in the 1894 season, however, at the start of a match which included the *Britannia,* the magnificent Cup challenger was sunk in the Clyde when the yacht *Satanita* stove her in amidships.

The *Vigilant* had her full of racing when she met the *Britannia,* almost a Watson counterpart of the *Valkyrie*. In seventeen races against the Prince of Wales's yacht the *Vigilant* lost twelve. "It wasn't the American defender which beat the *Valkyrie*," said British yachtsmen. "It was local conditions." Whether that was true or not, the time had come, thought Lord Dunraven, to make another try for the Cup.

9

HISS

THE VILLAIN—

VALKYRIE III

In October 1894 the Earl of Dunraven wrote to the New York Yacht Club to say that he was considering another challenge for the Cup. He suggested that some of the conditions which had applied to the preceding match should be modified. Among some other convincing and intelligent comments was "It appears to me somewhat unfair theoretically that a Challenging Club should be confined to one vessel, while the Challenged Club can select a champion from an indefinite number." He also liked the one-gun starting signal and wanted it retained. At the time he wrote, a commission had already been placed with George Watson for *Valkyrie III*. Two other lords and a commoner joined Lord Dunraven in underwriting the cost of the challenger.

The club committee was very agreeable to most of the
122

Earl's suggestions. It made an important concession by allowing a substitute yacht if the *Valkyrie III* failed to show herself as fast as her owners hoped her to be. But it could not accede to the request for a single-gun start. American yachtsmen had demanded a return to the crossing allowance of two minutes—"the feeling on this point is very strong." Before the crisscross of correspondence had ended, so much time had elapsed that the club accepted a challenge only eight months in advance of the date set for the Cup match. Again five races were arranged for, the best three to win.

The Earl's challenge had again come through the Royal Yacht Squadron. Once again that Club had argued against the strict maintenance of the deed of gift. Further, they stated, they did not really want the Cup if their representative vessel won it. The victory would be enough glory. The mere suggestion that the famous trophy was so unimportant to the club which had originally donated it outraged American feelings. The New York Yacht Club was very firm about it. If the Squadron's challenger did win, it "could not reject the custody" of the Cup. After a little reflection, the Squadron replied that it would accept the thing if occasion arose, provided that current modifications of the deed applied. That settled, American yachtsmen made ready for defense. There were many of them, and British yachtsmen, too, who were to regret that the 1895 match ever took place. It was to be dramatic theater, with percussion right out of Wagner's *Valkyrie.*

This time Boston stayed out of the contest for a defender. The commission naturally went to Herreshoff. The cost of the yacht was born almost entirely by William K. Vanderbilt; E. D. Morgan and C. Oliver Iselin each held one-tenth shares. The latter, a noted yachtsman, was appointed manager of the new boat, to be named *Defender.* What the commission called for was a sloop with a fin keel, the first of that type

123

used in defense. When completed, she had more the appearance of a cutter. Her bow was canoe-shaped, a style which was becoming fashionable in American waters.

Additional to novelties in design, Nathanael Herreshoff introduced another element in the building of a defender: the heaviest secrecy. In this he was not influenced by the elaborate concealment which had made the *Thistle* a thing of mystery. He seems by nature to have been a reserved man. Because of his taciturnity in public, he had been the victim of some galley yarns spun by reporters. After that he became even more clamlike when in the open. Insofar as the press was concerned, he was not on speaking terms with their news gatherers.

The *Defender* was loaded with metal and alloys: manganese bronze for bottom plating, aluminum (in which a little steel and nickel were mixed) for topsides, frames of steel, and bronze and steel fastenings. The Herreshoff idea was, of course, to produce as light a craft as possible. The idea was good but the combination of metals was bad in the laws of nature. The action of sea water on different metals in close proximity is to induce electrolysis—a scientific fact of which Herreshoff was obviously unaware. And, further, under the stresses of racing, aluminum was to prove structurally weak.

When the *Defender* was afloat, Captain Hank Haff, who was to be her sailing master, went looking for a crew. Suggestions had been made that the defense should be handled only by pure Americans—but not necessarily the noble red men. This may have been good patriotism but it did ignore the achievements of the skillful and energetic crew of mixed nationalities who had manned the *Vigilant*. Captain Haff went to Deer Isle, Maine, where, with the help of a local mariner, he hand-picked a salty group of American Vikings.

On the water the *Defender* showed, surprisingly enough, that her fine lines were more British than American. Her hull was deep and narrow (a beam of 23′ 3″), with easy bilges. With 124′ 2″ over-all length, she had a load-waterline length of 88′ 5″. Her draft was 19 feet and her total canvas spread 12,602 square feet. Herreshoff remarked to the syndicate for whom he had built her that he was especially proud of his use of aluminum. During her trials, however, it was rumored that the *Defender* was not a strong boat, and it was questioned whether her mast, under certain tensions, wouldn't go right through her hull. Manager Iselin vigorously denied the rumor. In a statement to the press he said that "the absurd stories that *Defender* is structurally weak [are] entirely false and unwarranted."

Meanwhile Watson had turned out *Valkyrie III*. It seemed almost as though he and Herreshoff had arranged a switch, for the challenger was as close to the American concept of a racer as the defender was to the British pattern. The challenger had, obviously, been designed to be raced in American waters and weather. *Valkyrie III* had a sloop's characteristics, with a broad beam (26.20′)—wider than any yet in a foreign Cup contestant; a pronounced sheer; shallow hull with hard bilges, and a deep keel (20′ draft). She was 129′ over all, with a load waterline of 88′ 10″ length. Her sail area was 13,028 square feet (3,000 more than the *Valkyrie II* carried). Her construction was wood over steel frames. She had experimental spars: a steel mast and boom, the latter hexagonal in shape. The mast was not used in the races—the steamer freighting it brought it over too late. What was used in the races on the *Valkyrie* was one of Oregon pine. As quickly as could be done, the *Defender*'s boom and gaff were unslung and replaced with steel spars. Her round boom was 700 pounds lighter than the one of wood it replaced.

The *Valkyrie* was as graceful as a yacht could be and quite as handsome as the *Defender*. There seemed, however, to be some uncertainty about her speed. In racing in England she had once beaten the great *Britannia,* but, on the whole, American experts did not think she was a boat about which the Cup holders need worry. She had come across the Atlantic in twenty-two days, jury-rigged as a North Sea ketch. Her hull appeared to have been strained in the passage and upon her arrival she went at once into dry dock. Both she and the *Defender* had been built purely for the purpose of a single match. As their type developed and became more refined, it was to become dangerous for a challenger to attempt the Atlantic passage.

The racers in the 1895 match opened up a period in yacht construction when seaworthiness was relegated to a secondary place and all the emphasis was on lightness and speed. Competent authorities were to point out later that the ninth Cup match brought in an era of "unwholesome boats," "a vicious kind of yacht, more of a curse than a blessing to the sport."

Though the trials to test the *Defender* were not easy on her, she was finally selected as the club representative. She ran aground twice and had a number of accidents which entailed new spars. Yachting commentators expressed apprehension over her ability to handle the defense, but manager Iselin's continued faith in her was reassuring. In the trials the recommissioned *Vigilant* and *Jubilee* and the *Volunteer* were entered. The rearguards of the pacers were frequently in violent protest because of alleged violations of racing rules by their rivals. The dailies and sporting journals gleefully opened their columns to the debate.

At the helm of the *Vigilant* was one not new to yachting honors, Captain Charles Barr. He made the trials exciting. His elder brother had skippered the *Thistle* and had been a teacher to Charles. The latter, too, was born in Scotland and had become an American citizen. His skill at the helm called for admiration. A historian of the Cup matches called him "probably the greatest skipper that ever trod the deck of a

126

racing yacht, an aggressive and magnificent helmsman." He was cool, calculating—and a master of the dangerous bluff. It was thought that sometimes his tactics were plain unscrupulous. Racing committees became very familiar with him, for he was frequently on the club dock explaining away some violations of the rules charged against him.

A few days before the date of the first race Lord Dunraven wrote to the committee in charge. He was taking the *Valkyrie* to the Erie Basin to be measured, he announced. There would be fifty-five persons on board, one bower anchor and chain and no water or other tanks. (He said nothing about the three mascots his crew had acquired: a yellow dog and a small black goat frisky as a bull pup, both of Brooklyn nativity, and a singing canary. The crew of the *Defender* were contented with a single mascot, a yellow cur, origin unknown.) Lord Dunraven asked that the committee "take every precaution to insure that the vessels sail on their measured load water-line length." That his lordship's suggestion was based on a suspicion of possible fraud was not obvious then. He seems to have heard some mean rumor that Iselin, manager and part owner of the *Defender,* had been responsible for the secret shifting of ballast on a racing yacht. The gossip was malicious, of course, but it appears to have had an effect on Lord Dunraven which was to prove most unfortunate.

The first race, September 7, 1895, was attended by the hugest pleasure-boat fleet yet seen. Its presence gave the contestants and the regatta committee no pleasure. On the more than 200 steamers and other craft which crowded the course were an estimated 60,000 paying passengers. This was far beyond the common-sense bounds of safety for many of the vessels. Twenty steam yachts had been assigned by the New York Yacht Club to try to keep the course clear enough for the helmsmen on both racers to see where they were going. It

127

seemed an impossible task at first; the club patrol had no authority over the good-natured, unruly fleet. By dint of urgent pleading they did finally get enough open water for the committee to decide that the race should begin. Both challenger and defender kept jockeying close to the starting line. They had no chance to come in for a fast crossing.

Though the *Valkyrie* made the line first—by four seconds— the *Defender* stayed with her. What wind there was remained too light to provide any real excitement. It was a pleasure, though, to see the two fine yachts in action. An hour or so after the start the boats went on a new tack almost simultaneously. As they nearly met, the *Defender* just barely slipped across the *Valkyrie*'s bow. She kept her lead thereafter. On a broad reach home the wind freshened and the sea kicked up a little. This helped to bring the *Defender* in 8 minutes, 20 seconds elapsed time ahead of the challenger.

The Cup and regatta committees received a startling announcement that night from Latham A. Fish, the club member on board the *Valkyrie*. Lord Dunraven had stated privately to him that additional ballast must have been secretly added to the *Defender* on the night preceding the race. That meant that she was not sailing on her measured load waterline, as she had acquired an extra foot of length. The Earl wanted both yachts remeasured and the waterline clearly marked. He also made a strong protest, by letter, to the regatta committee, about the intrusive mass of pleasure craft.

The committees, properly shocked over the imputation of fraud, maintained a discreet silence. In the early morning of the day following the first race, the requested measurement of both yachts took place in the Erie Basin. There was a nervous wait until the figures were announced. The change in waterline length between the measurement figures on the day before the race and the day after were negligible: one eighth of an inch longer for the *Defender*. It was expected then that that would settle the matter. It did not—but nothing happened at the time.

On the tenth, the day of the second race, the *Valkyrie* had on board Lady Rachel and Lady Aileen Wyndham-Quin, Lord Dunraven's daughters. A member of the famous family of sailmakers in Cowes, Thomas W. Ratsey, and the club's representative, Joseph R. Busk, joined them. At the challenger's helm was Captain Edward Sycamore, assistant to her sailing master, Captain William Cranfield. Both men were from the Essex coast, from Wivenhoe, whose reputation for breeding superior seamen equaled that of New England. Captain Hank Haff was at the wheel of the *Defender,* under command of C. Oliver Iselin. The weather was fair, with a light southerly breeze. In consequence, a much greater fleet of excursion boats than before showed up. As many of their skippers as could brought their craft to positions close to the starting line.

At the preparatory signal, both yachts, already across the line, went about and recrossed. Then, after a minute or two, both jibed ready to run for the line. That was the moment when one of the bigger excursion steamers, *Yorktown* of the Old Dominion Line, blundered right into the racers' paths. Perhaps her skipper thought the race course lay in the opposite direction and he'd just follow along! No sailor he. The indignant reporter for the *New York Times* called that steamboat man's action "one of the most unpardonable interferences ever seen in American yachting waters."

What happened then was that the *Valkyrie* managed to pass ahead of the steamer's bow, on her weather side. The *Defender* had to go astern of her and came out to leeward. For a minute or two the startled men on the committee tug did not know where the two yachts were. Then, with the *Yorktown* out of the way, they saw them, converging. They

129

were coming fast, too. As the *Defender* was on the starboard tack (and also close-hauled to leeward of the *Valkyrie*), she held the right of way. Captain Haff hauled his sheets to bring the *Defender* closer to the wind. The starting gun was still 15 seconds off and the challenger was getting too close to the line. Therefore, Captain Sycamore bore down, a tactic which, had it worked, could have back-drafted the *Defender* and given his own boat a few seconds' needed grace. But when he luffed sharply to straighten the *Valkyrie*'s course, the main-boom end was brought against the rival boat. The challenger's helm should have been more responsive or her hands should have brought the main sheet in faster as she started her luff. Whatever the reason, the shackle of the iron strap on the main boom, as the boom swung hard, caught for a moment on the *Defender*'s weather shrouds.

That was enough to part her taut topmast stay. With the topsail drawing, the topmast was sprung and the port spreader was carried away. The *Defender* was put in the wind while some hands went aloft fast. At that moment the starting gun was fired. Thirteen seconds afterward, the *Valkyrie* was across the line—and she kept on going. Behind her, the protest flag was displayed on the *Defender*.

Nothing that occurred in any Cup race caused greater astonishment than that the *Valkyrie* continued on her course. It seemed a clear case of hit-and-run, a violation of the age-old rules of safety at sea and, most amazing, everything considered, just bad manners. That, however, was not as Lord Dunraven saw it.

On the *Defender* her useless shroud was lashed and the jib topsail lowered. Then a temporary stay was rigged. The emergency work was done so fast that she went across the line only 1 minute, 15 seconds late. The first leg was to windward and Captain Haff handled the *Defender* with reasonable caution. On the second leg, when the wind freshened to 10 knots, a small balloon-jib topsail was set. Only an expert helmsman would have dared carry it. All the sail the boat needed was aloft on the reach home, for the temporary shroud was then to leeward. She came along so fast that she would have been ahead of the challenger had that last stretch lasted a little longer. The *Valkyrie* crossed first, 2 minutes, 18 seconds ahead, but it was not to be her victory. After the *Defender*'s starting time and her allowance were applied, the *Valkyrie*'s time was cut to 47 seconds.

Manager Iselin sent in a formal, written protest. On the eleventh the regatta committee reported that the *Valkyrie* had been disqualified in the race on September 10. Lord Dunraven placed the blame for the foul on the *Defender*. His arguments were that, after establishing an overlap, she had luffed, which brought her against the challenger; the *Valkyrie* had then luffed quickly to prevent an accident and to avoid hitting the committee boat; no protest flag had been visible to him—had he seen one he would have run up his own, and he was not aware of having violated any racing rule. He thought the regatta committee in error in allowing the protest but he felt he must accept their decision.

Photographic evidence was available which contradicted Dunraven's statement on the relative position of the two boats. These shots had been taken 30 seconds before and 5 seconds after the incident. But there had been no deliberate foul and no serious damage. The *Defender*'s manager dropped a note to Lord Dunraven offering another race. He could not have made the suggestion, he said, before the committee's decision. It was a fair offer but one which his lordship "quite properly" declined in two notes: "You would not have protested had you not believed that *Valkyrie* had caused a foul by committing a breach of the rules." He still could not understand the decision. And, in the second note: "Had the Committee ordered the race to be re-sailed that would have been a different matter; but how could I possibly agree to re-sail a race decided and given against me by the decision of the Committee?" Dunraven was criticized by yachtsmen and others for continuing the *Valkyrie* on her course after the accident. But there was no official comment about that.

Not everyone thought the decision of the regatta committee was what it should have been. The Cup committee, which lacked authority to order the race rerun, appears to have favored Lord Dunraven's explanation. An effort had been made to get Iselin to withdraw his protest but he had refused. "The Defender people were elated [at the decision]," the *New York Times* reported, not at all elated.

All the Summer they have almost regarded everything as theirs by right, and have shown a disposition to win by hook or crook, and they succeeded in beating Vigilant on two occasions by straining the yachting rules.

The consensus among "many fair-minded persons," it was stated, was that the regatta committee should have ordered the race resailed.

Dunraven was quite bitter about the sightseeing steamers. He put his complaint in a letter to the committee in which he said that, unless the course were clear of interference, he would not race on the twelfth.

To attempt to start two such large [yachts] among moving steamers and tugboats is exceedingly dangerous. I will no further risk the lives of my men or the ship.

At the start of the first race the crowding was so great that we could not see the mark-boat. . . . Today, on the reach home eight or nine steamers crossed my bow, several were to windward of me, and, what was worse, a block of steamers were steaming level with me, and close under my lee. I sailed nearly the whole distance in tumbling, broken water in the heavy wash of these steamers. To race under these conditions is . . . absurd.

132

Before the details of the 1895 match had been settled, Lord Dunraven had urgently asked the regatta committee to select any place rather than New York Bay for the races. He would have liked a course off Marblehead. The request had been denied. His lordship's urging had come partly from painful experience. When the *Valkyrie II* had been sunk in the Clyde, he was at the helm. The *Satanita* was racing the *Valkyrie* for the starting line when a boat loaded with spectators came across her bow. As she luffed sharply to avoid an accident, she rammed Dunraven's boat. There was nothing new about intrusive seagoing audiences. Commodore Stevens had made the observation at his Astor House speech in 1851: "We got off before the wind, and in the midst of a crowd that we could not get rid of for the first eight or nine miles; a fresh breeze then sprang up that cleared us from hangers-on."

No doubt about it; the Cup races off Sandy Hook had become a marine chaos with potentials of great danger. Yet there seemed to be nothing the club could do to ease the situation until restrictions were legally established. A special committee discussed the subject of his letter with Lord Dunraven, but they could only say they would do their best to keep the course clear. As an afterthought the Earl wrote the committee. He would sail on the twelfth provided that they would void the race if, in their judgment, the yachts were interfered with by the spectator fleet. If they would not accede to this, he would bring the *Valkyrie* to the line for the third race, give the *Defender* her start, and then withdraw.

This note, which went off at midnight, got to the committee before the time set for the race on the twelfth. Later, its members were to make the statement that a decision on Dunraven's demand was outside their authority. Some canny marine-news gatherers, their ears tuned to scuttlebutt, had reported to their city desks that the Earl of Dunraven was

133

hopping mad and might not sail. The suggestion appeared in some morning dailies. But as great a concourse of steamers and tugs with paying guests as ever before turned up at Sandy Hook. For the most part, however, their sea manners were better and they stayed farther away from the starting line.

The *Defender,* all dressed for a party, was playing around the starting line by the time the *Valkyrie* showed up. The challenger did not seem to be in a hurry or in a gay mood. All she wore were her working clothes, her big topsail in stops, her staysail stowed. She entered, however, into the usual maneuvers of a yacht making ready for the big moment of running for the line. When the signal came, the *Defender* shot across, with the *Valkyrie* close astern. Once across, the challenger luffed briskly. Down came her racing flag and up went the burgee of the New York Yacht Club, of which the Earl of Dunraven was an honorary member. Soon her tug made fast and towed the *Valkyrie* to her mooring off Bay Ridge. The *Defender* went on a lonely tour of the 30-mile course for almost five hours and, technically, was winner of what was planned as a race.

In such fashion the ninth challenge in the greatest of international yachting contests came to a bilious end. It was sour enough then—commentators gave it a slogan, "a fluke, a foul, and a fizzle"—but later events were to make it worse. The press, generally, hissed the villain; Lord Dunraven was "a quitter," "a poor sport," "a troublemaker." The young men about town, whose adulation had continued since 1893, abandoned his lordship and went in search of another hero, preferably not a yachtsman. Lord Dunraven stayed a while at Newport on a social round already arranged. He refused to discuss the Cup match openly. It was a relief to him, and probably to his hosts, when he went home.

It seemed to be tacitly understood that there would be no more challenges for the Cup. Perhaps it was just as well. The

134

matches had inspired as much bad feeling as good. Tiffany, which had advertised the Cup as on public display in its Union Square establishment, was advised to put the old trophy in its deepest vault, seal it, and forget it.

These opinions underrated the magic in the Cup. The dust from the Dunraven incident seemed hardly to have settled before another challenge was received. This came at the end of September from the Royal Victoria Yacht Club, acting for a member, Charles Day Rose. Rose, a banker, was better known as a horse fancier than a water sportsman, though he had recently acquired the *Satanita*. His extracurricular activities were, however, not important to the New York Yacht Club. They accepted his challenge for a match in 1896. The name of his yacht would be the *Distant Shore*.

Upon Lord Dunraven's return to England, he was interviewed by the noted yachting authority and editor Dixon Kemp, who reported that his lordship had expressed his annoyance that the challenge of "an American" had been accepted. "It is offensive to me for the reason that the American people have been assured by [their] press that the challenge is intended as a mark of censure upon me and a vindication of the action of the Cup committee." It was learned that Rose was not an "American," but Canadian-born, the son of Sir John Rose, an Englishman. Kemp then announced that the statement attributed to Dunraven, expressing his annoyance, was Kemp's own, but the retraction was generally doubted. During the interview, his lordship spoke in high terms of individual members of the Cup committee. He suggested a Mediterranean race between the *Valkyrie* and the *Defender* even though French rigging rules would greatly handicap the English yacht. It was clear, therefore, that he did not then regard the *Defender* or her manager, C. Oliver Iselin, among the untouchables.

Not long thereafter, over the towers of Dunraven Castle,

Wales, and Adare Manor, Ireland, storm signals were hoisted. They had been run up by Windham Thomas Wyndham-Quin, Earl of Dunraven. His lordship had been stung by the sharp criticism directed at him chiefly in the American press, and by those Britishers who had questioned the reasons for his withdrawal from the last race. It had seemed to him that everyone would approve of his fair demand that the spectator fleet be controlled or its interference taken into consideration. In his autobiography, published some time after the Cup match, Lord Dunraven wrote:

The London Stock Exchange cabled New York that they hoped that, when war was declared, excursion steamers would not get in the way of our fleet; and the New York Stock Exchange replied that in the interests of a fair fight they hoped our warships would be better than our yachts. All very funny, but not funny to me.

As was customary, Lord Dunraven had made an official report of the 1895 Cup match to the Royal Yacht Squadron, his sponsoring club. This was then published in pamphlet form. (The report had been sent over by the Earl while he was still in the States. It was to be shown later that he had requested that, if it were published, the portion relating to the *Defender*'s load waterline should be excluded. This suggestion did indicate that he must then have had a doubt on the subject or was unwilling to stir up a controversy.)

Portions of the pamphlet appeared in an article by Dunraven in the London *Field* on November 9, 1895. In it he stated openly details of what had been reported or discussed only privately before. This was the charge that a deliberate fraud had been committed through additional ballast secretly added to the *Defender,* which immersed her an extra three or four inches. As this had increased her load waterline a foot, her racing trim had been improved. The work, the Earl charged, was done by the crew of the *Hattie Palmer* (the de-

136

fending yacht's tender) the night preceding the September 7 race; the extra ballast was removed on the night of the race. Lord Dunraven and his associates had seen the *Hattie Palmer* tied up to the *Defender* on both occasions and had observed the tender's crew at work.

A week or so after publication of the charges in the *Field,* Lord Dunraven repeated them, with extensions, in a speech at Cardiff, Wales. He remarked that he had taken it as further proof of fraud that the regatta committee had ignored his request to put an observer on board the *Defender* directly after the first race on the seventh. The measurement of the American yacht on the morning of the eighth had, therefore, no value, as the extra ballast had by then been removed.

In his Cardiff address, the Earl remarked on "a storm of indignation passing over the United States at my treachery in formulating the new charge from the safe distance of three thousand miles." But, he went on, there was nothing new about his charge of fraud. If he had to, he would repeat it before the membership of the New York Yacht Club. The English and Scottish press gave prominence to his speech. Editorial reaction was highly critical of him for renewing the subject. Dunraven remained aggressively defensive. By then it was very probable that battered egotism had taken its usual form of stubbornness.

When the news of the Earl's charges reached the States, there was a chain reaction of violent protest. Most of the members of the New York Yacht Club expressed healthy anger and thought that Dunraven should be expelled forthwith from honorary membership. Yachtsmen generally rejected the imputation of fraud, and in angry terms. The gnashing of teeth resounded across the Atlantic. Even the New York Stock Exchange (but none of its shares) felt the impact of controversy. When James D. Smith, a former commodore of the New York Yacht Club, appeared on the floor of the Exchange to carry on his activities as a broker, he was soundly cheered. Trading was halted for half an hour, by tacit consent of the members. Speeches were made, Dunraven was hissed. Everyone then felt better and trading was resumed with renewed vigor.

The situation inspired by Dunraven was not one which could be ignored by American participants in the Cup match. C. Oliver Iselin, having first publicly called the Earl "a liar and a blackguard," calmed down long enough to write to the committees involved. He placed himself, Captain Haff, and all available members of the *Defender's* crew at the club's disposal for a full inquiry. Among other things he stated:

I was responsible for the proper officering and manning of the yacht. I personally examined the Defender's *hold and every part of her on the morning of the 7th, immediately before the race, and I know the absolute falsity of the imputation. I consider myself, therefore, as standing before the world solemnly charged by Lord Dunraven with an offence as base as could possibly be imputed to a sportsman and a gentleman, and which I indignantly resent and repel.*

He was particularly angry that Lord Dunraven

after a silence of more than two months makes this odious charge in a communication . . . to a public newspaper on the other side of the Atlantic, which it would be impossible for me to read or reply to before it had already made a deep impression on the minds of his countrymen.

A committee was promptly assigned to communicate with the Royal Yacht Squadron. In its reply that club refused to associate itself with the matter in any way as it had, by then, become "purely a personal affair of Lord Dunraven's." The general character of the reply gave a hint that perhaps there was something to his lordship's charge. This served only to make the whole affair more serious. It was thereupon decided by the New York Yacht Club to go into the subject so thoroughly that everyone concerned would be satisfied with the investigation and the correctness of the final decision. A committee of unusual prominence was appointed. Its members were Captain Alfred T. Mahan of the United States Navy (author of *The Influence of Sea Power Upon History, 1660–1783*), Edward J. Phelps, formerly American minister to Britain, J. Pierpont Morgan and some other yachting notables.

A representative of Lord Dunraven informed the committee that his lordship was prepared to come over and present his evidence. The Earl thought, however, that it would all be a pretty useless procedure, as the investigation was being conducted much too late. The committee nevertheless sent him a formal invitation. When he came, he was slipped off the liner at Quarantine and his quarters near the club were placed under police protection. His legal representative, who accompanied him from England, was an outstanding admiralty barrister, George R. Askwith, later knighted. Joseph R. Choate, then one of the best-known of American attorneys, and later ambassador to the United Kingdom, was Iselin's counsel.

The proceedings, which opened on December 27, 1895, began with the introduction of Lord Dunraven's pamphlet. His attorney made the statement that its public distribution had been necessitated as a matter of self-defense. The Cup committee of the New York Yacht Club had released a part of its report on October 24, 1895, to the American press. One New York paper, in its account, headed the news "Dunraven Cried Fraud." His lordship had been justified, therefore, in presenting his side to the press.

139

Dunraven had come over for just one day's meeting of the board of inquiry. (The proceedings took five full days.) He had, he said, pressing business at home and he left on the twenty-eighth. While a witness in his own behalf, he was completely self-assured and appeared stubbornly convinced of the justice of his cause. Under severe cross-examination he remained calm, showed a superior intelligence and a certain skill in parrying his questioner.

His major arguments were that his attention had been called to the "fact" that the *Defender* was visibly lower in the water on the day of the first race. Several people on the steamer which was the *Valkyrie*'s tender had first noticed the condition. That was factual evidence based on eyesight. Then there was that business about the *Hattie Palmer*'s crew busy on the *Defender* the nights before and after the race. And the refusal of the committee to put a representative on board the *Defender* after the race, as he had requested, intensified his belief that a fraud must have been perpetrated. (Latham Fish, the club member on the *Valkyrie* during the first race, emphatically denied later that Lord Dunraven had made such a request, and the regatta committee testified they had received no such message.)

Iselin's attorney gave a great deal of attention to a question which appeared to trouble him. If Lord Dunraven had thought a fraud was being committed, why had he not protested before the race on the seventh? His lordship replied that he did not believe a protest by signal was required under the rules. Furthermore, answering a question, Dunraven accepted the correctness of his attorney's statement that he did not want to disappoint "60,000 people who had collected to see the race." The suggestion that his lordship dearly loved commoners and was only too happy to entertain them did not satisfy Choate. He returned to the theme:

140

Q.—*You sailed that race that day, believing that some one was trying to cheat you, did you not?*

A.—*I sailed that race that day believing the* Defender *was immersed too deep in the water.*

Q.—*Yes, and believing that a fraud was being committed on you?*

A.—*If you like to put it that way.*

And, later:

Q.—*You were willing to sail with a fraudulent party, with a fraudulent rival under a Cup committee who refused you any opportunity to prove the fraud . . .*

A.—*Quite so, excepting, of course, your definition of the transaction as "fraud" and "fraudulent" all the time. I rather demur to that.*

Q.—*Well, you have concurred in it once or twice. Have you ever continued a sport of any kind after such a discovery by you, except in this instance?*

A.—*It never occurred to me before to have found myself in that position.*

When Dunraven left the club, his testimony over, two husky detectives saw him safely to his quarters.

The examination of American witnesses was painstaking. (The proceedings, when published, appeared in a stout volume of 555 solidly printed pages.) Herreshoff stated that any additional ballast would have diminished rather than improved the *Defender*'s speed. (She already had 85 tons of ballast in her keel.) Scientific evidence was adduced to disprove the possibility that the *Defender* could have been a foot beyond her proper waterline length. It was clearly shown that the alleged additional immersion of "three or four inches" to create that extra foot would have necessitated thirteen long tons more of internal ballast. At the waterline the *Defender*

141

displaced about three tons to the inch. (That was part of a body of technical evidence.) Proper stowing in a few hours of one night and the removal of those extra tons in part of another could not possibly have been done during the time the tender's crew worked.

There was no concealment about the activity of the crew. No one had been told that this was an undercover job and, therefore, top secret. The work had been done, true, but it was simply explained. As the *Valkyrie* had removed its water tanks, bulkheads and fittings, the removal of similar equipment was permitted on the *Defender*. That necessitated ballast to compensate for the lost weight. The pigs of lead ordered, about three tons weight, were oversize. They were cut on the *Hattie Palmer*'s deck at night and then stowed on the *Defender*. Riggers were also at work on bridles for main-sheet blocks on the same night.

In his excellent *Memoirs* (more than half a century after the Dunraven incident), C. Sherman Hoyt pointed out that there was probably a technical violation of the rule against any handling of ballast after 9 P.M. He also thought that the *Defender*'s management should have given notice to the Cup committee or to Dunraven about the necessity of "restowage of shiftable ballast." When it was done under cover of dark, it did appear to be surreptitious.

The proceedings completed, a full report went off to Lord Dunraven, the Royal Yacht Squadron and others concerned. The findings of the investigating board included:

Upon a careful consideration of the whole case, the committee are unanimously of the opinion that the charge made by Lord Dunraven, and which has been the subject of this investigation, had its origin in mistake; that it is not only not sustained by evidence, but is completely disproved; and that all the circumstances indicated by him as giving rise to his suspicion are entirely and satisfactorily explained. They deem it, therefore, but just to Mr. Iselin [partners, officers and crew] that the committee should express emphatically their conviction that nothing whatever occurred in connection with the race in question that casts the least suspicion upon the integrity or propriety of their conduct.

And the committee are not willing to doubt that if Lord Dunraven had remained present throughout the investigation . . . he would of his own motion have withdrawn a charge that was so plainly founded upon mistake, and that has been so unfortunate in the publicity it has attained, and the feeling to which it has given rise.

Lord Dunraven's stubborn adherence to his theme puzzled some good people. Believing that it was not actuated by petulance or malice, they thought that perhaps there was a reasonable explanation for his charge. They had not, however, accepted the contention that a fraud had been deliberately perpetrated. After publication of the club committee's report almost everyone accepted the opinion that the *Defender*'s management had been fully cleared. Some club members felt that, perhaps, Dunraven had not been fairly treated. It was reported that they were expelled or that they resigned under pressure. Meanwhile, in London, the press continued its unfavorable opinions of Lord Dunraven. Editorial writers thought the club had been "most commendable in passing no censure upon Lord Dunraven." It was suggested that he apologize for his "short-sighted delinquencies."

There was no apology. There was, however, a cable from his lordship to the club. In it he asked that further action be withheld until two of its members received letters already mailed by him. A motion had been made to request his resignation; he must have been aware of it when he cabled. When the two letters were received, it was found that their contents were merely a reiteration of his complaints—and a resumption of hostilities. After all, said he, his charge of fraud had been

143

"made on *bona fide* direct evidence of the eyesight—my own and that of competent men. . . . I cannot admit to a mistake in observing facts."

The club then took expected action: It expelled him from honorary membership, as he had "forfeited the high esteem which led to his election." Just prior to this step the Earl had resigned. The English press published his letter before it was received by the New York Yacht Club. Writing of the summary expulsion, many years thereafter, C. Sherman Hoyt remarked that

whether such action was taken prior to receipt, or after, as claimed by Lord Dunraven, of his rather dignified letter of resignation, is of little moment now, but at the time it added fuel to the bitter feelings on both sides of the Atlantic.

The notorious affair had brought international sports to their lowest level. During the height of the dispute, the challenge from the Royal Victoria Yacht Club on behalf of Rose was withdrawn. Rose took the step by cable: "Owing to the general impression that my challenge might be construed as an expression of opinion on the result of the last race . . . I must regret having to ask you to withdraw same." It was reliably reported that the Prince of Wales had been annoyed at Rose for issuing his challenge before he had discussed the situation with Lord Dunraven. Then, in November 1895, Sir George Newnes, owner of the *Strand Magazine* and *Tit-Bits* announced that he would challenge. In the following year, however, his club, the Royal London Yacht Club, refused to forward his challenge. They had already gone on record, they stated in explanation, that they were opposed to the third deed of gift which "was inimical to the sport of yacht races."

Although Dunraven retained an interest in yachting—he

had the first semi-Diesel yacht built for him when he was seventy-nine—after the 1895 match he retired, except occasionally, from active racing. In his autobiography he wrote:

I am not sure that I like international contests. . . . I think they tend to demoralize sport by turning it into a serious business in which national prestige is at stake, and to convert amateurs, playing a game for the game's sake, into professional specialists struggling for their country's sake.

Under the British rating rules *Valkyrie III* had to face penalties which put her at a disadvantage in matches with most British cutters. Her end came in 1901, when she was broken up. The *Defender* finished her career in the same year. Though almost entirely rebuilt in 1899 in order to participate in trials for a Cup defender, she was suffering from marine anemia. Electrolysis had done its stealthy work of corrosion on the hull of mixed metals, and her aluminum topsides could not take the strain of racing.

For some years after the Dunraven affair the topic could be depended upon to inspire violent argument. Perhaps the most vicious incident of the aftermath period was the publication of a pamphlet, *Which Was Right?*, in 1898. Its author used a pseudonym, Captain J. G. Johnston. In it an attempt was made to prove that the *Defender* was a "trick boat,"

so constructed that, by means of tanks effectually hidden from the view of even an expert and pipes leading thereto and a pump attachment, water ballast to the amount of 23,870 pounds or about 11 tons could be introduced and taken out at will.

As a part of its investigation, the special committee of the New York Yacht Club and Lord Dunraven's counsel (a maritime authority) had examined the *Defender* in her winter

145

quarters. There were, of course, no secret compartments nor could alterations have been made to conceal them had they been there originally. The offensive pamphlet was merely further evidence of the suspicions and animosities stirred by Lord Dunraven's unfounded charge of fraud.

THE LIPTON ERA

Valkyrie II losing the first of her spinnakers in her third race against Vigilant, October 13, 1893. From a drawing by L. A. Shafer, 1899.

Defender taking the lead from *Valkyrie III* in the first race of the
ninth challenge match, 1895. *From a water color by W. G. Wood.*

George L. Watson, designer of Cup challengers.

Captain "Hank" Haff, sailing master of several defenders.

As Americans saw the Earl of Dunraven, courtesy of *Harper's Weekly*, 1895.

As the British saw the Earl of Dunraven in his mellow later years. *A photograph by F. A. Swaine in Dunraven's* Past Times and Pastimes *(Hodder & Stoughton, London, 1922).*

10

"SIR TEA"—

AND *SHAMROCK I*

What must have been its most pleasant surprise in years came to the New York Yacht Club on August 6, 1898. It came in the form of a cable sent by an unassuming Irish yacht club, the Royal Ulster of Belfast. The club was challenging for the Cup on behalf of one of its members, Sir Thomas Lipton. It hoped that the suggestion for a match would be agreeable to the holders of the Cup.

Nothing could have been more agreeable to the New York club. An acceptance was made promptly and with enthusiasm. The suggested visit of the challenging club's committee was a splendid idea; "they will be warmly welcomed." The gloomy prophets who were so certain there would be no more challenges, that Cup matches had become only of academic interest, were wrong—again.

149

To the New York Yacht Club the Lipton challenge had novelty but no particular significance. No one could foresee— even Sir Thomas could not then know—how it was to develop. Before his time the Cup had been a provocation to the British, a symbol of a superiority they had long held and were unwilling to relinquish. And the nature of its defense had seemed to make the trophy more important than the sport for which it stood. In restoring it to its intended place, Sir Thomas did so by his almost invariable graciousness and generosity. He succeeded in the fullest degree in giving real meaning to the donors' original intention, that the trophy should inspire "friendly competition between foreign nations." In making it the Cup that cheers Sir Thomas was to become indelibly associated with a whole era in international yachting.

At the first meeting with the challenger's representatives the club committee was probably wary and protective. It wasn't at all necessary. Everyone was charming; no unreasonable demands were made. There was not a single problem to be settled. In the visiting committee was the noted designer, William Fife, Jr., who was following in the tradition of three generations of a yacht-building family at Fairlie, Scotland. The challenging yacht, he said, would be called the *Shamrock* and her waterline length was to be 89' 6".

The Cup committee expressed a natural curiosity about the challenger. They had all sipped the pleasant beverage almost synonymous with his name. They might now drink even more of it and try to understand the meaning of tea leaves. The committee was composed of noted yachtsmen, cultured men, and they were not too openly inquisitive about Sir Thomas. Fife and his companions told those surface details of the challenger's life which they assumed would interest hosts of such quality. The committee members tried not to appear astonished when they were told that Sir Thomas had

150

never been a racing yachtsman. He had never as much as had his hands on a helm. But he was owner of an exceptionally fine steam yacht, the *Erin,* on which he had traveled widely, and when on board he wore a yachting cap.

What the visitors from abroad left out in their account of their principal, perhaps through traditional reticence, was of far greater interest than what they told. It shows that he was an exceptional man, and it makes his role of persistent challenger more understandable.

Shortly before his birth in 1850 his parents had fled the misery of the potato famine in Ulster, Ireland, and settled in Glasgow. They were poor in their new home but they did not face daily hunger. Lipton's father found a place as a time-keeper in a warehouse. Out of a weekly wage of thirty shillings the thrifty man supported a family—there were four children—and saved a shilling now and then. Sir Thomas, in his memoirs, was to write with pride of those difficult early years in the cleanly little tenement flat on Crown Street, Glasgow. And he wrote with unashamed love—his lifetime love—of his mother, and of the respect he held for his father.

Young Lipton had no formal education after he was ten, except for a brief and casual acquaintance with the textbooks of a night school. That was enough for one who was to prove himself a commercial genius. He went to work, to "earn his keep and aid the family." By the time he was fifteen—a man—and after the sort of jobs a boy tries, he decided that his fortune lay in the glittering West. There was no holding him then. He asked for his mother's blessing and got it. When he reached New York the last shots of the Civil War were being fired.

There was no work in New York but he found employment in Southern tobacco and rice fields, then as a peddler of family portraits done on appointment, and as commander of a tramcar in New Orleans. He saw more of the States than most

151

immigrants do. When he ran out of money he found a berth, as a stowaway, on a coastwise steamer. He didn't wait to be caught. When he faced the captain (who had once been a boy), he was allowed to work out his passage in the galley—exactly what a hungry youngster would hope for. Back in New York he found his niche, clerking in the grocery section of a department store. At last he knew what he wanted to do: become a provision merchant.

At nineteen he returned home. He had with him some special gifts for his adored mother—a "darlin'" rocking chair and a barrel of flour. He lifted them to the roof of a cab he had hired. The fare would not be much, and it would not be missed out of the $500 he had saved. The hackman was instructed to hurry to Crown Street, where his folks still lived. Then he was to proceed, on the last few streets to the flat, at a most leisurely pace. Young Tommy was going to apply the most important lesson he had learned in the States: advertise! Leaning out of the cab, he shouted greetings to the astonished Crown Street folk on the street or at their windows. It wasn't often a cab came clattering over the cobbles. It was a triumphant day for him, a hero's return, and everyone suddenly remembered Tommy Lipton.

The tiny grocery store his father had recently opened, out of his savings, was not nearly big enough for an imaginative young man influenced by American business techniques. He was just twenty-one when he opened his own shop. By the time he was thirty he owned a chain of twenty. It was his flair for focusing attention on his wares and his remarkable sense of timing which gave momentum to his commercial success. Some overly enthusiastic admirers thought him the inventor of publicity. There was no question at all but that he made full use of it. What he did do which was novel in his locale was to introduce pictorial advertising and live promotion, a good deal of it in a vernacular and colloquial style. In the neighborhoods where these examples of homely wit were conspicuously on display, the neighbors had something to talk about for a week and more.

By the time twenty years had passed he weighed millions in the credit scale. During one of many interviews he was asked by a reporter about his politics. "It is very simple," he said, with his ready smile. "Open a new shop every week." By 1890 when one bought tea in the British Isles, one thought first of Lipton's. He was never too busy, when in Glasgow during the years of growth, to neglect his Sunday meetings with his parents and go with them to their little Presbyterian church. His brothers and sisters had died; then his parents went at good old ages. There was nothing to do thereafter but continue what he wanted to do: play intensely at his greatest hobby, his business, and to promote it through skillful advertising. His concentrated efforts developed a commercial empire.

A year or so after he had received a warrant (1895) as supplier of tea to the royal household, the Queen's Diamond Jubilee was celebrated. A member of the royal family thought it would be a good thing to provide meals for a full week to the dwellers in London's huge slums. Not enough people thought it a good idea and—an embarrassing matter to the sponsor—the plan was about to be abandoned because money just wasn't coming in. Sir Thomas heard of the impending failure and promptly donated £25,000. He was headlined for days thereafter. In 1898 he was knighted. The few intimate friends he had in England nicknamed him "Sir Tea." He had recently become an intimate of Edward, Prince of Wales, long a keen sailor. With such an association the new knight could hardly avoid yachting circles.

Yet when the Prince put his name in nomination for membership in the elite Royal Yacht Squadron, it became known that Sir Thomas would be blackballed. The Squadron was far too exclusive to admit a man without social rank, a mere purveyor of jams, sausages, teas. An Englishman's home was merely his castle; his club represented the ultimate in privacy. The Prince should really be more careful about his associations. Angrily protesting, the Prince withdrew Sir Thomas' name. The latter was far less annoyed about it than was his sponsor. At the urging of friends he had joined numerous clubs. By the time he was eighty he was paying dues to twenty-one, almost all of them including "Royal" in their name.

Once in a while he dropped into some neighborhood yacht club. The casual interest was a sentimental one. For, years earlier, he had participated in a regatta. It took place near the Crown Street tenement where he lived. The course lay in a large, rain-filled mud hole, ideal for homemade boats of miniature size. All the contestants were boys, not yet in their teens, and all members of the Crown Street Clan. There were no regulations; only the signal "Now!" At that, a contestant pushed his entry from the edge where he lay and blew might-ily on the sails of torn linen or heavy paper as long as he could.

The boat that got across the pond first was an undersize scow made from a wooden box. Its name was painted on its deck. It was *Shamrock*. As a reward for the great victory the designer, builder and owner had a small sign hung on him, inscribed "Comidore Crown Street Clan Yaht Club." He was Thomas Johnstone Lipton, age ten, and he never forgot that first yachting triumph. He recorded it in his memoirs and, in his maturity, he would delightedly tell about the incident to yacht-club acquaintances.

Most of his adult life took place under spotlights. A man of charm, with a ready native wit, he circulated chiefly among the well known, the well placed, the well fixed. A close friend remarked that it flattered his ego to collect celebrities. Gambling and its attendant luxuries were part of the behavior pattern of most of his associates. Yet Sir Thomas never gambled, never drank, never smoked. He was a tireless raconteur, yet no one ever heard him tell an even mildly risqué story. He entertained lavishly in a "hideous house," studded with trophies—a museum of bad taste. In consequence, his mansion at Osidge Park was more frequently referred to as "Sausage Park," a pleasantry which never failed to amuse the owner.

Some ladies, of varying degrees of charm, tried hopelessly to enter into a partnership with him. Among them was an English princess. (King Edward VII said "No!"—but Sir Thomas had never intended to say "Yes!") A Lady Lipton would have interfered with the really consuming passion of his life then, his business. And such a partner would undoubtedly have had a difficult time anyhow with a man whose concept of the perfect woman was his mother.

The notorious Dunraven affair had bothered Sir Thomas. There were too many people talking about it, blaming the New York Yacht Club and American yachtsmen generally. The association of Sir Thomas with American businessmen was very close. He admired them, and he had many friends in the States. His English acquaintances thought him more American than British. There must be some way, he thought, to smooth away the animosities stirred by the last match. Merely telling his British friends that Americans were not cunning, unscrupulous, and poor sports just wasn't enough. The tranquilizer had to be something dramatic. Suddenly he had it. Excitedly he told his friends, "I think I'll have a shot at the ould mug!"

Once he had decided on that, he had to make an even more important decision. He would have to restrain his impulse to publicize. That meant a self-control which would not be easy. For more than a quarter of a century his life had revolved around the widest public promotions of his business. He was his business. There was no question, though, about

155

his genuine intention to bring about more cordial relations between Britishers and Americans. He would be able to do that, he thought, if everyone understood clearly that that *was* his intention and that a challenge for the Cup was no mere advertising scheme.

His restraint during the long series of his challenges was highly effective. He seems never to have slipped in public. True, he had jokingly told a young lady at a Boston reception that he profoundly admired the city's forebears. Why? Because they had thrown tea overboard at a famous party in Boston Harbor, "as it wasn't Lipton's!" That was no advertisement, everyone agreed. Just further proof of the Lipton wit.

Then, after *Shamrock I* reached New York Harbor, a number of young men in their home-built catboat sailed around her at anchor off Tompkinsville, Staten Island. They had their hearts set on going on board and looking her over. They knew it wasn't going to be easy but they were prepared. They sailed over to the nearby *Erin,* where Sir Thomas was sunning himself. One of them held up a large canvas sign reading "We Use Lipton's Tea," while they played around the yacht. Sir Thomas signaled them to the accommodation ladder. They told him why they had come out. Very well, he would let them on the *Shamrock* if they would tear up that sign and not tell anyone about their scheme. (They kept that promise for years.) No advertising!

When he decided to challenge for the Cup, Sir Thomas offered the commission to a Belfast shipbuilder. What he hoped for was a racing yacht which would be Irish-built from the designs of an Irishman, and with an Irish crew. He was told that, eager as they were, the Belfast firm was not able to execute the commission. On their advice he gave the order to Thornycroft, a noted firm of shipbuilders on the Thames.

156

In turn, William Fife, Jr., was engaged as designer. Thorny-croft turned out a magnificent yacht. Fife had been influenced by Herreshoff's use of metals. The new boat, therefore, had manganese-bronze bottom plating and topsides of aluminum. (Proof was not yet fully available to show that the latter metal, as then constituted, was structurally wrong for racing yachts.)

The Lipton boat was designed to meet the American rule then in force. This still took into consideration only water-line length on even keel, and the square root of sail area. As a boat's sailing length was increased when she heeled under wind, long overhangs on a flat hull and a deep narrow keel with heavy outside ballast were standard form for racers.

The *Shamrock I* was 128′ over all with about 39′ overhang, a beam of 25′ and draft of 20′ 3″. From boom end to bowsprit tip she measured 189.13.′ (This is about the official length of a New York City block running north and south.) Part of the delicate engineering problems in the construction of racers was the staying of the mast. In the 1899 match the height of the single stick, with topmasts, was between 130 and 140 feet. (They were to become taller.) Steel spars and new, experimental metal for shrouds were then coming into more general use.

Both boats intended for the Cup match were constructed under conditions of elaborate secrecy. This had become established policy. Just why, no one seemed to know; the building of both challenger and defender was almost simultaneous. It would not have been in character for either Herreshoff or Fife to attempt to arouse curiosity through a system of calculated concealment. They did not need publicity. Nothing, indeed, was needed to increase the wide general interest over the planned match. Excitement about it had been genuine ever since it was announced. Journalists seemed most to enjoy

157

the current mystery. They were able to make imaginative use of their talents in filling space with predictions and salty gossip, and in playing the sleuth around the shipyards.

Herreshoff's creation, the *Columbia*, was launched in June 1899. She was the sole yacht built for defense and had been commissioned by J. Pierpont Morgan, heading a syndicate. C. Oliver Iselin was her managing owner. Her lines were more extreme than those of the *Shamrock*, with her 131' 8" over-all length, 89' 8" waterline and 24' 2" beam. Both boats had steel spars, internally braced. The masts were far from perfect. In one of her trial races *Columbia*'s snapped. That on the *Shamrock* kept her crew in a state of dither because it worked or buckled. Finding sails that would really set right on that temperamental mast was a problem. The *Shamrock* had six suits in her first year, and when the wind was on her not one was an ideal fit.

A challenging vessel had at last become so tender that she did not dare cross the Atlantic without a proper escort and strengthening. The distance between the Thames and the Cup was a long one and some of the passage might be difficult. The New York Yacht Club saw reasonableness in the request for modification of that part of the deed of gift which stated: "Vessels selected to compete for this Cup must proceed under sail on their own bottoms. . . ." If it were necessary, the *Shamrock* could be towed. She came across most of the Atlantic tied to the stern of the *Erin*. A storm broke her loose briefly but she went bravely through it under her reduced rig.

Sir Thomas, when he reached New York Harbor, was welcomed enthusiastically. (That was to be true of all his visits; the welcomes grew progressively greater.) The initial public reaction was something astonishing. Heretofore challengers had been received warily. Never before had Americans given voice to treasonable utterances, as many did now, that they

158

hoped the invader would take the Cup back with him. A delegation of prominent men and officials boarded the *Erin* shortly after she was anchored, to the frank delight of Sir Thomas. Fortunate chance was on his side; his visit could not have been better timed. The *Olympia,* with Admiral Dewey on board, had arrived earlier than was expected. She was sighted first from the *Erin,* then at Sandy Hook. The heroes of Manila Bay dined on board the Lipton yacht that night. Then the *Erin* took prominent part in the victory parade that steamed a little way up the Hudson a few days later. Receptions and parades kept the city in a gay mood. When the Cup races finally took place, they seemed a continuation of the carnival spirit which celebrated the triumph of American arms over Spain.

The *Erin,* back at her anchorage off Tompkinsville, became the scene of daily festivities. There was, of course, a bar and great quantities of properly brewed tea. It was open house for the numerous persons Sir Thomas had invited. They were conveyed to the *Erin* by a steamer he had engaged. After a few days of that, the really proper people began to find that they had other important engagements. It was the right thing to do, of course, to meet "Sir Tea," but not at the risk of being trod on by simply hordes of people not socially registered.

It had been decided that October would be a more dependable month for breezes than September. It was a wrong guess. On four occasions, beginning with October 3, the rival boats went hopefully out but light winds or no wind at all prevented racing. Then fog made it impossible even to start on four other days. Betting on the races had become feverish and stakes were high. It was said that everyone concerned with the planned races lived for nearly two weeks on chewed fingernails only. Sir Thomas had his own opinion on the maddening wait:

159

If the Book of Job were to be written again, a windless day off Sandy Hook while two yachts are waiting to pit against each other their vast expanse of sail might serve the purposes of an allegory.

Nearly two weeks after the date set for the first race it actually took place, on October 16. It was a disappointment. There was a choppy sea and an occasional drifting fog. At one time the fog was thick enough to require the service of a club tug as a guide to the outer mark. A breeze lifted the soupy mixture, and the run home was the quickest part of the race. The *Columbia* had been better able to meet the head seas on the beat out, a distance of 15 miles, which took almost three hours. She also showed that she could point higher than the *Shamrock*. Her elapsed winning time was 10 minutes, 14 seconds.

The turnout of sightseers had been large on each of the days a race was expected; on the sixteenth it was enormous. For the first time, however, since Cup challenge matches had begun, the spectator fleet was kept in line (although tugs and steamers were still dangerously overcrowded). Congress had finally agreed with American yacht clubs that there ought to be a law. In 1896 a special act "for the safety of passengers on excursion steamers, yachts . . . and all craft taking part in regattas" was passed. As a result, revenue cutters, torpedo boats, steam-powered yachts of the New York Yacht Club did an effective job in keeping sightseers at least a mile off the course. Skippers of the spectator fleet had copies of the law and for the most part they obeyed it. The few who stepped out of line were complained against by the commanding officer of the patrol. Faced with a loss of license, they promised to be good. Sea manners of marine observers at regattas have been correct ever since.

An interested observer of that first race between the

Columbia and the *Shamrock* was a twenty-five-year-old genius, Guglielmo Marconi. He was on the new coastwise steamer, *Ponce,* and in charge of the wireless transmitter. For the first time in history Marconi wireless was used to report a Cup race. The messages went to the inventor's clients, two New York newspapers. The less fortunate dailies had to content themselves with the slower methods of communication then in use and which thereafter could be abandoned. One of these had involved a cable ship anchored near the committee tug, which reported only the start and the finish. The other method was the use of tugs which would follow the racers for a while, then run close to the beach at Navesink on the New Jersey coast. There a strong-armed hurler on deck would throw a canister carrying a message shoreward. An expectant runner would then wade out, seize the container and take the report to a waiting telegrapher. Cold, wet work, but nothing was too good for the readers of daily newspapers. Carrier pigeons also were used on occasion.

As part of the mutual agreement before the 1899 match, it was decided that races were "no less a test of strength of construction of competing vessels, than of their sailing qualities." The first to be affected by this agreement was the *Shamrock*. In the race on October 17 her topmast snapped when a puff hit her big topsail. The challenger was put in the wind to see if she could be jury-rigged, but the damage was too great. The *Columbia,* under the rule, continued on her course while her rival was towed in. The defender, therefore, had two wins to her credit.

The only race in the series which was worth the while of spectators was the last, in a brisk northerly breeze on the twentieth. The *Shamrock* was fast—she hit 13 knots several times while on a reach—and spot bets favored her to win that race. That was partly because the *Columbia* was 1 minute, 1 second late at the crossing line. (As there was a 2-minute grace period at the start, that tardiness had no bearing on the final time calculation.) The defender came along so fast, however, that at the turning mark she was 17 seconds ahead of her opponent. She had started out without a topsail on the first leg, down wind, but she had broken out her spinnaker as she crossed the line. That sail very nearly gave the afterguard heart failure. After behaving for a moment as a well-trained spinnaker should, it suddenly collapsed as though it were a pricked balloon. Then, when it filled again, its boom buckled and soared to a dangerous height. Everyone waited tensely for the pole to snap but it remained in its half-circle. Temperamental though it was, the sail finally drew so well, the hands in charge just nursed it until the *Columbia* was ready for the beat home. Meanwhile, the topsail had been set and it was that which put the *Columbia* ahead on the run out. When the race was over, she was 6 minutes, 18 seconds elapsed time ahead of the *Shamrock*.

It had been a series marred by irritating delays, an accident, and not much excitement. For one person particularly it was a triumph. He was Captain Charlie Barr, skipper of the *Columbia*. The defender's manager, C. Oliver Iselin, had been scolded when he announced his choice of Barr. Indignant yachtsmen and most of the hands on the *Columbia* wanted only a "full-blooded American crew" on a defender— and Barr was a naturalized citizen. This was pretty silly business, of course, and narrow-minded. To Iselin's credit, he ignored the noisy meddlers, who became even more persistent when the *Columbia*, during her trials, had a number of accidents. After the series there was unstinted praise for Captain Barr. It was the general opinion that he had proved himself a better strategist and helmsman than any of the *Shamrock*'s afterguard.

The challenging vessel was at a disadvantage, as her designer had suddenly become ill and was confined to bed

throughout the series. He could undoubtedly have been help-
ful to the distinguished trio who were in the *Shamrock*'s
afterguard. They were Captain Archie Hogarth, a highly
rated professional skipper; Captain Robert Wringe, a helmsman of equal reputation, second in command; and Captain
Ben Parker, sailing master of the Kaiser's *Meteor II*. The latter was on board in a consultative capacity. Yachting authorities felt that the challenger had suffered from a divided
control, that any one of the trio would have been enough.

Yachtsmen converged on Sir Thomas to praise him for his
spirit, to offer counsel and even to murmur their sympathy.
Yet he was not downhearted. True, his yachting cap had been
tilted to port from starboard and his half-barnacle goatee
seemed to have retired in the cleft of his chin. But he was as
erect and gracious as ever. Several American yacht clubs indicated their esteem by electing him to honorary membership,
among them the New York Yacht Club. There was, finally,
the last of the farewell dinners. When he rose to speak he
announced, beaming, "Gentlemen, I shall be back." (That
was to become a familiar comment.) Thereupon his listeners,
after a spontaneous cheer for "the world's best sportsman,"
shouted the hope he would make it soon. When he reached
England he was greeted with as much enthusiasm as if he had
the Cup tucked under his arm.

11

"THREE
LEAVES TO
A SHAMROCK"

A year after the 1899 match the Royal Ulster Yacht Club again challenged on behalf of Sir Thomas. With a note of shyness which must have been new to him, Sir Thomas wrote to say that he had waited for someone else to challenge. As no other had come forward, he thought that he would try again. This evidence of modesty was greeted politely. But it was clear to everyone that he had contracted a habit-forming condition known as Cup-itis and that this was not easily curable. There was no hesitation on the part of the New York Yacht Club. They accepted the offer for a series of races in 1901. When Sir Thomas reached New York, just before the Cup match, he announced, "After all, the ould mug needs a change. A sea voyage would do it good."

George Watson was the designer of the second *Shamrock*.

Though the Irish-Scotch knight was his friend, Watson "needed a good deal of persuasion," the challenger was to comment later, to accept the commission. One of the things which interested Watson was a chance to experiment with tanks in order to produce "the perfect hull." (This was a new application for yachts. Tank tests had been applied only to steam vessels, for a number of years.) Every angle of heel, resistance to forward motion, and other factors came within Watson's elaborate study. The yacht he turned out, with its flat body and deep fin, was beautiful in the eyes of experts. When the marine editor of *Scientific American* saw her in the Erie Basin dry dock he wrote, "She has the most refined form ever seen in a Cup challenger." She was longer than her predecessor, with fine sharp lines: 137' over all, 89' 3" water-line, 24' beam and a draft of 20'. Her sides were plated with a new alloy (immadium), of great strength and rigidity. Her rigging was so skillfully arranged that, though she proved to be larger than the defender, calculation of her sail area brought her only a 43-second time penalty in the races. A wooden topmast was held by a socket in the head of her steel-pole mast.

Some of *Shamrock*'s experiences in her own waters were upsetting. They might well have given pause to a nervous owner or one inclined to superstition. On one of the rare days that Sir Thomas was on board any of his sailing yachts a sudden puff jibed the mainsail and a block off the steel gaff dropped to the deck. It missed Sir Thomas by inches. The next near-fatal disaster occurred in Cowes waters at the beginning of a trial race. After a luncheon party on the *Erin,* Sir Thomas took his guests, among whom the most distinguished was the fairly new King of England, Edward VII, on board *Shamrock II*. Everything should, of course, have been just perfect. As the yacht was running for the starting line an unexpected gust caught the mainsail wrong. Half of the steel mast went vertically overside, anchoring the yacht in the mud. Everything but her boom dropped to the *Shamrock*'s deck.

The King, luckily in the companionway, acted just as the knights and commoners on board did—he ducked his noble head. "All England gasped," wrote the reporters. Not the King. He retained his poise (after that single duck), directed some hands in rescuing those of their companions who had gone overboard—and then lit another cigar. Among those who had joined the party was George Watson. The accident was a puzzle to him, as that sudden puff, even though there was a chop in the sea, did not seem to have enough force to have created such havoc. It was around this time that the Kaiser, who had grown intensely jealous of his uncle, Edward VII— he called him "the old peacock"—made a remark very much in character. To someone who had mentioned the British King, the German monarch said tartly, "They tell me he has gone boating with his grocer."

While the *Shamrock* was, literally, undergoing trials, Herreshoff had built a new defender. There was nothing basically wrong with the two-year-old *Columbia,* but the syndicate which had commissioned Herreshoff hoped for an even faster boat. And, too, she had not had the advantage of tank tests. To everyone's surprise the "wizard of Bristol" had gone back to an earlier model, the *Defender,* as his pattern. The new yacht was the *Constitution,* and she became one of the most controversial of Herreshoff's productions. To some she was a "failure"—a rare term to apply to one of the master's creations.

Meanwhile, in Boston, a syndicate made plans to put their own candidate in the running. Thomas W. Lawson, a noted Boston broker and writer on financial subjects, finally became the sole underwriter of the project. His Cup hopeful, the *Independence,* was designed by Bowdoin B. Crowninshield.

It had become traditional for the burgee of the New York Yacht Club to be carried on defenders. The club was custodian of the Cup and was responsible for maintenance of the terms in the deed of gift. Nothing in the deed stated or implied, however, that only members of the club had exclusive rights to defend the old trophy. Yet the club made that interpretation promptly when Lawson offered to enter the *Independence* in trials against the *Constitution*. He was told that he must first become a member or charter his boat to the club as a possible defender. If not, it was hinted, he could go play with himself.

Everyone aching for a fight jumped in at once. As the debate became noisier the press had a fine time with it. Public sentiment, on the whole, was with Lawson. An expression of that sentiment appeared in *Mr. Dooley's Opinions*, accurately reported by Peter Finley Dunne:

. . . *no more gallant sailor rides th' waves thin hearty Jack Larsen iv th' Amalgamated Copper Yacht Club. "What ho?" says he, "If we're goin' to have a race," he says, "shiver me timbers if I don't look up th' law," he says. So he becomes a yachtsman. "But," says th' Noo York la-ads, thim that has th' Cup on their mantel-piece, "Ye can race on'y on two conditions." "What ar-re?" says Larsen. "Th' first is that ye become a mimber iv our club." "With pleasure," says he. "Ye can't," says they. "An' havin' complied with this first condition, ye must give us ye'er boat," says they. "We don't want it," they says.* [*Yet "Cap. Larsen" laid down impossible conditions for the use of his "expinsive raft." But he wanted a security bond, for*] *"Yachtin' is a gintlemans' spoort," he says, "an' in dalin' with gintlemen," he says, "ye can't be too careful," he says.*

The news got out that the *Independence*, a "colossal scow," was no champion yacht. She was too lightly built, too heavily canvased, and, though extremely fast on some points in light

167

airs, she was difficult to handle even with her balanced rudder. During a tow from Boston to Newport her defects became more apparent when she met a heavy sea. She opened up and leaked so badly that an extra pump was needed to get the water out. After repairs, the *Independence* got her first chance to test what merit she had when she went into six trials against the recommissioned *Columbia* and the *Constitution*. Her skipper was Hank Haff. The series had been arranged by the Newport Yacht Racing Association, which thought that, in all fairness, Lawson's boat should have her chance. She was a consistent loser, which eliminated her, to the particular relief of the New York Yacht Club.

Herreshoff's *Constitution* was the most expensive defender yet built, having cost a quarter of a million dollars. Except for one or two participants, the owners of Cup defenders were, of necessity, men of wealth. By the time of the tenth match, Cup contestants were being built specifically for participation in only one event. Quite a few of the racers before the 1890s had later done duty as cruising boats. Some had passed from "aristocrat to drudge" (a phrase of Alfred Loomis'), having been converted into trading vessels or freighters. But by 1900 the possibility that a Cup participant might be put to practical use after the match never entered into a designer's consideration. Cup racers were to become far more expensive than the *Constitution*. Additional to her initial cost, there were such expenses (hardly petty cash) of wages, crew maintenance, inevitable repairs and an item which took a good deal of space in the ledger: "miscellaneous costs." All this should explain to puzzled people why boats are given the feminine gender. As some wit remarked, "her rigging and her keep cost more than her hull!"

The *Constitution* was given a heavy workout in trial races. On one occasion, with Nathanael Herreshoff at the helm, a gust snapped her topmast and carried away part of the mainmast. (The smaller spar was fitted to house inside the steel mast.) The sailing master engaged for her was Captain Uriah Rhodes, a good man at the wheel. He was, however, faced with exceptional competition in the shape of Charlie Barr, who was handling the Cup-winning *Columbia*. That was bad enough. What made matters worse for Captain Rhodes was that the *Constitution*'s spars seemed to be delicate. That kept her crew nervous. As a well-known editor of *Yachting,* Herbert L. Stone, remarked, "All hands would turn a back-handspring to get out of the way whenever there was a snap aloft or the boom fetched up hard on the main sheet in coming about or jibing."

Captain Rhodes was a reliable skipper but a most cautious one. He felt, as did the boat's manager, that the *Constitution* was logically the new defender. Therefore everything must be done to save her from damage even when she was on the right side of the rules. Captain Barr and the *Columbia*'s temporary manager, C. Oliver Iselin, were well aware of how their opponents felt. As C. Sherman Hoyt observed, they "frequently appeared to disregard right of way rules." The *Columbia* responded more quickly to her helm than the *Constitution* did to hers and Captain Barr would just miss bringing the two together.

The cry of "foul" was heard frequently during the trials but Barr was penalized just once. The discipline was meaningless, for on that very day the *Columbia* was again chosen to defend the Cup, with Barr as her skipper. (E. D. Morgan, who purchased Iselin's share, was her manager.) Herreshoff was annoyed at the choice; he commented that he had never designed a faster boat. Many yachtsmen felt that, as the *Constitution* had been built to beat its predecessor, the club's selection was wrong. Each Herreshoff boat had been regarded as an improvement over any he had designed before. The situation was complicated by the fact that there had been

169

eighteen completed trial races; both contestants had won nine each. In four unfinished trials the *Columbia* had shown better form. It was this which had influenced the committee in its choice. Yet (a general opinion) had Barr been at the wheel of the *Constitution*, it is certain that she would have made a better showing.

Once again the *Erin* towed a *Shamrock*, strengthened with extra stringers and braces, across the Atlantic. The magnificent new yacht reached her berth in New York Harbor well in advance of the date set for the Cup match. By that time the *Columbia* had been selected as defender, a decision which encouraged Sir Thomas. What chance could an "old" boat have against his scientifically designed challenger? The sentiment was reflected by her crew, half of whom had not had the advantage of sailing the *Shamrock* in her trials. That was because some of her regulars had staged a small mutiny just prior to the *Shamrock*'s departure from England. Sir Thomas had made a fair offer of a bonus over wages but there had been a demand for more. The demand was met by a prompt refusal, and a quick selection of replacements by the *Shamrock*'s skipper, Captain Sycamore, who had commanded *Valkyrie III*.

The pleasure with which Sir Thomas had greeted the news about the *Columbia* and his enthusiastic expectation of victory were suddenly dimmed. On September 6, at Buffalo, President McKinley was shot. It was decided at once that the Cup races would have to be postponed. Though he would have been the last to admit it, Sir Thomas was then in a state of tension over the impending races. At that period in his career he was keen for victory. His anxiety was expressed in a manner which he probably regretted later. He said, excitedly, that the New York Yacht Club might try to use the attack on McKinley as an excuse "to get out of racing *Columbia* against my sloop [but] I'll see that it doesn't." What should be done if the President died? Well, naturally, there would have to be a postponement and he thought that a week's time would be formally correct. After all, life (of which Cup matches were a part) must go on. When McKinley did die, on September 14, it was decided to hold the races over until the twenty-sixth. No one paid too much attention to the remark Sir Thomas had made in a moment of stress.

The editor of *The Rudder*, Thomas F. Day, gave expression to a popular opinion when he wrote:

For the sake of the sport I would like to see Sir Thomas Lipton win. As it is, the contest is too one-sided, but if the Cup could be passed and repassed across the ocean it would be better for yachting on both sides. It was for this same reason that I would have been pleased to see Herreshoff knocked out, and the right and power to design a successful defender pass to another man.

The huge crowds that came to the first race were clearly Lipton partisans. They cheered every move of the *Shamrock* while she was jockeying for the start. She was beautiful in motion and she had been polished from truck to keel. As an instance of the exceptional treatment and loving care given the *Shamrock,* the topside paint of green had been removed. (Green was the standard color on all Lipton racing yachts, except for *Shamrock III.*) Her nursemaids were certain that this delicate operation would improve her speed by reducing friction. Captain Sycamore was superb at the helm, handling the 90-footer as smoothly as though she were a sailing dinghy. At his side was his "second captain," Robert Wringe, also a fine helmsman. There was no timidity in either of them and they met all of Captain Barr's bluffs, except once. That was when the *Shamrock* gave way in order to avoid a collision with the *Columbia.* The challenger's crew said later that Barr was clearly at fault but that Sycamore was determined not to

171

claim a foul just before the start of a race. When the race did take place it was unexciting. The wind dropped and became too light for the contestants to finish within the time limit.

The first completed race, on September 28, began well for the *Shamrock*. Captain Sycamore adroitly took his boat over the starting line seconds ahead of the defender. The *Shamrock*'s ability to sail closer to the wind than the *Columbia* in the beat out earned her 39 seconds on the first leg. No one had ever before seen a challenger outpoint a sound defender, and her helmsman was credited for the achievement. But on the run home, the old-timer, with less sail area than the *Shamrock* and without the benefit of improvements in design, overhauled her rival and won by 37 seconds elapsed (1 minute, 20 seconds corrected) time. That win came as a thorough surprise. Quite a number of people had prepared themselves for the expected moment when the Cup would be delivered to Sir Thomas.

On October 1 the challenger was well in advance of the *Columbia* when the race was abandoned because of an unseasonable calm. London, when it heard by cable how far ahead the *Shamrock* had been, celebrated as though there had been a final victory. The general expression was that "Sir Tea will lift the old mug this time for certain." Two days later, however, the *Columbia* showed what a flyer she really was. The race was over a triangular course; reaches on the first two legs; to windward on the last leg. The wind freshened on the beat home and it laid both yachts well over. It was more *Columbia*'s weather than *Shamrock*'s and she crossed the line 2 minutes, 52 seconds elapsed time ahead. The defender had been traveling fast. Her speed over the 30-mile course had averaged 9.31 knots. This was a record except for the questioned one of 9.9 knots credited to the earlier *Columbia* in the 1871 match.

172

The next race, which was to prove the last, was the sort for which everyone had been hoping. Both boats maneuvered so warily before the start that neither crossed the line within the two-minute grace period. Though the *Shamrock* was behind the *Columbia* at crossing, she was 49 seconds ahead of her rival when she rounded the mark. On the beat home the defender really went to work. She caught the challenger and stayed with her, and they raced for the finish line with almost even bows. A tense silence held the scene; spectators seemed as taut as the racing crews. Then the *Shamrock* seemed to leap across the line—seconds ahead. But she had not won. Because of her time allowance *Columbia* was the victor by 41 seconds.

Once again Sir Thomas had met defeat. Once again he accepted it as a gentleman sportsman. He was not ready to give up. "Next time, for sure," he announced. "After all, the shamrock has three leaves!" What stung, of course, was the defeat of the "scientific" *Shamrock* by a supposedly passé boat. Good as Captain Sycamore was, Captain Barr was conceded to be the smarter helmsman. The British seemed to think so, too. Not Sir Thomas. He told reporters that he thought the *Columbia* simply a more suitable boat for American waters. The value of that opinion is debatable. And, in his autobiography, Sir Thomas wrote, "The British boat was freely admitted to be the best and swiftest challenger ever sent over. . . . My boat lost to the American defender by an aggregate of only three minutes, 27 seconds actual time [over a] total distance of 90 miles." Of that total 40 miles was to windward.

Watson had unquestionably shown how imaginative a designer he was when he planned *Shamrock II*. Yet it was the British naval architects who seemed to be the most upset. What had been the use of those painstaking tank experiments

173

by Watson? "The trouble with them," one expert observed, "seems to be that Watson did not have the model of the *Columbia* to test also."

Back in England they gave Sir Thomas an affectionate reception. There was, quite naturally, much talk about Cup matches and the *Shamrock*'s defeat. A lady guest tried to be consoling. She did not really know Americans, but she had heard things. Said she, "Sir Thomas, I'm certain as can be that they put something in the water over there which makes you lose." "I completely agree with you, madam," was the reply. "It is a better boat!"

The *Shamrock* had gone to the Erie Basin for a winter's sleep. It occurred to Sir Thomas that, as long as she was already on the American side, a match might be arranged for 1902. But when the suggestion was made to the New York Yacht Club, it propped itself stiffly against the deed of gift and said "No!" It was written in the law, as represented by the deed, that no repeat challenge could be accepted until two years had expired or another contest had intervened. Sir Thomas made the usual conventional sounds of a gracious man in the face of intractable rules and the preservers of formalities. "But," he said grimly, "I'm still out to lift that mug unless some one else does it first."

There were angry protests over the club's decision. William P. Stephens, as fair-minded a man as George Schuyler had been, and more competent to express an opinion than most yachtsmen were, gave point to a reaction held by thoughtful people when he wrote in *The Yachtsman:*

In view of the construction of the new deed of gift in part and as a whole, and of the way in which it has been repudiated in actual practice by the New York Yacht Club, this decision is absurd. The new deed is a mixture of bad sportsmanship, bad law and bad English, made in a hurry by a little clique, and never

yet ratified by the New York Yacht Club. [Various provisions
having already been abandoned and others modified] it is childish
to fall back on the comparatively unimportant point under which
a vessel clearly eligible in every other way as a challenger is
debarred. . . .

The New York Yacht Club committees were, by now,
pretty case-hardened. They felt (as they had always felt) that
they had only done their duty; that the club members who
had built expensive defenders were no less than noble, and,
particularly, that the club needed no advice on deportment.
They just shut all ports, battened down the hatches and rode
to a sea anchor.

The storm of protest had hardly passed before attack came
from another quarter. This was in the form of a privately
printed limited edition, *The Lawson History of the America's
Cup*, 1902. Its underwriter was Thomas W. Lawson, who had
paid the costs of that unlucky candidate for Cup defense, the
Independence. Winfield M. Thompson, an outstanding
writer on yachting subjects, had done the research and done
it superbly. The volume was magnificent, eye-filling, and
enriched with exceptional illustrations. Lawson had provided
a supplement. In this he outlined the genesis of the *Independence,* broke down her costs—they came to over $205,000—and
explained why the big scow went under the wreckers' sledges
only three months after she was in commission. Lawson had
not produced his impressive *History* merely to provide enter-
tainment for readers among yachtsmen. His part of it pep-
pered the New York Yacht Club for its refusal to accept the
Independence in trials as a possible defender. The club
merely drew its stateroom curtains closer and signaled the
flying bridge, "Maintain your course."

It came as no surprise when a third challenge, on behalf
of Sir Thomas Lipton, Bart. (he had been elevated in 1902),

was received from the Royal Ulster Yacht Club. This was in October 1902 for a match in 1903. Sir Thomas added a private note to the formal challenge:

In thus desiring an opportunity of making a third attempt to obtain possession of the America's Cup, I hope I may not be deemed importunate or unduly covetous of the precious trophy so long and so securely held in trust by the New York Yacht Club.

The membership of the New York Yacht Club, for the most part, were not overjoyed at the challenge from this hardy perennial. Those who disapproved of Sir Thomas' persistence expressed their opinion in language more common to the fo'c'sle—a fact mentioned some time later by reporters on the scene. In its acceptance (how else?), the Cup committee conformed to the latest edition of admiralty etiquette. Its acknowledgment of the note from Sir Thomas corresponded to "Glad to have you on board, sir."

Had the club refused merely on the grounds that they were tired of having the new baronet around, there really would have been a howl. There could very well have been an army of pickets, with banners, "Unfair to Sir Tea" outside the magnificent home of the club on West Forty-fourth Street, new in 1901. The effect of his two attempts to win the Cup had enormously increased the popularity of Sir Thomas. Since his appearance on the scene, the great international contest no longer seemed a snobbish sport confined to exclusive yachtsmen. It is not certain that many yachtsmen liked the wide popular interest in Cup matches which Sir Thomas, more than any other challenger, had inspired.

True, the focus was on him, the "darling of the people," rather than the races. When he came to New York in 1903, he was the most important of current visitors and was effusively welcomed by most of the press. Wrote Dorothy Dix,

176

the heart specialist, dipping her golden quill in the finest imported perfume, Sir Thomas "was a three-volume romance bound in yachting flannels." She went on to give an inflammatory description of the *Erin's* "bedrooms—little dens all done up in dainty lace and silk like a beauty's boudoir." Under her ecstatic eye came the steam yacht's *objets d'art,* the music room—it had singing canaries and a harp, too—and the three thousand lamps which illuminated the exterior of the floating palace at night.

The British were not remiss in their expression of affection. It was being suggested that Sir Thomas would make an ideal ambassador to a certain backward country which had a certain Cup. The suggestion took the form of some pleasant sketches by press cartoonists who had been editorially briefed. *Punch* offered an out-of-season valentine which, for several issues, imaginatively described the baronet's supposed experiences in the former colony—among others, winning a walking race to Washington from New York and, when he reached the capital, painting the White House red. (Painting anything red was still permissible. He was, in fact, a guest of President Theodore Roosevelt, with his designer, William Fife, Jr. Neither had a paint brush.)

Then, as *Punch* had it, he called at Poloniville, Pennsylvania, "and is kissed at the station by 3,000 ladies, each of whom remarks" (as a studied routine), " 'This is a great day for Poloniville!' " Harvard, if *Punch* could be believed, made him an honorary D.C.L., the degree ordained for "Disappointed Cup Lifter." Naturally, he had to make an emotional speech of thanks, and each student who stayed to listen received "a portrait of Sir Tea in Okomagarin." In an earlier issue Sir Thomas appeared in an illustration as "Last of the Vi-Kings and the first of the Tea-Kings."

When *Shamrock III* came over at the end of the *Erin's* towline, she was accompanied by *Shamrock I,* towed by an ocean-

177

going tug, as a pacer. (*Shamrock II* was still asleep in the Erie Basin.) The latest *Shamrock* had a great deal of nickel steel, with a white enamel coating. This metal was regarded as structurally stronger than the immadium used in *Shamrock II*. The new challenger, 134′ 4″ over all, with 89′ 10″ waterline, had a fuller hull than *Shamrock II* with little less beam (23′ 4″). Lipton's third challenger represented a joint design effort of Watson and Fife, both of whom had been influenced by the lines of the *Columbia*. Unlike the cutters which had preceded her for many years, she was steered by a wheel (long before adopted for American sloops), and not with an oversize tiller. Her freeboard was low, and she had a racer's typical overhangs and fin keel. On the whole she was thought by yachting experts to be a more wholesome and better-constructed boat than *Shamrock II,* though she was still in the tradition of Cup-match dainties. John Scott Hughes, in his *Famous Yachts,* described the third *Shamrock* as "an exceedingly lively vessel and quite the most beautiful that had ever raced for the Cup."

In English waters the new challenger had an excellent racing record and she added to the growing yacht-trophy collection of her owner. She had had a serious accident in Weymouth Bay during one of her trials against *Shamrock I.* A puff had caught her wrong and her whole rig collapsed. Some of her crew were hurt and her steward drowned. Sir Thomas almost gave up. "This," he said, "is the first life that has been lost in my service. . . . I'd give the yacht sooner than lose a man!" Had it not been for that accidental death and the injuries some of her crew sustained, the loss of her spars and rigging would not have been regarded as noteworthy in the life of a modern racer.

Intelligent criticism of the "waste and extravagance" of Cup racers was to become more severe. Designers were warned by yachting authorities that they were promoting a trend

178

which would adversely affect the sport. They placed the blame chiefly on American rating rules which still excluded displacement. Challengers and defenders were being built as lightly as possible with the expectation that they would survive the strain of trials and of a Cup match or two. (The second *Shamrock,* for instance, fastest of the Lipton racers, was scrapped after her two-year lay-up. She had never again raced after the Cup match of 1901.) By 1902, over the dozen years since *Gloriana* had set a pattern, the inevitable development in design traceable to American rules had reached dangerous extremes.

A Cup contestant carried the weight of a Mogul locomotive, 90 tons or so, as ballast on its deep fin, and its mast and other spars grew excessively to support an abnormal weight of sail. The current conditions resulted, therefore, in a great advantage to an American defender. The challenger had twice to cross a body of water for which she was not constructed. That meant she had to be strengthened to face the Atlantic, unstep her mast (sent over as freight, usually), come and go under jury rig in case she did have to slip her tow, and be rerigged when she made port. Then, if she had the time to do so, she could start tuning up in the waters in which she would race. These conditions made the word *sport* a pretty doubtful one to use when applied to Cup matches.

The current rule applied, of course, to the new American defender. Herreshoff was again the designer and builder, having been commissioned by a syndicate of ten men in the top income bracket. Stubbornly adhering to his faith in his unsuccessful *Constitution,* Herreshoff made use of many of her features in his new creation, the *Reliance.* He went further by incorporating the basic elements of Crowninshield's *Independence.* The performance of that unfortunate scow in light airs had impressed the master designer and he understood how to eliminate her serious defects. The consequence was that the *Reliance* was the most extreme of "skimming dishes." In the opinion of William P. Stephens, she was "perhaps the most wonderful and useless racing machine known to yachting." And because she fully displayed the "absurdities of the type the rule produced," she was the last of her kind.

The biggest American yacht built to her time for defense of the Cup, the *Reliance* was 143' over all. Her beam was 25' 10" and her draft 19' 9". She was built to heel to her lee rail in as light a wind as 7 or 8 knots. This ran her bearing surface from her measured 84' 6" to around 130', an obvious advantage when racing. Yet she was steady in a breeze up to 12 knots. Her sail spread was enormous for a single-sticker: nearly 16,000 square feet. (This was an eighth more than on *Shamrock III*, twice that of the racers in the 1886 match.)

In order to carry this weight of canvas, one of the greatest in any American sloop, her topmast was well socketed into a powerful steel mast. When her club topsail was aloft, her "ceiling" was over 175 feet. Herreshoff left no room for discussion as to whether or not he had turned out a "sailing machine." The *Reliance* was studded with winches. All of her sheets and her backstays were trimmed from below decks. The master had never turned out a Cup-defense candidate which moved faster. In trials against the recommissioned *Constitution* and the *Columbia* she won them all with ease.

During the building of the defender Herreshoff maintained his usual tight security, a secrecy which yachting authorities and newsmen found highly irritating. The famed designer made no concession to critical opinion on his attitude, beyond a rare letter to the press denying some statement attributed to him. Reporters, in his book, were to be regarded with deep suspicion. A newspaperman out of Boston waylaid him, on an April day, just before the *Reliance*

180

"Sir Tea" before he began his pursuit of "the ould mug."

Sir Thomas Lipton, yachtsman, on board a *Shamrock* under sail. An experienced helmsman is lending a steadying hand.

PHOTO CULVER SERVICE

Erin I in New York waters (1899), open houseboat to numerous Lipton guests.

Maneuvering for the start in the first race of the 1899 Cup match. The lady is Mrs. C. Oliver Iselin; Captain Charlie Barr is the little man on *Columbia's* wheel; behind him (bending) is Nathanael Herreshoff; between the helmsman and designer is Iselin. *Shamrock I* was a far better-looking yacht than the artist, T. D. Walker, showed here. *From Harper's Weekly, October 1899.*

Just after the finish of the final race between *Columbia* and *Shamrock II*, October 4, 1901.

A well-behaved excursion fleet giving sea room to *Shamrock II* and *Columbia. Drawn by Charles Dixon for the London Graphic, Sept. 1901*

was launched. Herreshoff was on his way home to dinner. Quickly identifying himself, the eager reporter asked:

"What do you think of the *Reliance,* Mr. Herreshoff?"

"I have nothing to say."

"Will she beat the *Constitution?*"

Yankee silence.

"What is your opinion of *Shamrock III?*"

Continued silence.

"Good day, Mr. Herreshoff."

"Good day, sir." He walked away a pace, then turned. "Now please do not make this interview long. Do not print any more information than I have given you." He went, leaving a speechless and slightly stunned reporter.

Without benefit of Herreshoff's opinion, Sir Thomas knew what to expect. As he related in his memoirs:

We had not been long in America on this trip when it was borne in on us that, while we had a good ship in Shamrock III, *the genius of "Nat" Herreshoff had built a bigger and a better one in the* Reliance.

Captain Robert Wringe was at the *Shamrock's* helm in the first race, August 20. The wind was so light that it took the *Reliance* over 4½ hours to reach the outer mark, 15 miles to windward from the start. The *Shamrock* never made it, and when the 5½ hours' time allowed for the race expired, the *Reliance* was far from home. The canny, unbeatable Captain Barr was at the helm of the defender and in all races he handled her as though he were built into the craft. If the challenger were held by light airs, Barr found where even a hint of breeze was blowing. If the sea kicked up and bothered the *Reliance* (which it did), while helping along the more soundly built *Shamrock,* the defender's helmsman knew where they kept smoother water. What made victory certain for the

181

American yacht was the simple fact that, adroit as he was, Wringe found his opponent too great a Barr.

On two occasions the wind was too light to be of any use; on one day it blew too heavily (so thought the regatta committee) for the boats to go out. There was not much excitement in the first three completed races. *Shamrock III* lost all of them in a row: the first by 9 minutes, the second by 3 minutes, 16 seconds (both elapsed time—the *Reliance* allowed 1 minute, 57 seconds to the *Shamrock*), and in the last she was fogbound.

In that third race there had been only a light southerly. Barr's handling of the defender to windward was so skillful that his boat was over 11 minutes in advance of the *Shamrock* at the outer mark. Then the wind veered a couple of points eastward and shortly dragged in a thick fog bank. Everything afloat in the area was suddenly hidden in a mantle of gray. The committee boat's siren was started to help the contending yachts find their way home. Thereupon excursion steamers, tugs, and other craft, conforming with marine law, let loose with whistles, horns or bells.

On the club tug the committee waited in anxiety—but not in silence. They had just about decided to send out tugs to help bring the racers home when they heard a sail shaking. Peering through the gloom, they made out the white hull of the *Reliance* and recognized her mass of canvas. Captain Barr had felt his way to the finish in the dimout, 4 hours, 28 minutes after he had started. There was yet no sign of the *Shamrock*. Just as the tugs were leaving to find her, the fog rolled away. She was still in New York waters but to the northeast of the line and well off her course. Britishers are, supposedly, well used to fog, but this was an unexpected and dirty one which came out of nowhere just to spoil the fun. The crew of the *Shamrock* were not feeling very well anyhow. They had something to live down. In the first completed race, they had sent up a balloon jib with a turn in it. It shouldn't happen to amateurs! It took that hand-picked, experienced crew several precious minutes to bring the sail down and reset it.

Calling off the race set for August 29 (which would have been the third had it been sailed) because the wind seemed too heavy caused another storm. It hadn't been blowing even half a moderate gale. The boats of an earlier period would have had a single reef down and gone gleefully through it. Under mutual agreement, as allowed by the deed of gift, it had been decided that

if in the opinion of the Regatta Committee the weather shall . . . be, or threaten to be, of such severe character as not to afford a reasonable opportunity of fairly testing the speed of the two vessels [and] unless either contestant shall insist on its being started . . . the race may be postponed.

On both sides of the Atlantic there was protest over application of the clause and the "sissy" boats. William P. Stephens had, again, a sensible comment to make. His disapproval of a condition which made it necessary to tow a challenger from England for her safety had frequently been expressed. Now, he said, "It was time to call a halt when 135-foot yachts could not go out in a breeze of over 12 knots' strength without danger of losing the entire rig overboard." This type of criticism was too intelligent to be ignored. In a little while after the twelfth match there was a return to sanity in yacht design. The *Reliance,* having carried out her assignment, retired from racing. After a period of useless waiting, she was broken up.

Disappointed once again, Sir Thomas was more expressive than he had ever been. Taking home that "ould mug" had become an obsession. No matter what his original impulses had been or what emotional factors had then mixed with

183

practical considerations, by the time of his third try he was simply, unaffectedly out to win. He told the crowding, friendly reporters:

No one has any idea of how I have worried and fretted over this race. . . . I don't believe in gambling, but I would have been willing to bet the Erin *that I would win. It is the greatest disappointment of my life. What can I do? I have tried my best. I have spent months of sleepless nights worrying over the challenger. They tell me that I have a beautiful boat. I don't want a beautiful boat. What I want is a boat to lift the Cup—a* Reliance. *Give me a homely boat, the homeliest boat that was ever designed, if she is like* Reliance.

The people of the city, yacht clubs, business organizations, and officials overwhelmed him with tokens of esteem and expressions of sympathy and with farewell dinners. There were a dozen occasions on which he was able to say goodbye to the same people. The most sophisticated local magazine, *Town Topics,* very distrustful of hero worship and generally satiric about tender emotions, had made Sir Thomas the butt of frequent critical comment. They disliked his "*opéra bouffe* style of cup racing," and insisted that he outdid Barnum as "past master in the art of humbugging the public." But now they, too, were affected by the general sentiment. It was a great conversion of the blasé. In a "noble apology" one of the journal's "horse marines" wrote of Sir Thomas that he was

the most graceful loser we ever saw . . . none can help applauding, and while congratulating him on his successful advertising, we can also compliment him on his manhood and his sportsmanship.

12

THE END
OF AN ERA

The Cup match of 1903 was to be the last for a long time. Part of the reason was an unforeseen and universal casualty. Before that occurred another reason was the serious thinking which Sir Thomas had been giving to the conditions a challenger had to face. (There seemed to be a general understanding that any effort to retrieve the Cup by a Britisher was reserved exclusively to him.)

The criticisms of intelligent, progressive American and British yachting authorities had had his careful consideration. He agreed that, without a sound rating rule which would apply to both sides of the Atlantic, a foreign yacht had little chance against an American defender. It seemed wholly wrong to spend a fortune on a boat for one Cup match, a boat which could not race in British waters without heavy time penalties.

A change in American rating rules had followed the building of the *Reliance*. The history of measurement rules and of time allowances is a long and involved one. Only the final results need be mentioned here. Since the 1880s there had been a series of efforts to work up a rule which would result in a more wholesome type of boat. In 1903, chiefly as a result of Nathanael Herreshoff's urging and suggestion, a Universal Measurement Rule was adopted. It was based on a formula proposed by the Seawanhaka Yacht Club. (From that club had come the "Seawanhaka Rule" of 1883, which involved only the factors of length and sail area in figuring allowances and penalties.) After the Universal Rule was adopted by the New York Yacht Club in 1903 (modified 1905 and later), future Cup contestants had, for some years, a limit on waterline of 75 feet instead of 90. The factor of displacement was now included and excessive sail area was penalized.

The first International Rules to apply to the uniform measurement of racing yachts in European waters were agreed to during two conferences in London in 1906. The principle adopted was sound: "habitability with speed." No Americans were represented, though that was not because they had not been invited. William P. Stephens remarked, "The isolationists of that day were ingenious in methods of delay and in framing unconvincing excuses" to decline the invitation. Their arguments, in his opinion, were puerile. There were twenty delegates from sixteen nations, including Switzerland, at the London conferences. Thus, by 1906, two rating rules were in existence, both designed to produce sounder, fullerbodied boats. The Internation Yacht Racing Union, including yacht clubs from Russia to the Argentine Republic (but not the United States), was established in Paris in 1907. There was, however, no single organization set up in the
186

States to put the America Universal Rule into effective operation.*

Sir Thomas had maintained a casual relation with the New York Yacht Club through correspondence. In 1907, after it appeared that the Universal Rule was one by which the club would abide, he issued a tentative challenge. His condition was that the club race under the Rule, and that the waterline length of the defender would not exceed that of the challenger. Still stuffy about the deed of gift, the club refused to agree. In everything having to do with Cup matches, they reserved the right to decide on the boat for defense. That might have meant a modern form of a *Reliance* insofar as Sir Thomas understood their reply. He withdrew his offer.

But he was not going to give up yachting. He commissioned Fife to design a 23-meter cutter. It was to be called plain *Shamrock*. "I'm reserving number *IV* for Sandy Hook," the baronet announced. *Shamrock,* the best of all British cutters of her time, as a racer in home waters loaded her deck with trophies. It made Sir Thomas restless and eager again for the excitement of a Cup match.

The club refused a second tentative Lipton challenge, a repetition of that of 1907, when it was received in 1912. Sir Thomas wanted action, not a portfolio of letters received and copies sent. In 1913, with a justifiable touch of impatience, he suggested a race "just for the fun of it"—no conditions beyond common-sense ones. How could the club say no? There was no other challenger on the horizon and it

---

* Standardization of measurement and racing rules was not effective in America until 1926, when the North American Yacht Racing Union was in operation. By international agreement, the I.Y.R.U. measurement and sailing rules were accepted by American clubs in 1929. That put the American Universal Rule in discard.

was highly improbable that there could be one as generous.

It would have been mere sporting protocol for the club committees to have been as generous—and promptly. They were not. But they were temperamental. A defender, it was announced, would be built under the Universal Rule, but a decision on the waterline length would be decided by the club. That bothered the Royal Ulster Yacht Club, which had again sent over a challenge on behalf of Sir Thomas. In a cable it stated that "a contest between yachts of unequal size would be wasteful and highly unsatisfactory," and it assumed that the New York club would not go to a 90-footer. This brought no immediate change in the formally correct attitude of the committees. It was only after conditions for a match in September 1914 had been signed that the club announced it would select a defender with a 75-foot waterline length. That was the challenger's length and just what Sir Thomas had been asking for all along! It appeared as though the club committees had decided upon only one thing in advance: to worry the perennial challenger. It seemed, however, to have had no effect on Sir Thomas' good nature.

For designer Sir Thomas called on Charles E. Nicholson, a man who had turned out some successful racers but who was new to Cup challengers. *Shamrock IV* was given what the British called a "Marconi" mast. It had a socketed topmast. This device was not new but it was effective. The fourth *Shamrock* had some below-deck winches. She was 110.48 feet over all, remarkably fast in home waters, and a weatherly boat. The experts called her "a powerful scow," and a "hammer-head shark." Her designer thought her "the ugly duckling." Said Alfred Loomis of her:

. . . she was without doubt the homeliest yacht ever put in competition for the Cup. . . . Forward, she looked something like a cross between a tortoise and an armored cruiser . . . while aft
188

*she appeared to have been built too long and sawed off to meet
the rule of measurement.*

After the long pause, the old excitement over Cup matches
stirred the collective breast of the American yachting fraternity. Three candidates for defense were under construction all at once. A syndicate headed by Cornelius Vanderbilt
placed a commission with the prime American designer.
(Herreshoff did not know then that this was to be his last
defender.) Had it not been for that commission, Alexander
Cochran, heading another group, would also have turned to
the master. For Cochran was the owner of the 323-ton
schooner-yacht *Westward,* designed and built by the genius
of Bristol in 1910. She had invaded European waters and in
eleven starts she had won eleven races, on elapsed time. But
in early 1914 Herreshoff was too busy, so Cochran went to
William Gardner of Boston. Gardner was a novice as designer of a Cup racer but he had won enduring fame by pro-
ducing the exceptional and beautiful three-masted schooner
Atlantic. She had won the Sandy Hook to Land's End race
against ten other large yachts in 1905 in the record time of
12 days, 4 hours, 1 minute. Also in Boston, George Owen had
been commissioned to plan yet a third candidate. Owen, too,
was new to Cup defenders but he had designed some famous
racers under the Universal Rule.

At the individual christenings Herreshoff's yacht was
named *Resolute,* Gardner's *Vanitie,* and Owen's *Defiance.*
During preliminary workouts the *Resolute* was consistently
fast and dependable but *Vanitie* was no slouch. Just which of
the two was to be awarded the top honor of defending the
Cup—and it would be a difficult choice—would be decided by
the official trials. It was destined not to be settled then.

Shamrock IV was halfway across the Atlantic, mothered
again by the *Erin,* when Sir Thomas heard bad news. The

189

wireless officer on the *Erin* had cut into a message broadcast by a German cruiser. A war, which was to spread widely, had started. There was clearly more danger of capture or trouble if the two vessels attempted to reach a home port. They went on, temporarily to Bermuda, then to Brooklyn. The *Shamrock* was dry-docked "for the duration." Sir Thomas braved the added hazards of the Atlantic on the *Erin* and reached home without incident. For a while his famed steam yacht was converted into a hospital ship on the run from England to Flanders. Then she went to war as a patrol in the Mediterranean. Not long thereafter an enemy torpedo reached her and the beautiful craft sank with six of her crew.

Sir Thomas was seventy years old before the match agreed upon in 1913 was held. That was 1920. Temporarily, a new steam yacht took the *Erin*'s place. She was the *Victoria*. When she reached New York most of the population paused from their accustomed occupations to roar out a genuine welcome to "dear old Tommy." It was, even with a newer generation grown up, again a triumphal entrance, and very heartwarming to the genial invader. Once again his yacht was the hospitable meeting place of uncounted guests. The war was over; life was worth living; those good old days were back. Sir Thomas was at his expansive best. He talked his memoirs with all and sundry, told again how he had won the title of "Comidore" at the age of ten. Occasionally, as Sherman Hoyt (who had an affection for him) remarked, he put on an act "cleverly staged to impress the reporters with his wide familiarity with royalty."

On what might otherwise have been a dull day, Sir Tea created a sensation. He had invited a group of the most ravishing models, more comfortable in decorating the famous dressmaker's salon where they posed at work, to the shipyard in which the *Shamrock* was being reconditioned. This invasion of gorgeous frippery completely demoralized the workers and the yacht crews. But Sir Thomas, the perfect host, was not upset. He agilely led the little troupe of dainties in a tour of the yard, climbed a ladder or two to reach the *Shamrock,* and on her deck, amid squeals of admiration from his adoring audience, explained all about Cup racing in half a dozen simple sentences. "It was," said an interested observer, Sherman Hoyt, "the only time I saw Sir Thomas on board any of his various *Shamrocks!*"

The 23-meter *Shamrock,* unnumbered, which Fife had designed ten years or so earlier, had been brought over as a pacer for *Shamrock IV.* The challenger had not been as well taken care of as she should have been during her half-dozen years under wraps at City Island. She had to undergo some serious operations. Some of her spars, which had been destroyed by fire in the yard, were replaced in improved form. Among these was a streamlined topmast. On the other hand the *Resolute,* which had by then been selected as the defender, had had loving care.

While tuning up, each of the contestants displayed a novelty concealed until a day before their first race. Herreshoff had long been annoyed at the behavior of the mainsail gaff when the wind leaned on it. It sagged to leeward and thus some of the driving force slipped off the sail. He applied a vang to hold the gaff to windward, a most effective device which prevented the sag and made it possible to point higher. It did put a strain on the gaff when close-hauled but that was unavoidable and it did no damage. On the *Shamrock* her designer had added something new—a canvas cover which enveloped the mast the length of the luff. By streamlining this to the mainsail, the luff was kept free of wind eddies from the mast. (The streamlining of masts was to be adopted later by a number of designers.)

When, a little while before the first race, the committee waiting on the tug at the starting line had a close look at the

191

mast "petticoat," there was a suggestion for remeasurement.
(The official measurer may have decided it altered the *Shamrock*'s sail area.) It was too late then. The challenger's helmsman would gladly have acceded to removal of the gear (called
a "fairing canvas"). He had been brought up in the tradition
of sailors who eye the luff when sailing—an excellent training. It was not used again after the race.

The sail area of the *Resolute* (106′ 11½″ over all) was 8,775
square feet to the *Shamrock*'s 10,500. Additionally, the latter
had over 200 cubic feet more displacement. All this placed a
heavy time penalty on the challenger: 7 minutes, 1 second
(reduced to 6 minutes, 40 seconds with a smaller topsail).
Apparently, when designing the *Shamrock,* Nicholson had
such faith in a large sail spread—the ratio used was exceeded
only by that of *Reliance*—that he had practically disregarded
the new rule. In this he may have been influenced by the
fact that one of Herreshoff's greatest attributes was his ingenious evasion of or adaptation of existing rating rules.
Some authorities thought, however, that Nicholson was not
sufficiently familiar with the rule to apply his design advan-
tageously. Herreshoff knew it well—he had helped formulate
it—and when he planned the defender he kept the element of
time penalties in mind.

A new sail pattern had been adopted by racing yachts since
the last match—the most important and effective change since
Cup races began. (This was the "Marconi" rig, about which
more later.) It was stipulated by both parties to the 1920
match, however, that the contesting yachts would retain the
rigs for which they had been designed. One of the more
distracting novelties, when the races took place, was the
appearance of aircraft at a Cup match. Some spectators saw
the contest from seaplanes or dirigibles. The first aerial shots
of Cup races were obtained by the press. Regulations were
quickly enacted to keep the aircraft in line and away from
192

the racers' topmasts. There were some casualties and a rescue or two at sea. And passengers on the excursion fleet were at last being limited through strictly enforced safety regulations.

For the first time in Cup matches the helmsmen and almost all of the afterguards of both boats were amateurs. Sir Thomas had asked William P. Burton (later knighted) to handle the *Shamrock*'s wheel. Burton had acquired an enviable reputation as a racer of his own many big yachts. He was regarded as an exceptional tactician. He had accepted the important assignment as the *Shamrock*'s helmsman provided that he could have his wife on board as timekeeper. She had always called time for him in his long years of racing and he said it would upset him to have any other in that spot. A female on board, however expert, was well out of tradition in important racing events but Sir Thomas bowed his knightly head and welcomed her. There were forty persons on the *Shamrock,* all that the rules allowed; thirty-two were paid members of the crew. The *Resolute* had a professional skipper, Chris Christensen, who had been a mate of Charlie Barr. Her helmsman, and an unusually competent sailor, was Charles Francis Adams, later a member of President Hoover's Cabinet as Secretary of the Navy. Most of the *Resolute*'s afterguard, an expert group of Corinthians, came out of Boston's exclusive yachting circles. Sherman Hoyt represented the New York Yacht Club on the *Shamrock.*

Despite his considerable experience as a racing yachtsman, Captain Burton had never before been in a spot where the eyes of much of the Western world were on him. He must have been at least a little nervous; it was certain that he was too eager at the moment the first race began. For, after the usual jockeying, he was across the line before the man with his eyes on his accurate timepiece fired the starting gun. Burton seemed, at the moment, to be more interested in retaining his momentary advantage over the *Resolute.* While

193

he recrossed the line the signal came, and the defender went promptly about her job of beating her way out to the mark in a fluky wind. The *Shamrock* was two hundred yards astern of her by the time she again went over the line. But she was still within the two-minute grace period. She had only lost a tactical advantage. The only thing anybody on board the *Shamrock* noticed was that Burton's face was very red.

On the beat to windward the *Shamrock* showed how skillfully she had been designed. She began to make up for her tardy second crossing. Then, as unexpected as it was unwelcome, a summer squall with lightning effects and thunder percussion broke dramatically. Torrential rain hid the racers from view of the audience on the inevitable excursion fleet. Everyone expected the worst. Prudence and experience would have dictated to trained sailors that they quickly drop their topsail and mainsail during the miniature cyclone represented by a thunderstorm. Yet the two yachts continued to sail—a tribute to their helmsmen. The sun came out again as abruptly as it had gone when the brief storm started. By then the *Resolute* was seen well ahead of the *Shamrock*.

The defender would have won that race, and with ease, on the run home in a freshening breeze. But the sudden storm had done its dirty work. As the thoroughly wet mainsail of the *Resolute* began to dry, it put a strain on its throat halyard. Not far from the outer mark the taut rope rendered on the winch drum below deck, and the gaff jumped the mast owing to a broken gooseneck. The men sent aloft reported that a repair was impossible. There seemed to be no use in continuing with a sagging mainsail. The *Resolute* withdrew and took a tow. For the first time in a Cup match race, a defender failed to finish. There was, in consequence, sharp criticism of her afterguard. Her topsail, it was pointed out, was intact, she had her jibs, and had she rigged a spinnaker she would have "gone down fighting."

194

The *Shamrock*'s afterguard and crews had some nervous moments, too, for the masthead had come aft appreciably. Her jib topsail was brought down and under club topsail and working sails she was eased home. The afterguard, which included the yacht's designer, was unwilling to continue after they saw that the *Resolute* was in trouble. It seemed unfair to take advantage of a crippled boat which, up to that point, was well on its way to victory. But, by mutual agreement, it had been decided that a race was a test of a boat's capability as well as that of its men. After a little discussion, the *Shamrock* sailed on to a victory without glory.

Once before a challenger had won a race and not because it had outsailed a defender. That had been in the third contest of the 1871 match when, because the *Columbia* was disabled, the *Livonia* had crossed the finish line well ahead. Sir Thomas derived no pleasure from the result of the empty victory. (The race had not really been a test of the merit of either yacht.) True, *Shamrock I* had lost its topmast in the second race of the 1899 series and had withdrawn. Nevertheless, as the victory had been a fluke, Sir Thomas offered to write it off and suggested that the race be resailed. The offer was a generous one and sincerely meant, but the regatta committee quite properly rejected it.

For a day or two Captain Burton came in for a verbal keel-hauling. The man had committed the dreadful crime of bouncing across the line before the gun! The common scolds on the seaside porches which lined both sides of the Atlantic were noisy and indignant. The opinions of British yachting authorities were merely severe. One might have thought, from the volume of criticism, that a false start was something new. Actually, the finest helmsmen had done it before and, during the tense jockeying for a flying start, it has happened in races many times since. Burton's error had not actually put the *Shamrock* at a time disadvantage. Because of the din

195

made by the critics, it was rumored that Burton would be withdrawn as helmsman. At that Sir Thomas stepped in. "I do not countenance this discussion and I disassociate myself from it. [We did discuss] the sailing of the *Shamrock,* but there was no talk whatever of the suppression of Captain Burton. It is nonsense."

Sherman Hoyt, on board the challenger, had found Mrs. Burton "a pleasant shipmate . . . most unobtrusive." (His admiration for Burton, who had much to put up with, increased with each race.) But the professional crew on board, all hardened Essex fishermen, clearly resented the lady's presence. She was a lady Jonah, particularly in a yacht race, and the fo'c'sle's opinion was that she would look right pert in a rocking chair at home, sitting and knitting. The excess baggage had the effrontery to have her own ideas of where she belonged and what to do. It was to keep time—a remarkable strain on most women—and call it as the helmsman asked for it. She set herself right in the cockpit.

It had been observed that Captain Burton had other problems on board. The crew were not only disgruntled because of Mrs. Burton but openly irritated because there was no way in which they could brew a dish of hot tea during a race! (This was no oversight on the part of the outstanding tea merchant in history. If Burton had said, "No unnecessary equipment on board, not even a teakettle—and keep your mind on the race," Sir Thomas was not going to interfere.) Also, to add to the helmsman's trials, there was a superabundance of advice from the afterguard, chiefly expressed by the designer, Nicholson. He meant well, as did the others, but they confused Burton with unwanted counsel. The bickering became intense. After the race of July 17 was postponed because the wind was somewhere else, Burton insisted upon and received full command. A Sandy Hook pilot temporarily took Nicholson's place.

196

Proof that the judgment of Sir Thomas was sound in re-taining Burton and putting Nicholson on temporary shore leave came in the second completed race on July 20, five days after the first. Captain Burton was on his toes this time. He put his boat across the line first and, even though to leeward, the *Shamrock* was in an advantageous position. A New Jersey sailing man, Captain A. J. Applegate, had been shipped as adviser on winds and tides.

During the race the balloon jib fouled and would not fill. Some hands, in trying to adjust it, tore it and it was hauled in. Burton then had a spinnaker set to starboard but the wind was in the wrong place to make full use of the sail. Quickly a block was rigged on the mast and a light sail of small area was set flying. Just what to call it puzzled the experts; they finally dubbed it a "fiddler's jib." It did what Burton wanted it to do. The *Shamrock* won.

It was a most satisfactory victory, for it was won on merit. Burton's skillful maneuvering had brought the *Shamrock* in 9 minutes, 27 seconds (elapsed time) ahead of her opponent. It had taken about 5½ hours in baffling, light airs to complete the race. With time allowance deducted, the challenger had won by 2 minutes, 26 seconds. The spectator fleet behaved as though they were Britishers.

Sir Thomas danced the first few steps of a combination jig and fling. (He was, after all, an Irish-Scotsman.) "I'm the happiest man in the world." There had been thirty-three races in thirteen matches and never before had a challenging yacht come home first by outsailing a defender. One more race to win—and the greatest yachting trophy of them all would be awarded to the man who had tried to possess it during more than two decades.

The press photographers swarmed about the challenger on the *Victoria*. He posed tirelessly, "lifting the cup"—of tea. Lord Tom Dewar, better known for his brands of Scotch whiskies than for his close friendship with Sir Thomas, was a guest on the *Victoria*. He conferred with a group of reporters and told them a number of things in the strictest confidence—for immediate release. "If he wins one more race, the precious Cup will be divorced from America and married to Lipton. Sir Thomas told me a long time ago, if he ever took the Cup from America, he would take an American bride with it. . . . Like the America's Cup he's an institution."

When the third race began, on July 21, Captain Burton again put the *Shamrock* across the line first. It was to be a beat out for 15 miles. Half an hour after the start the challenger was a quarter-mile ahead. If she could have held that lead her heavy time penalty would not matter. But on each tack the *Resolute* continued to outpoint her opponent. The vang which Herreshoff had applied to the gaff was credited. At the outer mark the defender was ahead by almost two minutes. No crew ever worked faster setting a spinnaker than *Shamrock*'s as she went around the mark. (They were sailors first, tea drinkers later.) Nicholson, who had rejoined the party, cheered them lustily. Except for that, he was quite restrained. "There were," said Sherman Hoyt, "less arguments than usual."

Had that race been a mile or so longer *Shamrock* would undoubtedly have won it. She stepped along at such a pace on the run home that she caught the *Resolute*—and crossed the line 19 seconds in advance of her. This alone was a coincidence. She had been exactly the same time ahead at the start. What made the race unusual—the closest ever sailed for the Cup—was that it was a dead heat. Both yachts took exactly 4 hours, 3 minutes, 6 seconds to cover the 30-mile course. The *Shamrock* lost that third race only to the *Resolute*'s time allowance. And she lost the fourth, over a triangular course, on July 23. Both yachts traveled fast on the second leg, logging almost 12 knots each. Squalls hit them on the last leg, a close reach. First topsails were doused, then head sails, and when both came in with only mainsails, the *Resolute* was more than 3 minutes elapsed time ahead. The *Shamrock*'s time penalty had been reduced by 21 seconds, as she was carrying a smaller topmast and club topsail. (This also applied in the first and fifth races.)

It takes little imagination to understand the excitement which immediately followed that last race. The series was two-even now. It surprised even blasé reporters to see the crowds that gathered for the final contest. Droves of people in the New York area seemed to forget that they had jobs and took to the sea. There was a fantastic crop of fatalities among grandmothers whose funerals office boys simply had to attend. Trading in the marts and the exchanges was desultory. Business was as usual—but it could wait. Betting became furious and extravagant. From northern Maine to southern California expensive calls were coming in to city desks, demanding news.

Both yachts were at the starting line on the appointed days, ready and eager. But twice there was just enough wind to sail a canoe across a lake. People who had not been to church since they were carried in for christening prayed earnestly for wind. They were heard. A hard 25- to 30-knot sou'wester came tearing into the Sandy Hook area—whereupon the committee canceled the race!

Each of the contestants had gone out with shortened sail. Mrs. Burton, Nicholson, and the hired pilot had been left on shore. On that day, Burton remarked, he needed "beef," and the trio had been replaced with some energetic huskies. On the way out to the committee tug the *Shamrock* pounded heavily, and as Sherman Hoyt (still the club representative on board) noted in his account of the races, "her mast is all over the shop." There were two mates on board, one a supernumerary who was professional skipper of the unnumbered

199

Shamrock. This character had the singularly appropriate name of Diaper, for according to Hoyt, who held him in "particular detestation," he was all wet.

In his *Memoirs* Hoyt relates that, halfway out from their anchorage at the Horseshoe inside Sandy Hook, Diaper had created a near-panic by coming aft and shouting that Burton had better turn back before the yacht broke up. "Hell of a yellow performance!" Hoyt went below with Burton, at the latter's request, and found that water had shipped through the fore hatch. But there was no damage so serious as to warrant a demand for postponement in order to make repairs. Half of the crew appeared to agree with mate Diaper. They did not expect the *Shamrock* to hold together. But Burton made a "good speech" which cheered the men. Hoyt did not think that with the wind outside the bay it would have been safe for the *Shamrock* to go out, but the decision was up to the committee and the afterguards.

Wrote Alfred Loomis of the fateful moment of decision:

As starting time approached, the Race Committee signalled each yacht asking if it consented to a postponement. The affirmative signals went up so fast they burned the halliards.

When the news was conveyed to Sir Thomas on the *Victoria,* which was feeling the effect of the sea and wind, too, he ordered her over to the committee boat. His barnacled goatee was hoisted to an angle which spelled anger. Again, in a tense moment, he showed irritation over an unexpected delay. His biographer, Alec Waugh, states that "He was in a fury of red rage. . . . Bitter words must have been exchanged." On the basis of contemporary accounts, this seems an exaggeration.

But even if he had wanted to take vigorous action, there was nothing that Sir Thomas could have done. At that moment he was merely the owner of a Cup contender. The man in command was the skipper of the *Shamrock*. It had been mutually agreed that a race would not be held if, in the opinion of both skippers, the lives of the crew and the safety of the boats were in possible danger. "Yet," said Sir Thomas, "*Shamrock* had much worse weather than this coming over. True, she had her ocean rig and not her racing rig but there was no more protection for the crew then than now."

Men of better experience than Sir Thomas thought the danger was real. Among them was Frank Gray Griswold, who, in his *Clipper Ships and Yachts,* reported that it was then blowing a moderate gale. He observed that there was no rail for the protection of the sailors and that it was not safe to send out racing yachts in a thrash to windward in so rough a sea. It was the hazard to human life, not the question of whether or not the yachts could weather it, which had brought about the decision not to race. Had the contest taken place, had the *Shamrock* won and lives been lost, it would have been a victory Sir Thomas would have hated.

Later he was to express regret for his indignation and to say that the judges and afterguards were right. There were quite a few people, though, who thought his initial reaction was justified. The contenders, it was pointed out, were supposedly designed for seaworthiness. Both had lived through the turbulence of a thunderstorm with only minor damage, in the first race. The *New York Times* correspondent "noticed" that both yachts had had an impromptu race back to their moorings. (But that wasn't outside, where they would have had the full sweep of the Atlantic.)

Much of the sporting public, keyed to a higher pitch than was usual, expressed contempt for boats and crews. Most writers on marine subjects were in opposition to the committee's decision and on the side of adventure. They were caustic about the "paper-napkin sailboats," and, wrote one:

201

The wind-shy regatta committee and the skippers of the blown-glass [racers] were rewarded yesterday by weather exactly suited to their capacities. There was absolutely no danger at any time of . . . throwing spray over the well-polished shoes of the racing crews.

This was a typical exaggeration written by a man seated far from gales, probably with a fan going (for breeze) and a long drink (for inspiration).

There was wailing in the realm of Albion. British expectation of a Cup victory had been justifiably high after the second race. Some of the comment on the committee's decision was most intemperate. Wrote one English journalist that, on a course "sheltered on three sides by land" (he must have been looking at the wrong chart):

The Yankees have the frankness to ask the sporting world to be fooled by the calling off of the race because their cockleshell was unable to stand up against a summer squall in a sheltered bay, while the sturdy British challenger that had stoutly weathered Atlantic storms was not allowed to sail the course.

There were, of course, several things wrong with this fairly typical expression of British irritation. The course *was* on the open sea and in deep water, though not ideal for racing because of fluky winds and heavy traffic. The third deed of gift had specifically required that "all races shall be on ocean courses free from headlands." (The *Shamrock-Resolute* match, was, incidentally, the last to be held on the course off Sandy Hook.) And, had either skipper decided to do so, he could have sailed the course alone if his rival had refused to join him. It was Sir Thomas who, by his manner, calmed everyone down. The papers had paid no attention to his momentary explosion—they were, on the whole, always genial and affectionate in their treatment of him. Yachtsmen and the public generally esteemed him the more for refusing to become involved in the controversy and for speaking no more of his disappointment.

It was all over on July 27. What there was of wind was so fickle that the start was delayed for two hours. Nicholson was at the *Shamrock*'s helm most of the time, and he sailed her "beautifully." But he and Burton were again at odds on tactics, which hardly helped. Then, on the beat out when the challenger seemed to be doing well, a sudden shift in wind set her drifting and pushed the *Resolute* along. It happened again on the run home. Those two soft spots "killed us," was the comment of the challenger's helmsman. At the finish *Resolute* was 13 minutes, 5 seconds elapsed time in advance of her opponent.

At the club dinner which honored Sir Thomas, the expected, inevitable question was asked. Could they look for him again? He hesitated. He wasn't sure. But everyone knew he would renew his challenge if he could. How could he possibly give up so readily? It wouldn't be the same yachting world without him. His public was unwilling to give him up. Because of popular demand, he put the *Shamrock IV* on exhibit in the Hudson River, off Ninety-sixth Street, for a few days. It was a typically generous gesture. He made a speech of welcome to the first batch of visitors on board and willingly acceded to the request of some of the ladies who asked if they could inspect the "kitchen."

More than 35,000 people crowded on the challenger while she was briefly on display, roamed her deck, explored her "downstairs," caressed the wheel, asked innumerable questions, and then went away contented. The manager of the *Resolute,* though asked to do so, refused to exhibit the defender. "We can't be annoyed; our crew is too busy." His decision was "deplored" by more democratic yachtsmen. He might well have permitted a close look at the winner as a gaff-

203

rigged sloop. She was converted to a two-masted schooner in 1926, then showed up with a Marconi sloop rig in 1928.

There had been talk, directly after the defeat of the *Shamrock IV*, of a Canadian challenge for 1921 or 1922 from a Nova Scotia club. The New York Yacht Club indicated that it would be willing. The matter went so far that the name of an unbuilt challenger was made public: *Maple Leaf*. Plans were announced for a public subscription to set her afloat. The energetic managers of the proceedings asked Sir Thomas not to challenge in 1921 or, if he felt he must, to agree to a triple contest. Then, somehow, the ambitious scheme lost itself in the fogs off the north coast and foundered.

For the next few years, on his frequent trips abroad, Sir Thomas could depend upon the recurrent question: "When will you challenge again?" The general understanding was that, despite an occasional manifestation of ambition elsewhere, the right to challenge was now traditionally reserved to him. Indeed, quite a few people had adopted the habit of referring to the great trophy as the Lipton Cup. He had earned it. In November 1921 news came out of New Zealand that some of its yachtsmen were considering a challenge, but there was no particular enthusiasm over the idea. The little item found its place in the press file marked "Maybe."

Some of the baronet's questioners coupled the standard inquiry with a plea for action. Tempus, they told him, was fidgeting and he would surely win if he only tried once again. From 1922 on, each year for the succeeding half-dozen, there was an announcement in the press, from an "authoritative source," that Sir Thomas would challenge in the following year. Then, to his inquirers, he would reply, genially, that he was not quite ready yet. One account carried a brief report of an interview with Sir Tea: He had commissioned Fife for a new challenger. It didn't happen. But Sir Thomas stayed in the news. In 1925 he presented the mast of *Shamrock IV* to New York University. That institution planned to erect a radio broadcasting station, and the 113-foot steel mast and 56-foot wooden topmast were to serve as a support for the antenna.

During one of his meetings with the press, Sir Thomas remarked that his four challengers had cost ten million dollars and that he was ready to spend another million in a further effort for the Cup. That was in 1926. He had, he said, the most valuable collection of yachting trophies anywhere in the world, won by his various *Shamrocks* in British waters. But he wasn't satisfied; there was still that Cup.

Sir Thomas was not merely tantalizing his wide audience of admirers by any calculated scheme. What he had really been waiting for came in 1927. In that year a meeting of yachting associations, American and European, formulated a number of logical regulations for yacht construction and changes in rating rules. Undoubtedly on the counsel of such competent men as Colonel Duncan F. D. Neill (long his yachting adviser), Brooke Heckstall-Smith, one of the outstanding British authorities on the sport, and Charles E. Nicholson, Sir Thomas had been waiting for conditions which would improve the chances of a foreign vessel racing in American waters. Neither he nor his advisers could foresee what a challenger would have to face in the next contest.

In conformity with the new code, large yachts had to meet Lloyd's construction rules of scantlings. (Smaller yachts were covered by other Lloyd rules. The New York Yacht Club formally adopted the rules in December 1927.) That meant that a challenger would now be so strongly built and so seaworthy that she could sail across to the Cup without more than the normal hazards of Atlantic winds and seas. A yacht of the class designed for a Cup match (the "76 rating") would range in waterline length from 75 to 87 feet. Yet the applicable formula, which included waterline length, square root of sail and cubic root of displacement, left room for variations. The allowable modifications put a premium on a designer's imagination.

The only class designed to participate in Cup matches in the 30s was that called "J boats." They had appeared first as racers in 1928. Before 1900 it had been customary for American yacht clubs to prefix a letter to the measurement of boats in various classes. The latter was dropped after a while and the letter retained. American yachtsmen were slow in returning to the reasonable custom of using racing measurement to designate a class. The European system of number-with-meter had been in effect for some time.

It was May 1929 before the Royal Ulster Yacht Club sent over a challenge on behalf of Sir Thomas Lipton. (The baronet had announced, in 1920, that he was bequeathing a large sum to the Irish club as a challenge fund.) His latest challenge had been sent thirty-one years after his first; nearly nine had passed since *Shamrock IV* had almost won. The new Lipton centerboard cutter would be 77 feet on the load waterline and she would be called, as everyone expected, *Shamrock V*. Her designer was Charles Nicholson.

Meanwhile, a most important change in rig, referred to previously, had taken place. The developing science of aerodynamics had opened up an exciting new field to progressive yacht designers. As a result, the long-used topsail and gaff for racing boats were put on the shelf with other antiques. They were replaced with an impressive jib-headed sail, triangular in shape, which united the mainsail and topsail on a pole mast. The undivided sail had, in consequence, a higher hoist. The main boom no longer projected well past the stern. It now was inboard and inside of a fixed stay. With the sails being elevated, yachtsmen, too, felt uplifted.

The British called the rig Bermudian; sailors called it leg-o-mutton, and jib-headed. It was not new. It very prob-
206

ably was first seen in the Netherlands but it was so common in Bermuda from earliest colonial days as to give the reasonable impression that it was native to those islands. Originally it was loose-footed, with a sprit instead of a boom. The rig was popular in the Chesapeake Bay area from an early period. In the New York area William P. Stephens used a form of the sail in 1895 in a Seawanhaka trophy race. There were other experimental applications of the sail in the same locale but they were not successful. Then George Nichols, later a commodore of the New York Yacht Club, made an intensive study of gaff- and jib-headed rigs. His jib-headed *Carolina* won some important races in 1921. In consequence, the new sail plan received due formal recognition from the makers of yachting rules.

The apparently novel rig acquired a pictorial name in the States, a name which, after the 1930 match, received general acceptance among American yachtsmen: "Marconi." The great inventor was not responsible for the term. But in the 30s the landscape was dotted with tall Marconi wireless stations held in position by numerous wire ropes. As the single mast on J boats had gone past 150 feet, it required extra stays and spreaders. Its converging pattern, bow on, had the appearance of a typical Marconi station.

Chiefly because of the undivided mainsail, the few J boats in existence could step along at a pace equivalent to that of the heavily canvased *Reliance* of 1903. Yet they had half or less her sail spread of 16,000 square feet. (Under the rules the height of the Marconi sail plan was limited to 150 feet.) The gaff rig was not entirely abandoned, but for the most part racers adopted the new sail plan. Sails new in American waters were being tried out a few years before the 1930 match. One which became extremely popular, once yachtsmen understood how best to use it, was the two-sheeted "Genoa" or "Genoese" jib, more familiarly known as "Jenny." This over-

207

lapped the mainsail almost a third of its width. It was a remarkably efficient racing sail in going to windward. On the
J boats it had, usually, an 80-foot length.

The combination of improved construction regulations
and adoption of the Marconi mainsail created a new type of
boat. The lines were finer, the hulls more wholesome. The
new challenger and the candidates for defense were particularly pleasing to the eye. And they delighted the most critical
among yachting experts because they were solidly built while
designed for speed.

A syndicate of men who could well afford it (among them
Harold S. Vanderbilt) commissioned as designer a man whose
family name was an important one in Cup history. He was
W. Starling Burgess, son of the famed Edward. He was much
further advanced in the science of naval architecture than his
father had been, being a keen experimenter. (After the 1920
Cup match he had conducted a series of "secret" experiments
for the New York Yacht Club. They involved two model
sloops, each 9' long with 15' masts. The tests were run off
Provincetown, Massachusetts.) The construction of the Bur-
gess-designed yacht took place in the Herreshoff yard. The
old master had very much retired, after designing Cup winners over a twenty-seven-year period. Yet on such an occasion he could hardly stay away from his familiar surroundings
or refrain from dropping a hint which would be treated with
respect. The result was called the *Enterprise*. She was 120' 9"
over all, with 80' waterline and a 22' 1" beam.

The New York Yacht Club had, meanwhile, encouraged
other groups to build Cup-class boats. In consequence, three
new Js were turned out: the *Whirlwind,* the *Yankee,* and the
Weetamoe. They were lovely to look at, and fast. During one
of the trials the *Yankee* sailed a 30-mile triangular course at
a speed averaging 10.72 knots, with one leg at 13.3 knots—a
record. But the *Enterprise* had special qualities which en-
208

deared her to the committee. In her last completed trial race she stepped up her average 9.45 knots to 10.63. Of the four possible defenders she was the smallest. Her sail area, 7,583 square feet, was a fraction larger than the others. All of the quartet were Marconi-rigged and with triple headsails. (The speed of these boats convinced yachtsmen of the superiority of that sail plan over that of gaff-rigged, topsail sloops.) The *Vanitie* and the *Resolute,* both of whose sails and masts had been altered in 1928 to keep them in style, had joined the trials as pacers.

Sail areas, over all and waterline lengths of both the defender—she was to be the *Enterprise*—and the challenger were close, with the latter about 2½ feet narrower in the beam. The *Enterprise* had two centerboards, one for sailing on, one for sailing off, the wind. Everything that money could buy went into the defender. It was not surprising to the experts when they heard that her reported cost was $630,000, excluding "extras." Burgess had carried out experiments with a 15-foot, 600-pound model in the United States Naval towing basin at Washington, sail and rigging tests at New York University's wind tunnel, structural tests at the Bureau of Standards. Satisfied then, he created the *Enterprise* full scale. He turned out something astonishing. On the water it very definitely looked like a yacht. It had a hull and mast, sails and stays, and the usual equipment of rigging, lines, cleats. But the thing was described as a "box of clockwork," "a mechanical yacht," "a robust robot."

No old-time sailor worth the salt in his whiskers would have regarded her with anything but scorn. Beef used to haul the halyards and hang on to a sheet and it was a good, honest feeling in strong hands and shoulders. Now all that was done with winches, about two dozen of them, below decks in an almost hollow hull. That section was cleared of bulkheads, cabins and what is usually regarded as a minimum essential, a head. The winches were used for all running gear and back-stays, operated by an undercover crew of eight men who never saw a race. (When they were allowed topside they knew it had ended.) They were called the "black gang," and they followed the orders of the second mate, who bellowed them through a hatch. Did the afterguard want a stay slackened or tightened, a halyard hauled or a sheet eased, the command was relayed to the gang of winchmen: "Number three, slack off." "Ease number nine. Hold it." "Half-turn on twenty-one. Belay!" (This is not necessarily a verbatim report of the mate's lingo but it seems a reasonable guess.)

It was no longer necessary to smell the wind, look at the set of a sail or feel a stay. Now, because of a special mast, strains on headstays and backstays were measured by a shunt dynamometer (a device then more familiar to structural engineers). And a strain gauge was used to determine the degree of compression on the leeward side of the mast. Engineering had gone to sea on a racing yacht.

Quite apart from the winches and gadgets, Burgess had produced (or accepted) some remarkable innovations. Chief of these was the "Park Avenue" boom on the *Enterprise*. This was a hollow wooden triangular affair which tapered near its ends, in the shape of a boat, with ribs and a keel, flat on top. It was wide enough in its center section for two men to walk abreast, with flush transverse rails and adjustable stops. The thing weighed about a ton and a quarter, which was 365 pounds heavier than the boat's rectangular boom on which, as was usual, the foot of the sail was tightly laced. The foot of the mainsail could slide to leeward on the rails and thus assume its "correct aerodynamic curve." This was, therefore, a form of a loose-footed mainsail which seems to have developed from the idea of a sliding luff and the studies of Dr. Manfred Curry. It proved to be an effective device, as it low-

210

ered airflow resistance and reduced downdraught of the big mainsail to the deck.

The afterguard of the *Shamrock* made no objection to this curiosity, though they were startled by it. They had something new on their boat, too, but not so extreme a development. It was a boom which could be bent laterally. During the trials of defense candidates, however, the manager of the *Weetamoe* had questioned the legality of the Park Avenue boom. It was not a protest, but Vanderbilt, who was to be the defender's helmsman, felt that as the contraption had been questioned he should discard it. He requested an opinion from the proper committee of the club. They reminded him that the *Enterprise* had been selected with its new boom in place. Thereupon Vanderbilt decided to retain it for use in light winds. Many yachtsmen were of the opinion that, despite the committee's opinion, the boom did evade the rules.

The other most conspicuous invention on the defender was its "tin mast," 162 feet from keel to truck, tapering from 18 inches at the foot to 9 inches at its top. It was composed of two shells of duralumin, the first time in yachting history that a big mast was constructed of that metal. More than eighty thousand rivets went into it, which partly explains why its cost was triple that of a wooden spar. It weighed much less and had a smaller diameter than the hollow wooden mast on *Shamrock V*. The obvious intention in its design was to reduce windage. While strong transversely—it had to support the weight of more than a ton of canvas with wind in it—it was not as dependable fore and aft as a wooden stick.

Starling Burgess thought it a "work of art," though he conceded that exact pressure on the headstays and backstays had to be under constant watch. It was Charles P. Burgess, an airship designer and brother of Starling, who had created the

211

mast. Clinton Crane, designer of the *Weetamoe,* called it a "miracle." The real miracle, said Charles Burgess, was that the men on the *Enterprise* were able to keep it in the boat! Because of the necessary adjustment each time wind direction changed or the mainsail was trimmed, Starling Burgess, originally assigned as navigator on the defender, now became the "mast nurse." This was something new in marine jobs.

Quite as remarkable as his creation was the designer of the *Enterprise.* Born in 1878 and educated as a naval architect, he had acquired an outstanding reputation in the new field of powered flight. He flew the first plane in New England, won some coveted aviation trophies, and produced warplanes (on rush order) for England in World War I. His great love had always been the sea; an only slightly less one had been poetry. In his early manhood he had written verse, poems of love and mysticism touched by the sea. His poetry was good and several volumes were published in the decorative form of the period. One of the special mannerisms reported of him was his ability to stand on his head—no hands—long enough to recite a Swinburne ballad, with encores if requested. This was not a demonstration of a form of Yoga. It was the opinion of this acrobatic elocutionist that a rush of blood to the head made Swinburne clearer to him and that, keel upward, the words of the poet of passion had the proper melancholy intonations.

That is what was so astonishing, that a man with such delicate understanding of seductive poetry could have turned out so mechanical a yacht. He was to be scolded for it, and not only by conservatives. If an official stop had not been put to the multiplicity of winches and associated devices a dreadful advance was foreseen in mechanics applied to yachting. Marine commentators thought that, if technology took hold, boats would need no more crew than a cook and a steward.

212

Shamrock III astern of *Reliance*, 1903.   PHOTO MORRIS ROSENFELD

Shamrock V (on the starboard tack) and
Enterprise jockeying for the starting line.

PHOTO EDWIN LEVICK-FREDERIC LEWIS

W. Starling Burgess
PHOTO MORRIS ROSENFELD

Olin Stephens
PHOTO EDWIN LEVICK-FREDERIC LEWIS

Charles E. Nicholson

PHOTO EDWIN LEVICK-FREDERIC LEWIS

Sails would be hoisted, sheets trimmed by pushing buttons, stays adjusted through tuning knobs.

Shamrock V came over on her own. For five days she was separated from her convoy, hidden in mist and fog. But she made Horta Harbor in the Azores without trouble on her way to the Cup. Her record in English regattas had been superb. She was particularly good in light airs which were regarded abroad as characteristic of the American locale. American experts thought her a thing of beauty. Captain Ernest (Ted) Heard, out of Essex and renowned as a helmsman, was her sailing master. Among the other semiprofessionals in the challenger's afterguard were her designer, and her time-keeper, Colonel Duncan F. D. Neill, who had sailed on all the *Shamrocks* and on the *Thistle* in the 1887 match. It was expected that Nicholson would take a trick at the wheel. On the *Enterprise* all the afterguard were amateurs: her helms-man, Harold S. Vanderbilt, rated among the really great handlers of yachts, and such top men as C. Sherman Hoyt and Starling Burgess.

The appearance of Sir Thomas in New York dispelled, for a time, depression gloom in the broad areas in which he circulated. Those congenial party men, Mayor Walker and his aides, handsomely decorated with gardenias and tall hats, never put on a more extensive welcome. Jaundiced reporters, the people who had seen everything, and even those normally indifferent to celebrities from abroad, were infected by the current enthusiasm for "our Tommy." He was old and tired, but the outpouring of praise and genuine affection was heartwarming and stirred him to activities expected of a much younger man. Whenever he could, he accepted invitations, made addresses, shook thousands of hands in public streets and private clubs. He set up new trophies for yacht races, even going so far as to offer a prize for winners of outboard-

213

motor contests. A man could hardly have been more broad-minded; for years he had been trying to win just one prize with boats powered only by wind.

The first close view of the *Enterprise* was a profound shock to Sir Thomas and his yachting associates. They had brought over a sailboat and expected to race one. What they faced was a product of the machine shops, which needed only an engine to take it out of classification as a sailing vessel. In discussion with Sherman Hoyt, Nicholson thought that the *Enterprise* had too many winches, the *Shamrock* too few. The English designer found much to interest him in the strange boom and, later, adapted some of its principles to his own device of a flexible boom. And he gave unstinted praise to the mast as the most remarkable engineering advance in racing yachts.

The races, for the first time, were to be held off Newport. The entrance to New York Harbor was bustling with traffic, and the waters had been fouled with oil and refuse. Further-more, a J boat could not pass under East River bridges unless the mast was unstepped. British challengers, for years, had been asking for a course away from New York. It takes time, however, to agree to such a request—and discussion, commit-tees, membership votes. By agreement, for the pending match there were to be no time allowances and the series would consist of seven races, if required.

The new rules of 1927, new sail plan, the special char-acteristics of the *Enterprise* and associated matters had de-veloped into a body of information extremely important to racing yachtsmen and to yachting history. One might very well have expected that the wealth of preliminary details would be justified by the races in the fourteenth challenge for the Cup. Yet the preliminaries proved to be more inter-esting than the contest. Perhaps it was just as well that the Prince of Wales, the King of the Belgians, and Mussolini, all of whom had been invited with other notables, had prior engagements. The races were certainly not exciting to the spectators, for the Coast Guard fleet, destroyers, revenue cutters and lesser craft went to the opposite extreme of the good old bad days. Even the press boats, usually privileged, were kept far from the course. And the series was not particularly exciting to the participants.

The *Shamrock* was thought, by authoritative critics, to be so badly rigged that it was difficult to trim her sheets. This is astonishing when one remembers that she was designed by the top man in his field in England. It was also said that the challenger was inexpertly handled; that the *Enterprise* was better built, better sailed, and far superior in windward work. After the first race on September 13, Sir Thomas made the grim comment: "I'd be more optimistic of getting first prize if the last boat over the finish were the victor!" The defender won that race by 2 minutes, 52 seconds, which was the closest of the series. The third race showed the challenger doing better than she had, but it was not to be her day. Before the first hour of racing was completed, the main halyard parted and her mainsail smothered the deck. The damage, so they said, was too severe for immediate repair and the challenger was towed to her berth.

Of that occasion, wrote Alfred Loomis:

In 1920 the defender's main halliard let go and Shamrock IV *sailed on to win a race. America criticized the crippled defender for not trying to finish. In 1930 Shamrock V's main halliard parted and the defender sailed on to win a race. Her action was, in the eyes of many Americans, an infernal outrage. Thus, in sixty years of defending the Cup, inconsistency had become a virtue and sportsmanship was exalted. In the first race of 1870 we would have said such a mishap to the challenger served him good and right for attempting to steal our Cup.*

215

Harold Vanderbilt was at the helm of the *Enterprise* most of the time during the four races, and his control of her was brilliant. As a tribute to her designer he relinquished the wheel to Starling Burgess near the finish. It was the designer who brought the defender across the line in the fourth and final race. In his excellent account of the boat and the races (*Enterprise,* 1931), Vanderbilt reported his feelings in the final moments:

And Shamrock V, *where is she? We look astern. She is about a mile behind, a badly beaten boat. Our hour of triumph, our hour of victory, is all but at hand but it is so tempered with sadness that it is almost hollow. To win The America's Cup is glory enough for any yachtsman. Why then should we be verging on the disconsolate? Uppermost in our minds is a feeling of sympathy for that grand old sportsman, Sir Thomas Lipton. . . . The ambition of a lifetime, to achieve which he has spent millions, is perhaps never to be realized. . . .*

The victory was unpopular. "It was not easy," wrote a *New York Times* editor, "it was almost a thankless task to defend the America's Cup when thousands of [Vanderbilt's] countrymen were almost clamouring for failure." The British press had no such sentiments but gave expression to a general opinion: The Americans had not won fairly; "gadgets had beaten manpower." William P. Stephens agreed with that. He thought yachtsmen were quite unnecessary on the *Enterprise;* good handle-turners, such as Bronx hurdy-gurdy grinders, would have been suitable as a crew. Yet he wondered whether the crew's "snappy work with sheets and halyards" had not been helped by the drum winches. And he thought that the duralumin mast must have helped, too. Yet he was puzzled over the value of the mechanical contrivances—and he was not alone in his doubts.

Sir Thomas shook hands with a multitude of well-wishers

and reporters who came to his new *Erin* to cheer him up, to say goodbye, to urge him to try again. "It's no use," he said again and again. "I can't win. I can't win." He seemed really to be seriously depressed and some of his guests left tearfully. He was entitled to his moods. Only a few days before, after the loss of a race, he had called the *Shamrock*'s afterguard for a meeting on the *Erin*. They did not know whether he was annoyed or not but they looked as downcast as they felt. Sir Thomas grinned at them. "Gentlemen, I have to congratulate you for having kept the *Enterprise* in sight the whole day through!" That brought the relief of laughter and a toast to the challenger's health.

The popular Ring Lardner had expressed his objections to the Cup matches, saying that "chief among them is that they invariably cast a pall of gloom over the American people" because of the successive defeats of Sir Thomas. To help dispel that gloom, Will Rogers said he had a bright idea. The *New York Times* published it as a conspicuous item:

What do you say to this? Let everyone send a dollar apiece for a fund to buy a loving cup for Sir Thomas Lipton bigger than the one he would have got if he had won. . . . Send it to a Lipton Cup Fund in care of Mayor Walker. . . . Let Jimmy buy it and present it with an inscription along this line. "To possibly the world's worst yacht builder but absolutely the world's most cheerful loser." You have been a benefit to mankind, Sir Thomas, you have made losing worth while.

It was reported later by the knowing that the New York publicity adviser of Sir Thomas was responsible for the plan. Whether this was true or not, what really mattered was the response. In a little over a week, $16,000 in single bills came to the Mayor's desk. They came from the Governor's Mansion and the Old Sailors' Home, the Ritz and Delancey Street.

217

The fund went to Tiffany's, who put their top artisans to work on a masterpiece in 18-carat gold.

Sir Thomas was openly touched. He would come back for the cup as soon as it was ready, and when he did he would know when he would challenge again for that other Cup. "America's Cup-hunting," he noted in his autobiography, published when he was eighty, "has been my principal recreation for over thirty years. It has kept me young, eager, buoyant, and hopeful. It has brought me health and splendid friends."

He did return in November of 1930 for the golden symbol of friendship. It was a star piece in his collection of trophies, outshining the rest of the great array of cups won by his *Shamrocks*. It was inscribed "In the name of hundreds and thousands of Americans and well-wishers," a dedication in better taste than that originally suggested. In its design pattern was the private signal of Sir Thomas, shamrock leaves, the Royal Ulster Yacht Club's insignia, and—a thoughtful touch, though a provocative one—the America's Cup. When he rose to make his speech of acceptance at a well-attended affair, Sir Thomas was too moved to say more than a part of what he had intended. "Although I have lost, you make me feel that I have won. But I will try again. Yes, I will try again."

The 1930 match had hardly been concluded when an English paper, the *News Chronicle,* angrily asked why Britain's premier yacht club still denied membership to Sir Thomas. ". . . every reputable yachting club in the world delights to do him honour [yet] the Royal Yacht Squadron still deems itself too exclusive for Sir Thomas Lipton." They thought the situation "ridiculous," and they were not alone among Britishers in that opinion. Someone in the Squadron must have heard of what was being said, for the matter was taken under solemn advisement. In 1931, more than thirty years after he had been proposed by Edward, Prince of Wales, the Squadron decided that Sir Thomas was a sufficiently proper person for membership.

It was clear that the composition of the Squadron had changed, something perhaps that the *News Chronicle* had not known. Younger, more progressive men were now dominant among the membership. Time was when so trivial an affair as a challenge for the America's Cup was something hardly discussed. The secretary would, after the suggestion had gone through channels, forward a challenge on behalf of some ambitious member. But the dependable reserve of fine old gentlemen of the later Victorian era, some of whom may have been proposed for membership when the Squadron was born in 1815, were politely interested only in the regattas which ended in front of the castle on the Squadron's polished lawn. Seated there, in Bath chairs, in the proper yachting costume of the period, they would at the correct moment order their chair jockeys to lift and wave the yachting caps conventional to members. Then the old men would, in unison, emit a cheer. The caps being replaced, they were wheeled off to bed. Actually, the anonymous, forgotten yachtsmen who had threatened to blackball Sir Thomas so many years earlier could not have been nearly so interesting and valuable as members as the Prince's candidate. But it meant little to Sir Thomas to have the belated honor. He seems never to have bothered to visit the clubhouse at Cowes.

Because of his membership, however, *Shamrock V* was a permitted entry in the Squadron's regattas. (She had very nearly been lost in a gale in December 1930, on her voyage home.) The boat which had made so poor a showing against the cunningly devised *Enterprise* had a remarkably successful record in her contests with the speediest British yachts. She seemed unbeatable. Her designer had maintained his faith in her, insisting that she was as fast a boat as the *Enterprise* but

219

that she had lost to mechanical devices. Sir Thomas began once again to say, in essence, that he "was bloody but unbowed," and to speak of another challenge. It would come through the Royal Yacht Squadron. That might change his luck.

Discussion of a possible match, and of "gadgets" on Cup boats, was actually under way when, quite suddenly, Sir Thomas died October 2, 1931. He had once acknowledged two great failures in his full, exciting life: He had never found that perfect woman who could be his wife; he had not been able to "lift the ould mug." Which was the greater loss to him only he knew. The world which found yacht racing exciting, and many who only stayed on the sidelines, felt that his most conspicuous failure gave him his greatest success.

There were people who knew him well who wondered, near the end of his efforts, whether he really wanted to win the Cup. They accepted the sincerity of his original intentions. But with the development of his popularity as a sporting loser, particularly in America where it had become a national legend, some British associates were convinced that Sir Thomas saw a value in not winning. It enhanced his popularity. Nicholson had commented that "nothing pleased the old man more" than to be told "he was the greatest sportsman in the world," after the defeat of one of his boats. In actuality, of course, Sir Thomas had nothing to do with winning or losing. Every race was honestly fought, and the afterguard and crew on each *Shamrock* was determined to win. If, after a while, Sir Thomas was playing a game, that was quite forgivable, and to the world that cared about the sport it would have been quite unimportant. The whole business of yacht racing, as Sir Thomas saw it, and particularly the America's Cup matches, was an elaborate sport played by rich, grown-up boys, many of whom had once had great fun sailing homemade scows in mudholes.

220

There was a wealth of favorable comment on Sir Thomas following his death. Alfred Loomis said what most people thought and, as usual, said it well:

The amiable tea-vending Sir Thomas Lipton bridged a generation in which American sportsmanship reached maturity and wondered why it had been such a nauseating infant. . . . He helped us lift Cup racing from the level of a barroom brawl and establish it as a contest between architects, legislators, and sportsmen-sailors.

13

THE

ENDEAVOUR

OF THOMAS SOPWITH

Sound critical opinion on the mechanics of the floating robot represented by the *Enterprise* was to have a valuable effect. Despite the numerous unfavorable articles on the boat he had guided to victory, Harold Vanderbilt would not concede that she was merely a mechanized yacht. "She had no more [winches] than her share; many of hers had been used in *Resolute* in 1920 and in *Reliance* in 1903." They were, he pointed out, but a gradual and inevitable development of the first such device, the anchor capstan in the old sailing ships. (Yet this was an admission rather than disproof.) There were some others who defended the gadgets on the *Enterprise*. On the whole, however, sentiment was against their further use—certainly against their development. The basis of the criticism was a good one: fair play. That element was thought, by most

222

yachtsmen, to be more important than a determination to defend the Cup at all costs. Not as clearly heard, in an age of advancing technology, were those who loved the sea and the rare sport it offered and who despised the intrusion of machinery in an element which depended upon manly men.

As a result of conferences between the New York Yacht Club and British yachting authorities, the "mechanical yacht" was abolished. Underdeck winches to handle rigging, except for headstays and main halyard, and the centerboard were eliminated. The weight of a bare mast was set at 5,500 pounds minimum, a rule enacted to insure its strength. (This agreement meant that masts on J boats would be more than 1,500 pounds heavier than the duralumin mast on the *Enterprise*.) Living quarters for crews aboard racing yachts were required. The triangular boom was allowed. These revisions of the rules spelled a death warrant for the *Enterprise*. She ended in the yard of a junk dealer. Her mast went to support the Rhode Island State Police radio antenna at Scituate. The new rating formula which accompanied the regulations on physical condition was puzzling to some. The *New York Times* man thought that "To the non-mathematically versed, the new rule is worse than a Chinese puzzle or Professor Einstein's theory of relativity."

A few years after the Wright brothers made their famous first flight, an air-minded young Britisher was demonstrating the clear fact that he was plane crazy. This intense interest once took the form of buzzing the heroic statue of William Penn on the top of Philadelphia's City Hall. The skillful young aviator was trying to dust off the statue's hat without dusting himself off his plane. Several hours were spent in this hazardous solo game before he came back to earth. He had a menagerie of flying crates and was trying to find out what was wrong with one of them. He acknowledged to the reporters who had gathered that he was Thomas Octave Murdoch Sopwith. The combination of initials naturally invited everyone to call him Tom.

A year or so after disturbing the peace of Philadelphia Tom Sopwith was hard at work in England on the development and production of air- and seaplanes. He had started just in time. When the war broke he was quickly able to fill orders for pursuit planes his firm had created, which acquired fame under such names as Cuckoos, Snipes, Bugs, Camels, Dolphins. The war over, he went ardently into the sport of racing yachts. His competence was such that he was regarded as the best amateur helmsman in Britain. He had a spectacular ability to time his racers perfectly for a starting line. Having bought the *Shamrock V,* he raced her for a while and then, in 1933, challenged for the Cup.

He would have put in his bid perhaps a year earlier, but the approval of the admiral-commodore of the Royal Yacht Squadron had to be obtained. That official was also the King of England. It was his opinion that "with industrial conditions as they are in America and elsewhere . . . this was not an opportune time." Sopwith indicated, during the usual polite conferences, that there were three other yachts suitable for a Cup match and that their owners were eager to challenge. He would like to take steps which would at least assure him priority. After due reflection his royal admiral decided that Sopwith had a point, and the point was in the direction of the Cup. Thereupon the Royal Yacht Squadron sponsored his challenge, the fifteenth since the great international contest had begun. Seven races were proposed for September 1934. The J-class boat on which Sopwith's hopes were to rest would be called the *Endeavour* and she would be 83 feet on the waterline.

The designer of the last two *Shamrocks* was the obvious man to plan the new challenger. Nicholson created one of the

finest boats, certainly the fastest, ever sent over to bring back
the Cup. Her mast was of tubular steel; most of the rest of
her was of steel as well. The boom was a slight modification
of the triangular one on the *Enterprise*. It was novel in that it
did not have to remain parallel to the deck but was adjustable
through rotation about its long axis. The blue-hulled centerboard *Endeavour* was not only strongly built; she called forth
ecstatic adjectives, the least of which was "beautiful."

The challenger had a new form of headsail. This was a
jib, cut away on the leech and double-clewed with two sheets.
One sheet ran from the lower, the other (which led farther
aft and much higher) ran from the upper clew. The fore
triangle received a powerful impetus from the driving power
of the unusual jib, and backwinding was greatly reduced.
Sopwith had been trying out a combination of baby jib topsails on *Shamrock V*. Development of the new sail is credited
to an interested spectator who had newly become the owner
of *Shamrock V*. He was Charles R. Fairey, who tested it and
others in a wind tunnel built at his aviation plant in England.
Yachting experts named the four-sided sail a quadrilateral jib,
which seems logical. This was later reduced to "quad." But
the paid hands distinguished it by a name easier for anyone
to remember and which they felt more appropriate to the
svelte lines: "Greta Garbo." (The nomenclature of the sea
should be left to sailors.)

Because of a change in regulations the triple-head rig had
become impractical. A double rig (large jib and staysail) took
its place. It was difficult at first to sheet home the headsails
properly because of the narrow beam of the J boats, but
handlers finally learned the correct trim. The point from
which the head of the mainsail was measured had been raised.
J-class yachts were thus able to carry a larger mainsail than
those in the 1930 match.

The *Endeavour* went through her trial races in the Channel, after winning in a number of regattas. Her chief opponent, and a dangerous one, was the "steel-breasted beauty," the *Velsheda,* a J boat and another triumph of Nicholson's designing. Back in Cowes, the *Endeavour* was ketch-rigged for her Atlantic trip. With the last line in place, most of her professional crew decided the time had come to demand more money. Sopwith felt that he had been more than fair and was paying above-average wages and bonuses—an opinion which received press support. He promptly put the rebellious members of the crew on permanent shore leave, insofar as his yachts were concerned. The cook left and was missed, but the officers remained.

Days counted, and experienced professionals were not readily available. Sopwith turned to the Royal Corinthian Yacht Club to see if a crew could be rounded up. He was almost trampled in the rush of small-boat owners, all of whom were excellent sailors. From this starry-eyed group of Corinthians Sopwith selected the type of men who would not be lost on so large a cutter as his J boat. His choice proved to be admirable. Six of the substitute crew were promptly sent to Le Havre to join in a race of English J's and learn what they could of the ropes. Some stayed on the challenger until she reached the Azores. The *Endeavour* was then taken across the Atlantic's bounding main by professionals. The crew selected to handle her in the Cup match went over on the motor yacht *Vita.* The amateurs had an excellent workout when they handled the *Endeavour* during preliminary races off Rhode Island.

In the Herreshoff yard at Bristol, Starling Burgess was seeing his dream boat take shape. Her lines were derived from models tested at the Ann Arbor towing tank. The cost of a defender had now reached a bracket where no one was surprised to learn that a full dozen and a half of men of great wealth composed the syndicate which commissioned her.

226

Among them were some of the most conspicuous figures in the world of finance. Four of the syndicate were members of the Vanderbilt family. It was said that the boat cost "only $400,000," as good use was made of equipment from former boats and some expensive sails were borrowed.

The new defender, christened *Rainbow,* was thought to be well found—she could go cruising after the Cup races, if anyone could afford her. She was 126′ 7″ over all and 82′ on the water. Her lines were exquisite. The duralumin mast was the same height as that on the *Enterprise.* It was strong and stiff and streamlined. The *Rainbow's* chief other novelty was a plank-on-edge-flexible boom, a development of that on *Shamrock V.* This "bending boom" had been tried out on English J boats, but because several had snapped their use was not encouraged abroad. Through jackstays, struts, and winches—the latter requiring two members of the crew in watchful attendance—the desired curve of the boom could be obtained.

The *Rainbow,* in her trials, seemed to thrive on light airs. She was quick and dependable. An ecstatic commentator wrote of her as "moving on a zephyr's breath." Yet she represented a problem to the committee appointed to select a defender. The wonderful old *Yankee,* unsuccessful as a candidate in the 1930 trials for a defender, had undergone face lifting and some other alterations. She was the *Rainbow's* pacer, and, quite forgetting that, for a J boat, she was of advanced age, she bothered the committee by making it very difficult for the new yacht. Experts in the field jumped in to make a decision easier—they demanded that the *Yankee* be chosen. It was the *Rainbow's* performance in light winds which finally won her the honor of defending the Cup.

Sopwith had a sensitive situation to face in the States. After the "dynasty of Shamrocks" he was invading the emotional territory long ruled by that Glasgow-born Irishman over whose successive defeats Americans had dropped many a tear in a brew of Lipton's tea. No new challenger could expect a hearty welcome, with the memory of "our Tommy" still so ripe. Yet, despite his achievements, Sopwith was a quiet, modest man. If things went well he might not be resented as a mere intruder. They did not start well; they ended badly.

In line with custom the two yachts were inspected by their respective afterguards and club representatives. The group from the *Rainbow* found nothing contrary to regulations on the *Endeavour*. The challenger's inspectors, however, found cause for a reasonable protest. They objected because the defender had had all her cabin fittings removed, which lightened her. This was contrary to British practice. The protest was resented by the American yachting fraternity. This was a sour beginning; the shade of Sir Thomas must have stirred uneasily. Tension resulting from the disagreement was shortly eliminated when the race committee conceded that the *Endeavour*'s people were right. The challenger was thereupon permitted to be stripped of her furniture and a large part of her cabin fittings.

This delicate matter had hardly been settled before Brooke Heckstall-Smith, then in New York to cover the match for the London *Daily Telegraph,* reported that the *Rainbow* was only a racing machine with rough board partitions instead of cabins as such. He was a yachting authority of unusual prominence and his opinions were generally treated with deserved respect. He had a further major objection. It concerned the "enormous and powerful winch" by which the huge Genoa jib on the *Rainbow* could be hauled in, even in a strong breeze. It was his contention that, under the rules, no standing rigging was permitted to be operated from below the upper deck, excepting the fore- and headstays. He thought the presence of this winch, worked from above deck but with its gear below, was an evasion of regulations. American experts disagreed with him and with other Britishers who protested. They were insistent in arguing that the *Rainbow* did, in fact, meet construction requirements, as her winches were all on deck. The dispute remained unsettled.

The collection of controversies, which could have become unpleasant, was shortly forgotten when Gerard Lambert, owner of the lovely *Vanitie,* put that yacht at Sopwith's disposal during the *Endeavour's* tuning-up. This was the type of American sportsmanship which was expected and which Sir Thomas Lipton had done much to inspire. It had a noticeable effect in soothing the feelings of the British invaders and the American defenders. The *Vanitie's* big Genoa, a sail with which the challenger's crew had had little experience, was also made available. They found, on some sailing points, that this novelty was an improvement over their use of double-clewed jib and staysail.

There was to be a wealth of sails available to both yachts. Their tenders carried no less than four mains and a great variety of light sails. Additional to the Genoa, there were spinnakers larger than ever before, and a billowing one of the parachute type. Because of its magnificent arching front, this had been realistically christened "Mae West" by sailors who cared naught for scientific nomenclature. Quite apart from names for new sails there was other and more important knowledge to acquire: how best to handle Cup racers with double headsails, and the proper trim for parachute spinnakers, quadrilateral jibs, enormous Genoas. The huge parachutes, particularly, gave trouble even to expert trimmers. The newly adopted sails were to require some changes in racing tactics.

The big day, September 17, finally came. They had tried for it on the fifteenth but the wind just wasn't there. By the time the race was called the *Rainbow* was a mile ahead of the *Endeavour* and almost a mile from the finish. Among the disappointed spectators was President Franklin Roosevelt, a

229

guest on Vincent Astor's *Nourmahal*. But he stayed around a while. When the two yachts were ghosting along on the incompleted race several vessels got too close to the *Endeavour*, taking what little wind there was. Among them was the destroyer *Manley*, whose helmsman was being too kind to a group of motion-picture cameramen on board. It was reported that President Roosevelt requested the *Nourmahal*'s radio operator to send a message to the *Manley:* "Are you challenging the *Endeavour?*" The destroyer shoved off, and quickly.

As there was so little difference in hulls and rigs of the contestants, the decisive factor was going to lie with the helmsmen and the crews. What interested expert commentators was the skill of the *Endeavour*'s crew in handling the big Genoa in their first use of it. The challenger showed what stuff she was made of and how good the man at her wheel when she took the first two races. She won that on September 17 with comparative ease; the second was much closer. The triangular course of 30 miles in the latter, on the eighteenth, was covered in record time.

The defender had had serious spinnaker trouble in the first completed race, but she was well astern of the challenger at the time. In the second, Sopwith won the start and throughout the race showed himself as good a tactician as, if not a better than, Vanderbilt. There were cheers for his crew then, many of whom had had no experience with yachts of the J class. Yet they seemed thoroughly at ease in handling clouds of canvas. On board was Mrs. Sopwith, long her husband's dependable timekeeper during his years of racing. Light airs on the nineteenth brought two postponements, then a cancellation of the race. It was obvious to the committee that the contestants could not get through the 30-mile course in the 5½-hour limit. By then the challenger was a two-to-one favorite.

230

Again, in the third race, Sopwith won the start, and at the stake boat, 15 miles to leeward, he was 6 minutes, 21 seconds ahead of the defender. The course had been laid to leeward on the first leg, to windward on return. Because of a shift of wind the last 15-mile leg was a close reach. The loss of the first two races had increased the nervousness of the already tense man at the *Rainbow*'s helm. (He had had spinnaker trouble again.) Every race is a strain; it must have been acute to a man on whom the eyes of much of the world were then focused.

Ten minutes after rounding the mark, Vanderbilt asked Sherman Hoyt to take the wheel to see if he "could make the darned thing go." In his comment on that moment of discouragement, Vanderbilt wrote:

There did not seem to be anything I could do on deck at the moment, so I went below with Sir Ralph Gore, the representative of the Royal Yacht Squadron on board Rainbow, *to drown my sorrows in coffee and sandwiches . . . as far as I was concerned, the America's Cup was on its way back to England. [He thought that might be a good thing for the sake of the sport.] Still I hated to go down in history as the first skipper to lose it.*

British yachtsmen and others who had seen Hoyt engaged in his favorite pastime, sailing a powerful yacht, held him in high esteem. One authoritative opinion classified him as "undoubtedly the finest helmsman in the world and as a seaman without a peer." Additional to this exceptional skill was a cunning appraisal of an opponent's characteristics. He knew that Sopwith's behavior pattern in a yacht race was to keep a rival covered, regardless of the mark. When Hoyt took the wheel the *Rainbow*'s afterguard could not see where the finish lay. They knew, though, that they were fetching it; Professor Zenas Bliss was navigator, and he said so. That was enough. Hoyt decided to try a bluff. He luffed the *Rainbow*

231

well past the *Endeavour*'s weather, guessing that the challenger would follow suit in order to keep between the defender and the line.

Hoyt wrote later: "The bluff came off! Tommy tacked . . . right into a calm patch. Immediately I bore away and sailed right through *Endeavour*'s lee."

That fatal tack toward the *Rainbow* cost Sopwith the race. He came about four times; the *Rainbow* fetched the line without a single tack. Yachting critics jumped on the challenger for permitting himself to be outfoxed by Hoyt. (The tactics of that race were discussed for years.) Had the challenger kept his course, only an accident could have lost him that key contest. Now it was his turn to feel discouraged. Some felt that the incident, and the unfavorable comments of yachting critics, unnerved Sopwith and affected his sailing ability. That was part of the guessing games which involved a multitude of deep thinkers throughout the series.

It was the fourth race, on September 22, which was to cause the greatest unpleasantness since the Dunraven incident. As they were maneuvering for the line at the start there was a near-collision. Each helmsman was then (and thereafter) of the opinion that the other was at fault. The *Rainbow*'s afterguard had been requested by the Cup committee to do everything possible to avoid making a protest. Yet they very nearly did run up the grievance flag before the actual start because the *Endeavour* seemed so openly the offender. In Sopwith's written protest to the committee, however, he stated in part that the *Rainbow* had been the overtaking vessel. And Vanderbilt's maneuvers had forced the challenger, after she had jibed, to bear away to avoid a collision.

The standard red flag of protest was not hoisted by either contestant at the moment. Yet the fiction grew, and persisted, that it did appear on the *Rainbow*. The error can be traced to the showing of the flag on both boats in the last race of the match. The English *Daily Express* correspondent, in reporting on that display, commented that "Mr. Sopwith made the startling allegation that Mr. Vanderbilt hoisted his protest flag in anticipation that *Endeavour* would protest against his action." The statement was picked up by the British press. A further dramatization of the episode was created by the *Daily Mail* correspondent who cabled home that the *Endeavour*'s designer was "so disgusted, especially with Mr. Vanderbilt's move in protesting before Mr. Sopwith who had, it seemed to him, been fouled" that he was sailing for home at once. These reports unintentionally created a flag which Vanderbilt had *not* hoisted in the fourth race. The annoying ghost, flickering over the pages of various books, has been haunting Cup historians ever since.

The defender went across the line ahead of the challenger by 23 seconds. Sopwith may have been outraged at the incident before the start but it did not affect his helmsmanship. He handled the *Endeavour* so superbly, on the first leg (to windward) of the 30-mile triangular course, that he brought his boat around the mark 27 seconds in advance of the *Rainbow*. There then occurred the second controversial incident of the race, one which, in view of the disturbance it created, can only be described as earth-shaking. As the challenger was starting for the second mark, her crew was setting the unfamiliar Genoa and taking in her quad. The *Rainbow* rounded the stake with her Genoa already set and came out on the *Endeavour*'s weather side. Sopwith promptly luffed to force his opponent to give way, a permissible little game according to the rules book. Vanderbilt, however, held his course. A noted "sea lawyer" (in its best sense), he had earned great respect as an authority on the rules of yacht racing.

Sherman Hoyt, at that moment, shouted "Luff! Luff!" But Vanderbilt, quite sure of his position, answered "No, he can't hit me forward of the main rigging." (Under the current

233

rules a leeward boat, "within risk of collision range," had to be in a position as she luffed to be able to hit the windward boat forward of the leestays or amidship shrouds. This puzzling rule put a strain on helmsmen. They had to guess the approximate point of possible contact.) Vanderbilt was very sure that Sopwith had begun his luff past his time to do so, and he refused to yield. Yet he assumed that Sopwith would hold the *Endeavour* in her luff long enough to decide where his boat might possibly contact the *Rainbow* if she continued on her course.

The boats were a yacht's length apart when the challenger bore away. The *Rainbow* was thus in the enviable position of being able to sail on while the *Endeavour* was coming out of stays. While making ready for the stern chase—not in this case the long chase—Sopwith asked the opinion of the New York Yacht Club representative on board whether he should hoist a protest flag. Under British racing rules then, the flag did not have to be displayed with the race committee boat so far off. The American observer thought that the challenger could wait until he was closer to the finish. That was not the way the committee saw it. (What followed, as a result, will be told in a moment. It would mean another luff, to interrupt the race and tell it now.)

On the third leg, in hot pursuit *Endeavour* came along like an angry grampus, traveling at a fine burst of speed. When she was only about 200 yards astern of the defender, Vanderbilt decided it was his time to play luff. He went into the wind slowly, forcing the *Endeavour* off to windward. This tactic went on for a little while. The challenger would fall behind, catch up a little, fall off again as the boat under his lee luffed. This interruption of the contest, so doubtful a tactic to old-fashioned, ordinary people who think that boats in a race should just race and not play games, succeeded in putting the *Rainbow* well ahead. Sopwith had lost his second

234

luffing match in that day's contest but this time he had no grounds for protest.

The defender won that fourth race by 1 minute, 15 seconds, making it two-all. It was said that strong men among yacht owners and marine reporters broke down and wept. Sopwith had, said they, "practically tossed the race away." The *Endeavour* had clearly shown that she was the faster boat to windward and in reaching. The critics cried that she had been mishandled and that among other tactical errors Sopwith had kept his staysail set inside his Genoa. This slowed him up at a crucial point in the chase. And Sopwith had admitted that English yachtsmen were not sufficiently familiar with the correct use of a Genoa.

Sopwith's handling of the *Endeavour* at the start of the fifth race hardly bore out the opinion of those who thought him unnerved by the upsetting incidents in the two preceding races. The echo of the starting whistle had hardly died before he had his boat over the line and ahead of the defender. But he did not steer as good a course as he had previously. And the failure of his crew to set correctly the parachute spinnaker (frequently a temperamental sail) brought the *Endeavour* home later than she had ever been before.

There was trouble on the *Rainbow,* too. Her parachute spinnaker split, but another was quickly set. Then, during a jibe, an experienced man, the bos'n, was jogged overside by the main boom. (The racing rules include a solemn injunction: a yacht must finish with the same number of men on board that she had when she started out.) Vanderbilt was about to execute a "man overboard" tactic. The man overboard had just unhooked a backstay whip, and he retained a powerful grip on it while dragging in the lee wash. A quick-thinking sailor (modest enough to be still anonymous) hauled on the wire stay and, with the help of others, swung the

235

dunked man above the deck. As the *Rainbow* straightened up, he landed feet first on the deck. (Later they read him the owners' simple rule: no swimming off a boat during a race!) This little incident had not hampered the defender in her forward course. She won handily.

Both boats went over the line in the sixth race—the *Endeavour* almost a minute ahead—with protest flags aloft. The cause for protest had occurred shortly after the five-minute whistle. On the second leg of the triangular course the *Rainbow* was well ahead. The last leg was a broad reach to the finish line. The crew of the defender had set a wrong parachute, one borrowed from the *Weetamoe,* and the error had added to the tension on board. *Endeavour*'s spinnaker had a stubborn stop around it which refused to open, and precious minutes were lost in getting the powerful sail to draw. (The hands of most of her amateur crew were badly damaged from handling sheets and stays.) Then the challenger moved so fast that she soon came abreast of the *Rainbow,* wide on her weather beam. "It looked all over for us," Sherman Hoyt reported in his *Memoirs,* "and Vanderbilt, highly nervous, asked me to relieve Parkinson at the helm and went below leaving me in charge." (The dean of the British experts observing the races had commented that Hoyt was the backbone of the successful direction of the *Rainbow.*) There was no time and no chance to bluff now; skillful sailing was what counted. It was a close race. Only a few lengths separated the boats as they boiled across the line. The *Rainbow* won—by 55 seconds—thus bringing the fifteenth challenge match to an exciting end and keeping the Cup where it had long rested.

Just before the *Endeavour* crossed the line, a sailor sent aloft by Sopwith—he still had his sense of humor—held a protest flag well out. The challenger said later that he wanted to be certain that the committee on the club boat could not

236

miss seeing it. He was cheered by the men on the press boat. But there was no hearing on the double protest in the final race. Sopwith withdrew his, saying, "My protest concerned a violation at the start, but inasmuch as I won the start and lost the race fairly, I feel I should not go on with the protest." Vanderbilt followed suit and the incident was forgotten.

Sopwith's protest in the fourth race was a vastly different matter. The race committee had promptly refused to entertain it. They pointed out that the flag was displayed on the *Endeavour* three hours after the alleged violation at the start and two hours after the second stated cause for protest. The rule required that the flag be displayed immediately after the incident protested. "While at first impression the rule may seem purely technical, and one which a race committee must feel justified in disregarding, this is not the case." The committee was explicit in its reply to Sopwith. It suggested that the rule of promptness also applied in Britain. Sopwith's failure to display his flag at the time of the "foul" before the start deprived Vanderbilt of an equal right to do so. Sopwith's reply was terse. He thought the committee was making too much of a "very trivial technical formality."

No one else seems to have been terse. The British press was quite bitter about "Yankee cunning." It was clear to its writers that the *Endeavour* had lost because after the protest was disallowed, before the fifth race, "Sopwith went to pieces," and "his crew was dispirited." That was part of the exaggeration that went with a new flare-up of national animosities. While the venerable *Times* of London deplored the ill feeling and hoped that good will would be restored, it could not resist a dig, perhaps partly based on the nonexistent Vanderbilt protest before the start of the fourth race. "One plain fact is that Rainbow won. . . . It is possible that the superiority of Rainbow over Endeavour included a certain smartness in running up a certain kind of flag."

237

After the fourth race Vanderbilt had requested an important opinion of his afterguardsmen, Charles Nicholson, and the American observer on the *Endeavour*. He wanted to know where they thought the challenger might possibly have hit the defender had Sopwith maintained his luff after the *Rainbow* had rounded the first mark. All agreed, except Sherman Hoyt, that *"Endeavour's* bow would have hit us aft our main rigging," Vanderbilt recorded, in *On the Wind's Highway*. Nicholson commented, however, that "irrespective of the point of contact," *Rainbow* should have kept clear. Had a hearing been held, Vanderbilt could have claimed that Sopwith bore away at a point when the *Rainbow* still had time to respond to the *Endeavour's* luff. Nevertheless Vanderbilt was dismayed at the committee's refusal to hear Sopwith's protest. The veteran Heckstall-Smith stated (as did Sherman Hoyt) that Sopwith had followed the old English custom in displaying his protest flag when he did. The committee's decision, he remarked, "would be regarded by all English yachtsmen as an action utterly non-judicial. The merits of Sopwith's protest will never be heard."

The opinions of experts in yachting matters were collected by a major American newspaper. The consensus was that Sopwith should have had a hearing, and the general attitude of the club itself was criticized by a noted authority. For the most part the American press was on Sopwith's side. As an evidence of that opinion one article was captioned "Britannia rules the waves but America waives the rules."

There was no question about the almost painful conscientiousness of the race committee. The suspicion arose later that perhaps the reasons for denying Sopwith's request for a hearing had not been publicly expressed but were sound. It was pretty generally agreed by objective observers that the *Endeavour* had, in actuality, fouled the *Rainbow* in the first instance on which Sopwith's protest was based. Photographic evidence was available to support this opinion. Therefore, had a hearing been held and the *Endeavour* found at fault on the first count, she would have had to be disqualified, and her second protest would, in consequence, have been invalid.

The controversy (which raged for years) might well have become more bitter at the time had Tom Sopwith been less a sportsman. He had, in an angry moment, said that "Americans seemed completely to disregard the fundamental rules of yacht racing," and "the Cup races are run as big business." That was about all, however, that was publicly heard. He seems to have been responsible for curbing Nicholson's freedom to express himself, radioing a request to him on October 3 not to discuss the committee's decision. The designer had preceded him to England and while en route had indicated his intention to "blow the lid off" when he landed. Sopwith calmed everyone down.

Vanderbilt, equally a good sportsman, helped. He gave unstinted praise to Sopwith's gallant effort, to the splendid *Endeavour,* and to the exceptional achievements of her largely amateur crew. The unpleasant incidents of the 1934 match had disturbed him. After a series of discussions with responsible yachting authorities he issued a pamphlet (1936) on suggested revisions of right-of-way rules in yacht races. That had not been his first constructive effort to formulate logical racing rules, and he was finally listened to.

The disputed incidents in the famous fourth race and the race committee's decision continued, of course, to remain a subject for intense discussion. It was implied in British yachting circles that anyone who challenged for the Cup again would be quite mad and might possibly even be a traitor. For a time the splendid spirit of sporting give-and-take which Sir Thomas Lipton had evoked with such ease seemed to be lost in the windy debate.

14

PRESENT,

PAST, AND FUTURE

The holders of the Cup may have thought that, after the effort and excitement of the 1934 match, they were entitled to a rest. That was not the way some Britishers saw it. They ignored the bitter criticism of American yachting ethics and discounted the objections to any further challenges. A discussion among a group of British owners of yachts developed into an idea. It took the form of a proposal to the New York Yacht Club early in 1935. That came from Charles R. Fairey, the "friendly rival" of Sopwith. Fairey was interested in challenging with a boat in the K or the L class. The former would be 75 feet waterline, the latter 65.4, which would be just over the minimum requirement. Would the club give consideration to the suggestion?

It was not said so by Fairey but the news had got around

that the Royal Yacht Squadron would not have sponsored his challenge. That elite club was reported to be angry at the New York Yacht Club for its "inexcusable discourtesy" in not sending an official copy of the report on Sopwith's protest. Then, to make Americans angry as well, Charles Nicholson published in *Yachting World* a most serious charge. An interpretation of immersion marks, made to the Yacht Racing Association by the New York Yacht Club, had been printed in the technical press. The appearance of the article gave Nicholson an opportunity to say out loud a few of the things he had discussed only privately. Among them was the statement that the *Rainbow* had increased her speed illegally by adding ballast and that if the weight of her crew (two and a half tons en masse) had been officially taken into account, the defender would have been penalized by having to sacrifice some of her sail area.

The subject of live ballast on a racing yacht was not new. During the inquiry into Lord Dunraven's charges it had been shown that a boat's head trim would be lowered by $2\frac{1}{2}$ inches when thirty men moved together up forward. When, therefore, the first *Columbia-Shamrock* match was under discussion, the number of men on board was limited to three for "each five feet of measured racing length."

Nicholson was at particular pains to say that the stated violations were not the fault of individuals or committees. He said, and earnestly, that American yachtsmen were a splendid lot. The responsibility lay with the "autocratic control by a few persons in the New York Yacht Club." Sopwith, Nicholson went on, had thought that rules for construction of Cup racers and racing rules, too, had been violated by the club. The friction was most unpleasant to so good a sportsman as Sopwith. In an effort to prevent any further unpleasantness after the ruling on his double protest, he had disregarded the more serious charges which Nicholson now brought forward.

241

American reaction to the designer's disturbing comments was mild. He was disagreed with by the club's official measurer and other responsible authorities. Nicholson was, however, regarded as a fair-minded man, and far too important in the yachting world to be ignored. His charges came late, and while public notice was at first thought to be unfortunate, it was perhaps a good thing that they had been brought in the open. For it gave an opportunity to the Americans most concerned to show that, in actuality, there had been no violations, nothing illegal. There was, though, a difference in the American and British methods of measuring freeboard. Nicholson had been basing his arguments on a variant interpretation. As a result of conferences between the New York Yacht Club and the Yacht Racing Association, an agreement was reached on measurement and immersion marks. During that period friendly relations were re-established with the Royal Yacht Squadron by the club. Thereupon everyone concerned breathed easier.

What may have been thought a little incident had great influence in further easing the tension between yachtsmen on both sides of the Atlantic. It occurred when Gerard Lambert took the *Yankee* over for the English regattas in 1935. Many years had passed since an American yacht of her quality had raced in British waters. Lambert had a most soothing effect upon yachtsmen prepared to be hostile or aloof. His wide popularity did much to renew cordial relations. The members of the proper yachting clubs began to suggest to each other the interesting possibility that there were some decent sportsmen left in the States!

Meanwhile Fairey's idea about a smaller boat in Cup races had been converted into a challenge. It was sent on his behalf by the Royal London Yacht Club, of which he had become commodore. The challenge was for a boat in the K class. It would measure around 107 tons. (J boats were about 40 tons more.) The New York Yacht Club, at first glance, did not favor the idea. There were no K boats in the United States or Britain and proper tests could not, therefore, be run for challenger or defender. If yachtsmen were encouraged to build them, it would mean the end of J boats. And there was not enough difference in length between the K and the J class to warrant the former. Harold Vanderbilt, too, was not enthusiastic over Fairey's suggestion though he thought that the L class might be more practical. (He had recently purchased the *Rainbow* from the syndicate of which he had been a member.)

The consensus then among American yachtsmen, and many Britishers, too, was that only the largest and fastest yachts should race for the Cup. That was traditional. (Economic conditions were going to force a radical alteration of such sentiments.) Yet, while the club was discussing Fairey's challenge, everyone involved in big-yacht racing conceded the great practical advantage smaller boats would have over the J's. A racer in the K class would cost only about $100,000, exclusive of sails, extra parts, wages of crews—and running expenses. ("They do not run," complained a yachtsman. "They gallop.")

Before he had conceived the notion of challenging with a K- or L-class yacht, Fairey had inquired about the possibility of racing 12-meter boats for the Cup. That was really reducing racing length for the most famous of international contests. The inquiry inspired the noted designer of small boats, Uffa Fox, to get into the act. He cabled the club in October 1935. If smaller craft were under consideration for a Cup match, would the club accept his challenge for a contest with sailing canoes? The club was not amused and the request was tossed in the lazarette.

Sopwith had, meanwhile, commissioned Nicholson for another centerboard J boat, 87' waterline. He had been pretty

243

certain that the New York Yacht Club would not favor
Fairey's idea. There had been some annoyance in Britain
over Fairey's challenge. It had been generally assumed that
an unwritten law would apply in Sopwith's case: first right
to a second chance. Sopwith had, in fact, asked the Royal
Yacht Squadron to forward his challenge in 1935, again naming the *Endeavour*. Other considerations apart, the Squadron
had been unwilling to sponsor a defeated yacht. And while
Fairey's challenge was under discussion the New York Yacht
Club could not deal with another. Sopwith sold the *Endeavour* for a fraction of its cost. The terms of sale included the
right of repurchase if the new J boat which Sopwith had
commissioned proved slower than his original challenger.
The *Endeavour* had acquired unquestioned title to "the
fastest yacht afloat"—and Nicholson might not be able to
improve on it.

Late in November 1935 Fairey withdrew his challenge.
Then, in 1936, Sopwith presented his, through the Royal
Yacht Squadron, without naming his boat. The New York
Yacht Club accepted his challenge, and accepted it gener-
ously. If his new yacht did not prove as fast as the *Endeavour,*
Sopwith would have the right a month before the first race
to substitute the latter. Races were to take place in July and
August 1937 under the same conditions as the preceding
match. The club tried then to promote interest in the building of a defender. It had difficulty in forming a group willing
to meet the high expenses of a J boat. Finally tired of waiting, Harold Vanderbilt decided to go it on his own, underwriting all costs. It was calculated by the knowing that a
J-class sloop could not then be built under $400,000.

Two men were called on for a design, Starling Burgess and
an equally imaginative though younger man, Olin Stephens.
The latter, among other splendid achievements in naval
architecture, was responsible for one of the most famous of

244

PHOTO EDWIN LEVICK-FREDERIC LEWIS
Start of the fourth race in the 1934 match with *Rainbow* leading *Endeavor I*.

PHOTO MORRIS ROSENFELD

Thomas O. M. Sopwith at the helm of *Endeavour I*.

Harold S. Vanderbilt giving *Ranger* a workout.

PHOTO MORRIS ROSENFELD

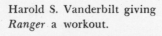

PHOTO EDWIN LEVICK-FREDERIC LEWIS

Ranger astern of *Endeavour II* before the
start of the third race in the 1937 match.

Mrs. Harold S. Vanderbilt

TWO LADY TIMEKEEPERS
IN TEMPORARY ROLES

Mrs. Thomas Sopwith

yachts, *Dorade,* the magnificent. It was agreed between them that they would keep secret whose model was chosen. After the 1934 match, Burgess and Nicholson had exchanged the lines of their Cup entrants. This helped the American designers greatly in the creation of two pairs of hull models with potentially greater speed than *Endeavour*'s. Under direction of Professor Kenneth Davidson of Stevens Institute of Technology, tests were run in the towing tank at Stevens.

As a result, the most promising model was selected, and production of the J boat based on it began at the Bath Iron Works, Maine. Its president, W. S. Newell, was persuaded by Burgess to do the major part of construction on a near-cost basis, as a patriotic and sporting gesture. The defender, to be called the *Ranger,* was to be an all-steel yacht with welded hull, 87 feet on the waterline. (It was the first time in forty-four years that a candidate for defense had not been built in the Herreshoff yards at Bristol.)

There was some criticism, by yachting experts and by builders, of tank tests. They pointed out that Watson's experiments with *Shamrock II,* when he conducted such experiments, had helped not at all, and that Nathanael Herreshoff had scorned such devices. But Vanderbilt remarked, after the 1937 match, that the *Ranger* was not merely a product of the tank. That elaborate mechanism only selected a model already designed by Burgess or Stephens. Furthermore—and this was important—the speeds predicted by tank-test calculations were fully met by the *Ranger* in her trials and the Cup races. After the tests in the Stevens tank, another series of experiments was run in the Navy Department tank at Washington.

No one seemed in the least surprised to hear that both the defending and the challenging yachts parted from their masts before they got down to the business of racing each other. While being towed from Bath, Maine, to Newport the

Ranger ran into a jump of sea. Her 165-foot mast could not take the heavy roll and snapped just above the deck. A new one of duralumin was turned out at top speed by the Aluminum Company of America. During her trials in England, Sopwith's new challenger, *Endeavour II,* lost her mast twice. She was finally ready for her transatlantic crossing and came over under tow. *Endeavour I*'s new owner made that splendid racer available as a pacer for number *II.* She, too, was hauled at the end of a cable from a power yacht. Several hundred miles off the American coast a full gale struck and *Endeavour I* parted from her convoy. She was unreported for a full week but she came through heavy seas, under jury rig, undamaged.

Not long before the arrival of the two *Endeavours* in American waters a number of English yachting authorities descended upon the North American Yacht Racing Union and the major associated clubs. The group included Charles Fairey and Major Brooke Heckstall-Smith. They were interested in converting the Americans to the idea of of an L-class boat for Cup races. The arguments they presented were practical. The proposed boat would require only ten paid hands, a J boat at least twenty-two. The L boat could be built and raced for a year for $125,000, the bigger yacht not for less than $500,000. There was a time in the swanky yacht clubs when one could mention a sum such as half a million to build a boat—and not hear an echo. But now, when one spoke of that amount, it set up most unpleasant vibrations. Yet the English visitors could get no further than a serious promise to give their proposal careful consideration. Meanwhile it went on the shelf marked "Pending."

The trials, in which the *Ranger* participated with the *Rainbow* and the *Yankee,* made the tank-proved yacht the obvious choice. A few days before the first race of the Cup match was run, *Endeavour* entered the trials. The *Ranger* won the first, the *Endeavour* the second in a fluky breeze. Yet betting odds favored the new defender three to one to win the first race, two to one to win four straight.

With both *Endeavours* available, Sopwith had been trying them out off Newport in a manner which exasperated yachtsmen and marine reporters. The criticisms of his tactics were frequently in bad taste and unreasonably harsh. Sopwith was, after all, as keen a yachtsman as any afloat and he was taking the business of realistic tests—and of winning—with the utmost seriousness. Instead of determining the speed of the two J boats by racing them under varying weather conditions, he kept them near each other and on the same headings. He tried on various occasions to put the second *Endeavour* in a disadvantageous position in order to study her "escape" behavior. Contact was maintained between the boats by wireless telephone. Various sail plans were experimented with. The two magnificent vessels seemed to be equal in speed when running free, but *Endeavour II* was obviously superior in windward work. She was nominated by Sopwith as the challenger.

The experts who had been present at the *Ranger*'s launching thought her ugly and her lines unconventional. They revised that opinion when they saw her again, in full dress. She then looked graceful and one born to win. Among other novelties, she had an amazing parachute spinnaker, the largest single sail ever seen on a yacht. It had an area of 18,000 square feet. It was not too big for the *Ranger*'s exceptional helmsman. By an ingenious arrangement of two booms (one attached to the spinnaker, the other on the mainsail side), Harold Vanderbilt was able to jibe his boat with that mountain of canvas set. Through his new method the spinnaker was not collapsed in a jibe. Instead of the usual time of 4½ minutes required by the older routine, it could now be done in 1½ minutes, so little way was lost. The race committee, however, after a jaunt on the *Ranger* said, "No, Mr. Vanderbilt." Their argument was technical: the rule stated that a spinnaker could not be set without a boom. For only a moment the sail was not attached to its pole, and Vanderbilt would, therefore, have to return to the conventional method. Sopwith had made no objection to the new style of changing a spinnaker's position. Vanderbilt appealed the ruling, pointing out that his use of two poles was actually safer. He was overruled. (Later the "antiquated" rule of the club was revised. Vanderbilt had been right—but he was premature.)

One other new sail, made of artificial silk, was to prove of inestimable value to the *Ranger*. It was a novelty in that it might have been a Genoa but its leech was cut off. It might have been an "isosceles parallelogram" or a gnomon, but it wasn't. It was a—well, for the time being the big quadrilateral jib was "the new quad."

The races took place in the presence of a spectator fleet so large that it seemed the depression was really over. Two lady timekeepers were on board the contenders, Mrs. Harold Vanderbilt on the *Ranger*, Mrs. Tom Sopwith on *Endeavour II*. As was frequent, Sopwith won the start but it did him no good. There was only a hint of breeze. Vanderbilt set his new quad on the beat out, his big light sail on a broad reach home. The *Endeavour* was beaten by the embarrassing time of 17 minutes, 5 seconds, one of the worst defeats in Cup racing. She did even more poorly in the second race. Thereupon she was hauled out for a look at her bottom. There was nothing wrong. Her record in the next two races was much better and closer to what had been expected of her. But, despite the speed born in her, she never won a single race in the match. Light winds and the *Ranger*'s powerful sails gave the defender the first four without a break.

After the uninteresting match, the contestants went on the

ways. That gave designer Nicholson a chance to look over
the defender at close range. He commented that she was "the
most revolutionary advance in hull design in fifty years." It
was a gracious salute to Burgess and Stephens, to Professor
Davidson of Stevens Institute, to the towing tank. (Twenty
years after her creation, because he had been publicly credited
with the design, Olin Stephens acknowledged that Burgess
was responsible for the hull selected. There was no longer
any need to keep the secret. Burgess had died in 1947.)

Sopwith said it was a fair win and had no complaints
except that he would have been happier had British breezes
blown in American waters. The two *Endeavours* went home.
On the way back the older boat, again towed by *Vita II,* had
an even worse time than on her passage to America. A hurri-
cane parted the cable. *Endeavour I*'s skipper, Captain Ted
Heard, and a crew member were swept overboard. They were
smart enough to be hanging at the moment on some lines
which were most useful in hauling them back on board. The
yacht was lost sight of for a dozen days. Then she came into
Gosport, battered and tired but whole. The *Ranger* was not
on the scene long. After a brief rest she went to the junk
yard; sale price $10,000. She was the last J boat to be built
in defense of the Cup. It was to be a long, long time before
another match would be scheduled.

For more than two Biblical generations, with pauses to get
their wind back, Englishmen, Canadians, Scotsmen, Irishmen
had contested for the Cup. Irresistibly drawn by a glittering
symbol, enchanted by the "wind's song"—or the siren voice
of ambition—romantic and sometimes daring, they deserted
their accustomed routines for the most dramatic of international competitions. They came to American waters with
magnificent yachts, eager to display their skill and to test the
triumphs of the designer's art. They had poured money and

249

sweat into the great endeavor. In fifty races, fair weather and foul, the finest of boats had gone across the line, rounded the mark, and raced home. Yet, except for its effect upon spectators and participants, not a dozen of those races had any real excitement in them. In restrospect it must be clear that the events preparatory to the matches (and some of the aftermaths) were far more interesting and significant than the races themselves.

During the later years of the Cup races, the yacht which had started the international excitement seemed all but forgotten. Her owner, General Butler, had cruised her and raced her. Then, in 1876, she went aground, lost her keel and damaged her garboards. Edward Burgess looked her over, and as a result of his planning she was practically rebuilt in 1880. Five years later General Butler commissioned Burgess to modernize her. The operation gave her a new look. But she was still the *America,* still the hull that had brought home the Cup. Then, in 1917, she once again changed hands, but that was not the time for cruising or racing. The lead keel Burgess had given her took other form, a contribution to the war effort.

She was afloat again a few years thereafter, with the Eastern Yacht Club at Marblehead as her owner by right of gift. They loved her at Marblehead, loved her memory, but they felt she belonged to the nation. The *America* was offered to the Navy. The very top of brass thought about it and then announced that regulations prohibited her acceptance as a gift. But they could afford to buy her with a piece of engraved paper backed by the credit of the United States. The paper read "One Dollar." That was not a large enough sum to warrant a Congressional investigation, yet its acceptance by the owners would keep everything legal and most shipshape.

An impressive ceremony was held in 1921 at her old home, Annapolis. The ambassadors of the yacht club sold the memorable vessel to Admiral Henry Wilson, representing the Navy. She was ready for the Old Sailors' Home after a hard, rich life of seventy years. A comfortable bed was prepared for her in the Dewey Basin and plans were considered to convert her into a permanent museum.

Years passed before someone came across her record in a lower file drawer. Thereupon she was surveyed and found to be badly in need of repair. The report finally reached the Secretary of the Navy. Then bids were asked for cost of restoration. These things take time, of course; just why so much time no one seems to know. It was 1940 before funds were appropriated for surgery and blood transfusion.

Meanwhile a shed had been placed over her. It was not a very good one. A heavy snowstorm hit the area and the undue weight of snow collapsed the shed. The *America* collapsed, too. They went to work on her then—with sledge hammers, to make the destruction complete. *Vale America!*

All that is left of her now, beyond a few souvenirs from her old timbers, are the rudder and the fine spread eagle once on her stern. The former is a prize display in the Marine Historical Association's museum, Mystic Seaport, Connecticut. The ornamental eagle had been discarded by one of her English owners, undoubtedly Viscount Templetown. It was acquired by the keeper of the Eagle Tavern at Ryde, Isle of Wight. There it was caged, swinging from an iron bar outside the door. For more than fifty years it hung in that spot as a publican's sign. That was long enough for the Royal Yacht Squadron to hear about it. Its committees conferred on what should be done and then made a noble proposal to the membership. They would like to buy it and present it to the New York Yacht Club. The idea was greeted with "Hear! Hear!" That was in 1912. The historic emblem, at which the Squadron fleet in 1851 had had too long a look, now hangs in the entrance hall of the club's magnificent building in New York.

A dozen years after Sopwith's second endeavor the club had the Cup dug out of Tiffany's vaults. It was set on an old oaken table and securely bolted with a wrench of a special type. The wrench then went into the club's safe, with the deeds of gift. It had to be used in 1951 when the Cup went back to England—on loan. It seemed a friendly thing to do, to permit the British to see the Cup for which their yachtsmen had yearned and which had so often inspired their challenges. The occasion was the Festival of Britain and the famous trophy was put on conspicuous display with lesser sporting memorabilia in Hutchinson Hall, London. In that year, too, the New York Yacht Club presented a silver bowl to the Royal Yacht Squadron to commemorate the *America*'s victory just a hundred years earlier. The bowl was in the style of a famed American silversmith, Paul Revere, the same who had once taken horse to cry the midnight alarm, "The redcoats are coming!"

Back in the club's treasure room, the Cup stands rich with memories, inscribed with triumphs. It seemed, for a time, that there would be no more challenges. None, certainly, for J boats, for not a one is left. But it was not the intention of the club that so great a prize should remain merely a museum piece. It applied for legal approval to alter part of the terms of the last deed of gift, a revision of one devised more than a century earlier. In December 1956 the New York State Supreme Court allowed the requested change. The alteration meant that twelve-meter boats, around 69 feet over all, 44 feet waterline, would be acceptable as challengers. (The former minimum had been 65 feet load waterline.) Sloops or other types with a longer waterline would not, however, be rejected should such a boat be proposed in a challenge. By due process a foreign vessel no longer has to make the hazardous crossing of the Atlantic on her own bottom. If her owner so decides, she can come over in the hold of a freighter or liner or even be tucked under steamer robes on deck.

Only months after the good news reached England, yachts-men dipped their quills in sea water and sent off a challenge. It came through the Royal Yacht Squadron for a syndicate of nine members. Races were proposed on courses off New-port, the first for September 20, 1958. The New York Yacht Club was prompt in saying yes.

The English syndicate invited the four top naval architects in Britain to turn out two designs each. It was announced that models would be tank tested and no expense would be spared to produce a boat to win. The selected challenger was the *Sceptre,* a twelve-meter boat. With that sleek, frisky type the British feel that they have vastly improved their chance to win against the American best. The American best, at this writing, is being made ready. Though there are a number of superb twelves still on the active list, three syndicates were formed, each underwriting the cost of candidates.

To those who saw the great matches of the early twentieth century, races with the small, neat twelves may seem tame. No more the towering masts, the white clouds of sails, the long, keen hulls. But for those who compete and those who watch there will still be some of the old enchantment during the supreme trial in the "friendly competition between foreign nations."

The time may come when the club which has so long and so ardently protected it may have to surrender the Cup. If that day comes, there will be no moaning at the bar. The special wrench will just be kept handy, the old oaken table marked "Reserved." For each member knows that if they must relinquish their most famous trophy because of a chal-lenger's victory, they must also have it back. They and their forefathers have been patting it caressingly for a hundred years. The treasure room, the club itself would not be the same without it.

There is magic in the America's Cup. That will never be lost no matter who wins it.

CHALLENGE RACES FOR THE CUP

DATE	YACHTS (Challenger 1st)	COURSE
Aug. 8, 1870	Cambria [1]	N.Y.Y.C. inside [2]
	Magic	35.1 miles
Oct. 16, 1871	Livonia	N.Y.Y.C. inside
	Columbia	35.1 miles
Oct. 18, 1871	Livonia	Off Sandy Hook Lightship
	Columbia	20 m. to windward and return [3]
Oct. 19, 1871	Livonia	N.Y.Y.C. inside
	Columbia [4]	35.1 miles
Oct. 21, 1871	Livonia	Off Sandy Hook Lightship
	Sappho	20 m. to windward and return
Oct. 23, 1871	Livonia	N.Y.Y.C. inside
	Sappho	40 miles
Aug. 11, 1876	Countess of Dufferin	N.Y.Y.C. inside
	Madeleine	32.6 miles
Aug. 12, 1876	Countess of Dufferin	From Buoy 5 off Sandy Hook
	Madeleine	20 m. to windward and return
Nov. 9, 1881	Atalanta	N.Y.Y.C. inside
	Mischief	32.6 miles
Nov. 10, 1881	Atalanta	From Buoy 5 off Sandy Hook
	Mischief	16 m. to leeward and return
Sept. 14, 1885	Genesta	N.Y.Y.C. inside
	Puritan	32.6 miles

[1] *Cambria* 8th on elapsed; 10th on corrected time
[2] The course is described on p. 52
[3] Length of course questioned; probably 30 miles
[4] Disabled

254

ELAPSED TIME	CORRECTED TIME	WON BY	IN
h.m. s.	h.m. s.		m.s.
4.34.57	4.37.38.9		
4.07.54	3.58.21.2	*Magic*	39.17.7
6.43.00	6.46.45		
6.17.42	6.19.41	*Columbia*	27.04
3.06.49½	3.18.15½		
3.01.33½	3.07.41¾	*Columbia*	10.33¾
3.53.05	4.02.25	*Livonia*	15.10
4.12.38	4.17.35		
6.04.38	6.09.23		
5.33.24	5.36.02	*Sappho*	33.21
5.04.41	5.11.44		
4.38.05	4.46.17	*Sappho*	25.27
5.34.53	5.34.53		
5.24.55	5.23.54	*Madeleine*	10.59
7.46.00	7.46.00		
7.19.47	7.18.46	*Madeleine*	27.14
4.48.24½	4.45.29¼		
4.17.09	4.17.09	*Mischief*	28.20¼
5.36.52	5.33.47		
4.54.53	4.54.53	*Mischief*	38.54
6.22.52	6.22.24		
6.06.05	6.06.05	*Puritan*	16.19

CHALLENGE RACES FOR THE CUP (CONT.)

DATE	YACHTS (Challenger 1st)	COURSE
Sept. 16, 1885	*Genesta* *Puritan*	Off Scotland Lightship 20 m. to leeward and return
Sept. 7, 1886	*Galatea* *Mayflower*	N.Y.Y.C. inside 32.6 miles
Sept. 11, 1886	*Galatea* *Mayflower*	Off Scotland Lightship 20 m. to leeward and return
Sept. 27, 1887	*Thistle* *Volunteer*	N.Y.Y.C. inside 32.6 miles
Sept. 30, 1887	*Thistle* *Volunteer*	Off Scotland Lightship 20 m. to windward and return
Oct. 7, 1893	*Valkyrie II* *Vigilant*	Off Sandy Hook Lightship 15 m. to leeward and return
Oct. 9, 1893	*Valkyrie II* *Vigilant*	Off Sandy Hook Lightship Equilateral triangle, 30 m.
Oct. 13, 1893	*Valkyrie II* *Vigilant*	Off Sandy Hook Lightship 15 m. to windward and return
Sept. 7, 1895	*Valkyrie III* *Defender*	3 m. N.E. of Seabright, N.J. 15 m. to windward and return
Sept. 10, 1895	*Valkyrie III* [5] *Defender*	Off Sandy Hook Lightship Equilateral triangle, 30 m.
Sept. 12, 1895	*Valkyrie III* [6] *Defender*	Off Sandy Hook Lightship 15 m. to windward and return
Oct. 16, 1899	*Shamrock* *Columbia*	Off Sandy Hook Lightship 15 m. to windward and return
Oct. 17, 1899	*Shamrock* [7] *Columbia*	Off Sandy Hook Lightship Equilateral triangle, 30 m.

[5] Fouled *Defender;* disqualified
[6] Crossed starting line and withdrew
[7] Damaged; withdrew

ELAPSED TIME	CORRECTED TIME	WON BY	IN
h.m. s.	h.m. s.		m.s.
5.05.20	5.04.52		
5.03.14	5.03.14	*Puritan*	1.38
5.39.21	5.38.43		
5.26.41	5.26.41	*Mayflower*	12.02
7.18.48	7.18.09		
6.49.00	6.49.00	*Mayflower*	29.09
5.12.46¾	5.12.41¾		
4.53.18	4.53.18	*Volunteer*	19.23¾
5.54.51	5.54.45		
5.42.56¼	5.42.56¼	*Volunteer*	11.48¾
4.13.23	4.11.35		
4.05.47	4.05.47	*Vigilant*	5.48
3.27.24	3.35.36		
3.25.01	3.25.01	*Vigilant*	10.35
3.26.52	3.25.19		
3.24.39	3.24.39	*Vigilant*	0.40
5.08.44	5.08.44		
5.00.24	4.59.55	*Defender*	8.49
3.55.09	3.55.09	*Valkyrie III*	0.47
3.56.25	3.55.56		
—	—		
4.44.12	4.43.43	*Defender*	—
5.04.07	5.04.01		
4.53.53	4.53.53	*Columbia*	10.08
—	—		
3.37.00	—	*Columbia*	—

DATE	YACHTS (Challenger 1st)	COURSE
Oct. 20, 1899	*Shamrock* *Columbia*	Off Sandy Hook Lightship 15 m. to leeward and return
Sept. 28, 1901	*Shamrock II* *Columbia*	Off Sandy Hook Lightship 15 m. to windward and return
Oct. 3, 1901	*Shamrock II* *Columbia*	Off Sandy Hook Lightship Equilateral triangle, 30 m.
Oct. 4, 1901	*Shamrock II* *Columbia*	Off Sandy Hook Lightship 15 m. to leeward and return
Aug. 22, 1903	*Shamrock III* *Reliance*	Off Sandy Hook Lightship 15 m. to windward and return
Aug. 25, 1903	*Shamrock III* *Reliance*	Off Sandy Hook Lightship Equilateral triangle, 30 m.
Sept. 3, 1903	*Shamrock III* [8] *Reliance*	Off Sandy Hook Lightship 15 m. to windward and return
July 15, 1920	*Shamrock IV* *Resolute* [9]	Off Ambrose Channel Lightship 15 m. to windward and return
July 20, 1920	*Shamrock IV* *Resolute*	Off Ambrose Channel Lightship Equilateral triangle, 30 m.
July 21, 1920	*Shamrock IV* *Resolute*	Off Ambrose Channel Lightship 15 m. to windward and return
July 23, 1920	*Shamrock IV* *Resolute*	Off Ambrose Channel Lightship Equilateral triangle, 30 m.
July 27, 1920	*Shamrock IV* *Resolute*	Off Ambrose Channel Lightship 15 m. to windward and return

[8] Fog-bound; did not finish
[9] Damaged; withdrew

ELAPSED TIME	CORRECTED TIME	WON BY	IN
h.m. s.	h.m. s.		m.s.
3.44.43	3.44.43		
3.38.25	3.38.09	Columbia	6.34
4.31.44	4.31.44		
4.31.07	4.30.24	Columbia	1.20
3.16.10	3.16.10		
3.13.18	3.12.35	Columbia	3.35
4.33.38	4.33.38		
4.33.40	4.32.57	Columbia	0.41
3.41.17	3.39.20		
3.32.17	3.32.17	Reliance	7.03
3.18.10	3.16.12		
3.14.54	3.14.54	Reliance	1.19
——	——		
4.28.00	4.28.00	Reliance	——
4.24.58	4.24.58	Shamrock IV	——
——	——		
5.22.18	5.22.18	Shamrock IV	2.26
5.31.45	5.24.44		
4.03.06	4.03.06		
4.03.06	3.56.05	Resolute	7.01
3.41.10	3.41.10		
3.37.52	3.31.12	Resolute	9.58
5.48.20	5.48.20		
5.35.15	5.28.35	Resolute	19.45

CHALLENGE RACES FOR THE CUP (CONT.)

DATE	YACHTS (Challenger 1st)	COURSE
Sept. 13, 1930	*Shamrock V* *Enterprise*	Off Newport, Rhode Island [10] Leeward-windward, 30 m.
Sept. 15, 1930	*Shamrock V* *Enterprise*	Off Newport Equilateral triangle, 30 m.
Sept. 17, 1930	*Shamrock V* [11] *Enterprise*	Off Newport Windward-leeward, 30 m.
Sept. 18, 1930	*Shamrock V* *Enterprise*	Off Newport Equilateral triangle, 30 m.
Sept. 17, 1934	*Endeavour* *Rainbow*	Off Newport Windward-leeward, 30 m.
Sept. 18, 1934	*Endeavour* *Rainbow*	Off Newport Equilateral triangle, 30 m.
Sept. 20, 1934	*Endeavour* *Rainbow*	Off Newport Leeward-windward, 30 m.
Sept. 22, 1934	*Endeavour* *Rainbow*	Off Newport Equilateral triangle, 30 m.
Sept. 24, 1934	*Endeavour* *Rainbow*	Off Newport Leeward-windward, 30 m.
Sept. 25, 1934	*Endeavour* *Rainbow*	Off Newport Equilateral triangle, 30 m.
July 31, 1937	*Endeavour II* *Ranger*	Off Newport Windward-leeward, 30 m.
Aug. 2, 1937	*Endeavour II* *Ranger*	Off Newport Equilateral triangle, 30 m.
Aug. 4, 1937	*Endeavour II* *Ranger*	Off Newport Windward-leeward, 30 m.
Aug. 5, 1937	*Endeavour II* *Ranger*	Off Newport Equilateral triangle, 30 m.

[10] Start and finish 9 miles S.E. (magnetic) from Brenton Reef Lightship
[11] Damaged; withdrew

ELAPSED TIME	CORRECTED TIME	WON BY	IN
h.m. s.	h.m. s.		m.s.
4.06.40	Time allowance		
4.03.48	discarded for	*Enterprise*	2.52
4.10.18	this and all fol-		
4.00.44	lowing races	*Enterprise*	9.34
—			
3.54.16		*Enterprise*	—
3.15.57			
3.10.13		*Enterprise*	5.44
3.43.44		*Endeavour*	2.09
3.45.53			
3.09.01		*Endeavour*	0.51
3.09.52			
4.39.00			
4.35.34		*Rainbow*	3.26
3.16.53			
3.15.38		*Rainbow*	1.15
3.58.06			
3.54.05		*Rainbow*	4.01
3.41.00			
3.40.05		*Rainbow*	0.55
4.58.20			
4.41.15		*Ranger*	17.05
4.00.05			
3.41.33		*Ranger*	18.32
3.58.57			
3.54.30		*Ranger*	4.27
3.11.26			
3.07.49		*Ranger*	3.37

INDEX

274

ABOUT THE AUTHOR

JEROME E. BROOKS *is never so content as when poking the nose of a sailboat into harbors along the Long Island and New England coasts. When at work he is a specialist in research writing, chiefly in the industrial field. He is, additionally, an authority on rare books and manuscripts, a subject on which he has written many hundred articles; the author-editor of an encyclopedic history of tobacco and author of the standard popular book on that subject. Among his less known but highly praised achievements is his invention of a potent punch, accurately labeled "Devil's Hoof," a brew designed especially for storm-tossed yachtsmen with asbestos throats, iron stomachs and India-rubber legs.*